"This very clear book deepens our experience of autism and Asperger syndrome in adults, where it can be harder to detect and where partners may be managing and even camouflaging it. It is a valuable contribution, laden with advice that will make such couples feel less alone and know where to turn for help."

—*Simon Baron-Cohen, FBA, Professor of Developmental Psychopathology, Director, Autism Research Centre, Cambridge University, UK*

"Many individuals with Asperger syndrome have a desire to establish and maintain relationships with others. As with most couples, finding a balance between their own personality and character and meeting their partners' needs and expectations is challenging. This complex balance is explored in *The Partner's Guide to Asperger Syndrome*. The valuable information and tools provided in this book will help partners better understand one another, respect their differences, and work together to achieve fulfilling and long-lasting relationships.

The book explores topics of communication, intimacy, and parenting along with other types of interpersonal relationships with regards to individuals with Asperger syndrome. This book will be useful for partners and professionals but mostly, its positive outlook will bring inspiration and encouragement to the entire AS community."

—*Isabelle Hénault, author of* Asperger's Syndrome and Sexuality: From Adolescence through Adulthood

"Part of me cried when I read this book. I wish my mother had been able to read it when she was a young non-spectrum woman married to my father, a much older Aspie. It would have fundamentally changed her life—for the better. *The Partner's Guide to Asperger Syndrome* is more than a guide, it is a lifeline for any marriage mixed with AS. In fact, it is the lifeline this Aspie woman, married for 26 years to a man with many AS traits, absolutely needed to finally understand the complexities of our interpersonal dynamics."

—*Liane Holliday Willey, Ed.D, author of* Safety Skills for Women with Asperger Syndrome *and* Pretending to be Normal

"Adults with Asperger Syndrome (AS) have traditionally had difficulties with relationships but today more and more of them are getting involved in long-term commitments. Although this is a positive development and a real sign of how far so many have come, these relationships are not without their challenges for both the people with AS and also for their partners. Until now there have been few guidelines or resources for partners to help them understand some of the differences that they observe daily in their partners and to know how to respond to them. This book is an important step toward helping those partners to understand and live more comfortably and happily with their partners who have AS... Readers trying to manage these relationships, those trying to help them, and others who just want to understand what it is like to be involved with these charming, but often challenging partners, will find the insights of the authors and the partners to be intriguing, thought provoking, and a remarkable learning experience. This book is a must-read for anyone interested in intimate relationships involving individuals with AS."

—*Gary B. Mesibov, PhD, Professor Emeritus,*
The University of North Carolina, USA

The

Partner's Guide
to Asperger
Syndrome

of related interest

The Complete Guide to Asperger's Syndrome
Tony Attwood
ISBN 978 1 84310 495 7 (hardback)
ISBN 978 1 84310 669 2 (paperback)

Asperger's Syndrome
A Guide for Parents and Professionals
Tony Attwood
Foreword by Lorna Wing
ISBN 978 1 85302 577 8

The Asperger Couple's Workbook
Practical Advice and Activities for Couples and Counsellors
Maxine Aston
ISBN 978 1 84310 253 3

Connecting With Your Asperger Partner
Negotiating the Maze of Intimacy
Louise Weston
Foreword by Tony Attwood
ISBN 978 1 84905 130 9

The

Partner's Guide
to Asperger
Syndrome

Susan Moreno, Marci Wheeler
and Kealah Parkinson

Foreword by Tony Attwood, PhD

Jessica Kingsley *Publishers*
London and Philadelphia

First published in 2012
by Jessica Kingsley Publishers
116 Pentonville Road
London N1 9JB, UK
and
400 Market Street, Suite 400
Philadelphia, PA 19106, USA

www.jkp.com

Library of Congress Cataloging in Publication Data
Moreno, Susan.
The partner's guide to asperger syndrome / Susan Moreno, Marci Wheeler, and
Kealah Parkinson ; foreword by Tony Attwood.
p. cm.
Includes bibliographical references and index.
ISBN 978-1-84905-878-0 (alk. paper)
1. Asperger's syndrome--Popular works. 2. Asperger's syndrome--Social aspects--
Popular works. I. Wheeler, Marci. II. Parkinson, Kealah. III. Title.
RC553.A88M66 2012
616.85'8832--dc23
2011026561

British Library Cataloguing in Publication Data
A CIP catalogue record for this book is available from the British Library

ISBN 978 1 84905 878 0
eISBN 978 0 85700 566 3

Printed and bound in the United States

Contents

Foreword

Relationship Problems of Adults with Asperger Syndrome

Tony Attwood

Adults with Asperger syndrome (AS) have difficulties acquiring relationship skills due to the defining characteristics of the syndrome, experiences with peers during childhood and the expectations of their partner. However, an increasing number of adults with AS do achieve long-term relationships.

Children with AS have significant difficulty developing peer relationships and have difficulties in knowing what someone may be thinking or feeling. Such individuals also have a conspicuously limited ability to have a reciprocal conversation or communicate emotions, and have special interests that can be unusual in terms of intensity or focus. They can also have an extreme sensitivity to particular sensory experiences. All of these characteristics will affect relationship skills throughout childhood and eventually an adult's ability to achieve a long-term successful relationship.

While an adult with classic autism may appear content with a more solitary lifestyle, this is often not the case with adults who have AS. Clinical experience has identified that the majority of adolescents and young adults with AS would like a partner, and that those who do achieve a relationship have problems maintaining the relationship. However, there is remarkably little research examining this aspect of AS, and very few strategies to facilitate successful relationships. This foreword outlines the difficulties in acquiring relationship skills experienced by people with AS, based on the defining characteristics of the syndrome, clinical experience, autobiographies and the descriptions of partners. This foreword also provides some preliminary suggestions to encourage a successful relationship and indicate areas for future research.

Factors inhibiting relationship skills

From early childhood, people with AS are less likely to recognize and understand the thoughts, beliefs, desires and intentions of other people in order to make sense of their behavior. They are also less competent in theory of mind (ToM) abilities (Baron-Cohen 1995). This adversely affects the development of the important relationship skills of empathy and trust, as well as the ability to repair someone's emotions and to share thoughts and responsibilities (Attwood 2004b). By comparison, typical children have a natural ability to achieve an age-appropriate ToM and have practiced relationship skills with family members and friends for many years before applying them to achieve a successful relationship with a partner.

In order to achieve a successful relationship, a person also needs to understand and respect themselves (Lawson 2005). Self-understanding and self-reflection can be particularly difficult for people with AS (Frith and Happé 1999). Self-respect often is adversely affected by being rejected, ridiculed and tormented, or otherwise bullied, by peers (Attwood 2006). Adolescents with AS can be gullible and vulnerable to being given misinformation on relationships by fellow teenagers. This can include instances of being deceived and "set up" that could lead the person with AS to be accused of inappropriate social or sexual behavior.

Clinicians recognize that people with AS have difficulty understanding and expressing emotions, are prone to develop an anxiety disorder or depression and have difficulty managing anger (Attwood 2003a). These characteristics can have a detrimental effect on the ability to develop friendships throughout childhood and relationships as an adult.

Further, a common characteristic of AS is emotional and social immaturity, which can influence the person's age preference for friends. This can be of particular concern when an adolescent with AS prefers the company of much younger children. In such instances, the relationship motivation of the person with AS could be interpreted as being more than platonic and thereby lead to accusations of stalking, molestation and so on.

Not surprisingly, love is a confusing emotion to many with AS. Typical children and adults enjoy frequent expressions of affection and know how to express affection to communicate reciprocal feelings of adoration and when to repair someone's feelings by expressions of affection. Children and adults with AS may not seek the same depth and frequency of expressions of love through acts of affection, or may not realize that an expression of affection is expected in a particular situation and would be enjoyed by the other person. They can be bewildered as to why others appear to be "obsessed" with expressing love for each other.

Indeed, someone with AS may perceive expressions of affection as aversive, and consider a hug an uncomfortable squeeze that restricts movement. They can become confused or overwhelmed when expected to demonstrate and enjoy relatively modest expressions of affection. We generally have a wide "vocabulary" of expressions of affection, but someone with AS may have a more limited vocabulary and problems with the intensity of expression. One of my adult clients with AS said: "We feel and show affection but not often enough and at the wrong intensity."

Another of the diagnostic characteristics of AS is the development of a special interest that is unusual in terms of the focus or intensity. In adolescence and adult years, the focus can be a person, which might be interpreted as a typical teenage crush, but the intensity and some of the associated behaviors might lead to accusations of stalking or harassment.

The predisposition to develop a special interest can have other effects on the development of relationship knowledge. Special interests have many functions for people with AS, and one of these is to acquire knowledge to understand bewildering aspects of their experiences (Attwood 2003b).

Teenagers with AS are often eager to understand and experience the social and relationship world of their peers, including relationships and sexual experiences, but there can be problems regarding the source of information on relationships. Adolescents with AS usually have few, if any, friends with whom they can discuss and be informed about relationship topics such as romantic or sexual feelings and the codes of sexual behavior. Unfortunately, the source of information on relationships for adolescents with AS can be pornography and television soap operas. The person with AS can assume that the actions in pornographic material provide a script of what to say or do on a date that could lead to being charged with sexually inappropriate behavior (Ray, Marks and Bray-Garretson 2004). Some may use television programs and films as source material to learn about relationships, and fail to recognize that the actions and themes are not an accurate portrayal of how to achieve and maintain a relationship in real life.

Clinical experience indicates that previously unpopular and socially excluded teenage girls with AS have, after the physical changes that occur at puberty, become flattered by the attention of teenage boys. Due to her naivety, the adolescent girl may not recognize that the interest is sexual and not a way for the boy to simply enjoy her personality, company or conversation. Because their daughter has no female friends to provide advice on dating and the social and sexual codes, parents may become concerned about her vulnerability to promiscuity, sexual experiences and rape.

Difficulties at every stage of relationships

There is a relationship continuum from being an acquaintance to a partner. People with AS can have difficulties at each stage on the continuum. The social circle of adults with AS can be remarkably small, especially if the person is unemployed and tends to stay at home to avoid social situations. The person may have few acquaintances. To progress from an acquaintance to a friend, the person with AS needs to have age-appropriate skills in the pragmatic aspects of language, the art of conversation. Adults with AS often have difficulties with initiating, maintaining and ending a conversation, and show a lack of reciprocity or conversational balance and a tendency to be pedantic and to have an obsession with excessive and tedious detail (Attwood 2006). We also recognize problems with empathy, limited conflict resolution skills, an inclination to criticize and rarely compliment and a tendency to show little interest in their friends' experiences and emotions. Adults with AS may talk a great deal about their special interest, but not be proficient with social chitchat, the art of attentive and empathic listening or recognizing what might be of interest to the other person.

To progress along the relationship continuum from a friend to a boyfriend or girlfriend, an adolescent or adult with AS needs to understand the art of flirting and romance, to read accurately the signals of mutual attraction and to understand the dating game. These abilities are not intuitive for people with AS.

I am often asked by teenagers and young adults with AS: "How do I get a girlfriend/boyfriend?" This is not an easy question to answer. Adults with AS often want to be a friend and lover but have little idea of how to be either (Jacobs 2006). One of the difficulties for people with AS can be how to interpret correctly someone's intentions. An act of kindness or compassion can be perceived by the person with AS as a signal of a deeper level of interest or more personal than was intended. I have had to explain to men with AS that the smile and personal attention of a female member of the cabin crew on an aircraft are signs of courtesy, not an indication of a desire for a relationship.

Despite the problems in relationship skills experienced by many people with AS some adults can progress along the relationship continuum and are able to experience intimate personal relationships, even becoming a lifelong partner. To achieve such a relationship, both partners would have initially noticed attractive qualities in the other person. What are the characteristics that someone would find attractive in an adult with AS?

Attractive qualities of a person with AS

Men with AS

Men with AS have many qualities that can be attractive to a prospective partner (Aston 2003). When conducting relationship counseling with one or both partners having the characteristics or diagnosis of AS, I often ask the typical partner, "What were the characteristics that made your partner attractive when you first met him/her?" Many women describe their first impressions of their partner with AS as being someone who was kind, attentive and socially or emotionally immature. The term "silent, handsome stranger" can be used to describe someone who seems relatively quiet and good looking. The man's lack of social and conversation skills can lead to his being perceived as the silent stranger whose social naivety and immaturity can be transformed by a partner who is a natural expert on empathy, socializing and conversation.

I have noted that many of the partners of men (and sometimes women) with AS have been at the other end of the social and empathy continuum. They are intuitive experts in theory of mind, namely understanding and empathizing with someone else's perspective. They are naturally gifted in the ability to understand the world as experienced by the person with AS, much more than a person of average theory of mind abilities. They are understanding and sympathetic, and provide guidance for their partner in social situations. Indeed, these are the characteristics that adults with AS recognize that they need and would find desirable in a partner. They will actively seek a partner with intuitive social knowledge who can be a social interpreter and is naturally nurturing, socially able and maternal. However, while a socially insightful and empathic partner may understand the perspective of the person with AS, the person with AS is usually unable to understand the perspective of their typical partner.

The attractiveness of a man with AS in a prospective relationship can be enhanced by intellectual ability, career prospects and degree of attentiveness during courtship, although the attentiveness could be perceived by others as almost obsessive. The person's history of special interests is viewed as typical of many men and initially endearing. The partner may share some of the enthusiasm for the interest, for example learning foreign languages or wine tasting.

The person can be admired for speaking his mind, even if the comments may be perceived as offensive by others, due to his strong sense of social justice and clear moral beliefs. The fact that he may not be "macho" or wish to spend time with other men can also be appealing for some women. The person with AS can be a late developer in terms of relationship experiences; there is no previous relationship baggage. I have also noticed that many women have described to me how their partner with AS resembled their father. Having a parent with the signs of AS may have helped determine their choice of partner as an adult.

Women with AS

What are the characteristics that men find attractive in a woman with AS? The attributes can be similar to the characteristics that women find appealing in a man with AS, especially the degree of attentiveness. The woman's social immaturity may be appealing to those men who have natural paternal and compassionate qualities. There can be an appreciation of her physical attractiveness and admiration for her talents and abilities. Unfortunately, women (and sometimes men) with AS are not very good at character judgments or identifying relationship predators. Women with AS often have low self-esteem, which can affect their choice of partner in a relationship. They can be the victim of various forms of abuse. As a female client explained to me: "I set my expectations very low and as a result gravitated toward abusive people."

Problems in long-term relationships

Oscar Wilde suggested that "women love men for their defects," but defects that were initially attractive can become a problem in a long-term relationship. The courtship may not provide an indication of the problems that can develop later in the relationship. Hans Asperger stated: "Many of those who do marry, show tensions and problems in their marriage" (Asperger 1944). Some partners have explained that the real persona became apparent only after they were married.

The initial optimism that the partner with AS will become more motivated and able to socialize and develop empathy and the ability to meet their partner's need for affection and intimacy can gradually dissolve into despair that these abilities are not going to be achieved easily, if at all. A common problem for the non-AS partner is feeling lonely. People with AS can be content with their own company for long periods of time.

Conversations may be few and the opinion of the person with AS is that a conversation is primarily to exchange practical information. They may not notice, recall or want to talk about information of significance to their partner.

In a successful relationship there is the expectation of regular expressions of love and affection. Chris Slater-Walker, a married man with AS, explained that:

> I have an enormous difficulty with the verbal expression of affection. It is not just a case of feeling embarrassed or self-conscious with it. I understand that this may be difficult for anyone else to understand, but it takes a great deal of effort of will to tell my wife how I feel about her. (Slater-Walker and Slater-Walker 2002, p.89)

His wife Gisela added her comments regarding her husband's infrequent words and gestures that communicate feelings of love and affection:

> Chris told me once that he loved me. I have since discovered that it is not necessary for the person with AS to repeat these small intimacies that are frequently part of a relationship; the fact has been stated once, and that is enough. (Slater-Walker and Slater-Walker 2002, p.99)

The non-AS partner can suffer affection deprivation, which can be a contributory factor to developing low self-esteem and depression. A survey of women who had a partner with AS included the question, "Does your partner love you?", to which 50 percent replied, "I don't know" (Jacobs 2006). What is often conspicuously missing in the relationship are daily expressions of love for the other person. For the person with AS, this frequent reiteration of the obvious or known facts is illogical and unnecessary.

During moments of personal distress, when empathy and words and gestures of affection would be anticipated as a means of emotional repair, the typical partner may be left alone to "get over it." This is not a callous act. For the partner with AS, the most effective emotional repair mechanism is often solitude, and he or she assumes this is the most effective emotional repair mechanism for his or her partner. The partner with AS may also not know what to do, or may choose to do nothing, because of a fear of doing something that could make the situation worse.

Partners have reported problems with sexual knowledge and intimacy. Adults with AS tend to be at the extremes of sexual knowledge, having either remarkably little information on sexuality and few sexual experiences, or a great deal of knowledge from pornography or being sexually abused. Partners with AS tend not to be naturally skilled in the art of romance, foreplay and sensuous touch.

Sensory sensitivity in general and tactile sensitivity in particular can affect both everyday and sexual relationships. An intense sensitivity to specific aromas can affect the tolerance of perfumes and thus proximity to other people. Due to tactile sensitivity, gestures of reassurance or affection, for example a touch on the forearm or a hug, can be perceived as an overwhelming, restricting and unpleasant sensation. The typical partner may resent the obvious lack of enjoyment in response to affectionate touch and the avoidance of tactile experiences during more intimate sensual or sexual moments. The aversion to touch is due to problems with sensory perception rather than a lack of commitment to the relationship. The sexual script of the person with AS can be described by their partner as rigid, repetitive and unimaginative with a relative lack of sexual desire.

Having a relationship with a person with AS can affect the partner's mental health. A survey of the mental and physical health of couples where the male partner in the relationship had AS indicates that the relationship has very different health effects for each partner (Aston 2003). Men with AS stated that their mental and physical health had greatly improved due to being in a long-term relationship. They were less stressed than when single and the relationship brought considerable personal satisfaction. This was in contrast to their partners, who reported that their mental health had deteriorated due to the relationship. They described feeling emotionally neglected and physically exhausted and depressed.

They may resent their partner for being emotionally inarticulate and feel trapped by the relationship. The physical exhaustion can result from the partner with AS not sharing the workload at home for domestic chores or caring for children. Adults with AS can have organizational problems such that their partner has to be an "executive secretary," taking responsibility for budgeting and planning. In modern western society we have tended to replace the terms husband and wife with the word partner. Women today expect their partner not only to share the responsibilities but also to be their best friend and provide emotional as well as practical and financial support. Sharing and being a best friend are not attributes that come easily for the person with AS.

Strategies to improve relationship skills

People with AS will require guidance in relationship skills at each point on the relationship continuum and probably throughout their lives. Children may need guidance from a speech and language therapist in the art of conversation, and strategies to improve friendship skills throughout the school years from a teacher or psychologist. The development of friendship and relationship skills must be a priority for educational services that support a child with AS, as greater maturity and ability in friendship skills will improve self-esteem, reduce incidents of being teased or bullied, lay the foundations for adult relationship skills and encourage teamwork abilities for successful employment (Attwood 2006). Adolescents will need accurate information on attraction, the dating game and sexuality. While this information is easily available for typical teenagers, often from friends, parents, classroom programs and gradual experience, this information and experience may not be as easily available for a teenager with AS. The lack of peer guidance, group discussion and practice will inhibit the development of relationship skills. Fortunately, we now have programs on relationships and sexuality specifically designed for adolescents with AS (Hénault 2005), advice from fellow teenagers with AS (Jackson 2002). In addition, some family planning organizations are developing resource material and expertise in teaching relationship skills to adolescents and young adults with AS. The education ranges from improving knowledge on dating etiquette and dress sense to ways to identify and avoid sexual predators. A valuable strategy is to have a socially perceptive friend or relative meet a prospective date to determine whether the person appears to be of good character, before developing a relationship.

Young adults will need encouragement to make acquaintances and friends. This can include joining a hobby or interest group that is associated with a special interest, such as attending a *Star Trek* or *Dr. Who* convention, or an application of a talent, such as a natural ability with animals and joining an animal protection group. There can be opportunities to make friends at community activities such as a local choir, taking a class or renewing old acquaintances. It may be wise to avoid trying to meet people at pubs and clubs due to the risk of meeting a relationship predator, access to alcohol and drugs, and the practical difficulty of trying to have a conversation in a noisy and crowded environment. Local AS support groups for parents have established support groups for young adults with AS. This can provide an opportunity for someone to address the group and provide discussion and guidance in relationships. The group can also be an opportunity for relationships to develop between group members. The relationship that developed between Jerry and Mary, two adults with AS who met at a support group in Los Angeles, has been the subject of a film, *Mozart and the Whale* (2005), and a book (Newport and Newport 2007). Some adults with AS have used the internet and dating agencies to meet people, but this method of introduction can also be used by relationship predators and an adult with AS needs to be aware of relationship risks using this strategy.

Do all individuals with an autism spectrum disorder seek a partner?

I have noted that adults who had clear signs of autism in early childhood (that is, language delay, learning difficulties and avoidance of social situations), and who in later childhood progressed to a description of high functioning autism, are often less motivated to seek a long-term relationship. They are more likely to be content with solitude and celibacy and having acquaintances rather than friends. A sense of self-identity and personal value is achieved by having a successful career and being independent. Temple Grandin (1995) is a well-known example. Some adults with AS have also decided not to seek an intimate relationship with someone for sensible reasons when one considers the characteristics of AS. Jennifer explained her rationale: "Can I deal with sharing a house with someone who might possibly touch my model airplane collection?" and "Model airplanes do not decide that they want to be built by someone else who is more attractive or less needy" (Myers 2006, pp.109, 112). Her life does include moments of intense personal satisfaction. She states: "I can assure you that being in love and having special interests are much the same feeling" (Myers 2006, p.112).

Not having a relationship can be a positive choice for some adults with AS who enjoy pursuing their special interests, such as wildlife photography or a career in information technology. They are content not to be swept away by the cultural belief that marriage or a long-term relationship are the only ways to achieve happiness.

What makes a successful long-term relationship?

When a person with AS is in a long-term relationship, clinical and relationship counseling experience suggests that there are three requisites for both parties to enjoy and benefit from the relationship (Aston 2003). The first requisite is that both partners acknowledge the diagnosis. Assuming the partner with AS has not been given a diagnosis in childhood, the non-AS partner is usually the first to recognize the signs of AS. The signs may have been recognized from information on AS in the media or a relative (sometimes a child of the relationship) being diagnosed. AS often occurs within and between family generations.

Recognition that a partner has AS can be a revelation. There is now an explanation for behaviors that have been confusing or infuriating. The non-AS partner's emotions, circumstances and experiences are finally validated. However, his or her acknowledging the diagnosis and becoming knowledgeable about the nature of

AS can be the end of hope that the AS partner will easily achieve improved relationship skills and will acquire insight into someone's thoughts and feelings. The acceptance of the diagnosis is also important for AS partners to recognize their relationship strengths and weaknesses and relationship skills that need improvement.

The second requisite is for both partners to be motivated to acquire and apply strategies to improve the quality of the relationship and to change their behavior, abilities and routines. There is usually greater motivation and flexibility in adapting to change from the non-AS partner, who already has a good foundation of relationship skills and is more adaptable to change. The partner with AS may be more content than his or her partner with the existing relationship pattern and may not recognize there will be sufficient benefits to justify a change in the relationship.

The third requisite is access to relationship counseling, modified to accommodate the profile of abilities and relationship experiences of the partner with AS, with a counselor knowledgeable in how AS affects a relationship. Conventional relationship counseling with a counselor who is not knowledgeable about AS is unlikely to be successful. A survey of couples with one of the partners having AS found that the majority were dissatisfied with the relationship counseling they received (Aston 2003). They reported feeling misunderstood and their problems disbelieved or trivialized.

There is literature that provides guidance on relationships written by couples with one partner who has AS, and by specialists in AS (Aston 2003; Attwood 2006; Edmonds and Worton 2005; Jacobs 2006; Lawson 2005; Rodman 2003; Slater-Walker and Slater-Walker 2002; Stanford 2003). There are also internet-based support groups such as ASPIRES (www.aspires-relationships.com). In recent years there has been the development of local support groups, such as ASPIA (www.aspia.org.au) in Sydney, Australia, specifically for partners, to provide practical and emotional support.

There are constructive strategies to assist non-AS partners, who can feel that they are gradually absorbing the characteristics of AS in their own personalities. The development of a network of friends can reduce the sense of isolation, and he or she may choose to participate in social occasions without the presence and responsibility for a partner with AS, who can be a social liability rather than asset. A friend or relative who has the intuitive ability to provide empathy and repair emotions can become a supportive soul mate, and an occasional escape or holiday with friends can provide an opportunity to regain confidence in social abilities and enjoy social rapport.

Parenting

When the relationship evolves into being parents, the partner and now parent with AS often has little understanding of the needs and behavior of children (Attwood 2006; Snyder 2006). Having a parent with AS can sometimes cause children to feel that they are "invisible" or a nuisance and deprived of the acceptance, reassurance, encouragement and affection that they need. The child feels noticed and valued only for his or her academic achievements and can be embarrassed by the behavior of a parent with AS in public and when inviting friends home. The non-AS parent has to compensate for the lack of parenting skills of his or her partner, and can feel like and function as a single parent. They may have to explain their partner's behavior to the child to prevent resentment, and mediate in disputes. They also have to provide guidance and encouragement to the parent with AS regarding what a parent is expected to do and say in order to have a successful relationship with their children. When one of the children has AS, there can be either a natural attachment or antagonism between the parent with AS and the child who has the same diagnosis. Parents recognize the daily challenges faced by the child from their own experiences and become social mentors. This may be an ideal relationship between parent and child, but often the enforced proximity of two inflexible and controlling characters with AS can lead to animosity and arguments. A metaphor for the relationship between a parent and child with AS is the poles of two magnets that either attract or repel each other.

Developing new strategies for successful relationships

We know that adults with AS have considerable difficulty progressing along the relationship continuum, but we lack research that provides quantitative and qualitative data on the relationship abilities, circumstances and experiences of adolescents and adults with AS. Research on the friendship abilities of children with AS has been reviewed (Attwood 2006), but very little research on boyfriend and girlfriend relationships and sexuality. Clinicians who specialize in relationship counseling suggest that the sexual profile of adults with AS is different from typical adults in terms of lower body image and fewer sexual experiences, although sexual interest usually develops at the same time as it does in adolescent peers. There can also be a more liberal attitude to sexual diversity such as homosexuality and bisexuality, and a rich fantasy life and sexual imagery. There may be less concern regarding age and cultural differences in a relationship. However, clinical impressions need to be substantiated by research that includes the administration of standardized assessments for relationship abilities and sexuality (Hénault and Attwood 2002).

We also need to develop and evaluate strategies to improve relationship skills. Much as cognitive behavior therapy has been modified to accommodate the unusual profile of abilities and experiences of people with AS, modifications will also be needed for conventional relationship education and counseling programs. There is a growing demand for access to professionals who are able to provide guidance for people with AS who are seeking a relationship and those who want to improve an existing relationship. This is due to the increasing number of people being diagnosed with Asperger syndrome and the knowledge from research studies that the same characteristics, although to a lesser degree, can be identified in the relatives of someone with AS (Bailey *et al.* 1998; Cederlund and Gillberg 2004; Volkmar, Klin and Pauls 1998). Clinicians may diagnose a young child with AS and recognize a ghosting of the characteristics in a parent or grandparent. That family member may benefit from relationship education and counseling, which would help the whole family.

Acknowledgments

We would like to thank Tony Attwood for his enthusiasm and encouragement while we were writing this book, as well as his contribution of the Foreword, which highlights his work with NS-ASD couples.

We are grateful to all the NS partners who shared with us in our group meetings and in individual correspondence and verbal exchanges. Often they had to drive hundreds of miles and make elaborate arrangements for children and family members in order to attend meetings and groups. They are an exceptional group of individuals who encouraged us to share their stories in the spirit of supporting and helping others. Many of them are still in contact with us and their fellow NS spouses through regional meetings, correspondence and an internet chat group. You are a remarkable group.

Special thanks to Aimee Polk and Dr. Kevin Mooney for sharing their perspectives and editing suggestions. Aimee is a regular at our spouse group meetings. Kevin is Susan Moreno's former graduate school professor and mentor.

Colleagues from MAAP Services for Autism, Asperger syndrome, and PDD, Inc., and the Indiana Resource Center for Autism must also be thanked. Special thanks go to Cathy Pratt, the director of the Indiana Resource Center for Autism, Brenda Smith Myles from the MAAP Advisory Board, Stephen Shore of MAAP's Board of Directors and author Kristi Sakai for their encouragement and belief in this book. Thanks also to Kirsten McBride and Keith Myles for their many helpful suggestions.

Thanks to the great crew at Jessica Kingsley Publishers, especially Jessica herself, for their encouragement and expertise.

Finally, we acknowledge and thank our spouses, Marco, Phil and Christian, who offered their support for this project.

Preface

This book is written for those in a relationship who are seeking understanding, help and hope for a successful relationship with someone who has been diagnosed with an autism spectrum disorder (ASD) or is suspected of having Asperger syndrome (AS), autism or pervasive developmental disorder-not otherwise specified (PDD-NOS). (Though we do not explain the diagnostic criteria directly, the characteristics commonly encountered by an individual on the autism spectrum are discussed.)

The non-spectrum (NS) partners who share their stories are all eager to help and support those in similar relationships. They represent various backgrounds, income levels and lengths of relationship. In most cases, they made the initial contact with us in an effort to seek understanding and help by attending our workshops, or by email, written or phone exchanges.

Many fear their partners with an ASD will suffer the loss of a job, friends or status within their communities, should their challenge be exposed. Therefore, we have taken great care to disguise situations and identities, without skewing the validity of the information.

We are honored that Tony Attwood, one of the world's foremost authorities on autism spectrum disorders, prolific author and practicing clinical psychologist, has volunteered his professional experience on this subject within our book. His foreword, "Relationship Problems of Adults with Asperger Syndrome," sets the context for the rest of the book. We think you will find that his words are a wonderful introduction to what follows. As we've heard so often from individuals on the spectrum and their families, "Tony really *gets* it!"

This book is meant to help non-spectrum spouses as they move along their journey. We hope it will reveal to the partner on the spectrum the experiences and perspectives of the NS partner. There are no formulas for success. Each couple faces unique challenges and triumphs. Finally, we hope this book empowers you to move in the direction that is best for you and your relationship.

Introduction

Until the mid to late 1990s, the common belief in the United States was that men and women on the autism spectrum did not get married. Most families were told by professionals that their sons and daughters on the autism spectrum would not be interested in intimate relationships. It was speculated that because of the social and communication differences inherent in the condition, even in the unlikely case that a person on the autism spectrum *was* interested, he or she would not be able to pursue a relationship with the opposite sex.

As an example, Temple Grandin, PhD—who wrote one of the first books about living as an individual with autism and is internationally known as both a livestock engineer and a speaker on autism, and recently as the subject of an Emmy award winning documentary (*Temple Grandin*, HBO Productions, 2010)—relates that her life is very full with her important pursuits and her work and that she is not interested in a romantic relationship. Such personal relationships to her are totally confusing and beyond her interest or needs.

Since Temple Grandin is one of the most recognized names worldwide in terms of being a successful and independent person with autism, many people assume that how Temple feels on an issue is how a majority of people with autism feel about that issue. This stereotyping of any category of person is usually inaccurate. For instance, all Italians love opera; or all Germans love beer; or all short stature people have Napoleonic complexes.

No wonder, then, that until recently, most families and the general public have failed to recognize the possibility that individuals with an autism spectrum disorder might be interested in pursuing intimate relationships. Yet we authors have all heard the heart-wrenching struggles of people with an ASD who long to find a life partner and true romance.

Fortunately these days, a larger number of people have now realized that not all ASD individuals are of the same opinion as Dr. Grandin. This is largely due to movies like *Mozart and the Whale* (2005), which is based on Jerry and Mary Newport's relationship (see Newport and Newport 2007). Another important factor in this enlightenment is a growing interest in autism spectrum challenges from the world's media.

Some ASD individuals pursue intimate relationships. Indeed, not only do such relationships exist, but also they are becoming more common than previously believed. (Autism spectrum disorder has the highest incidence rate in the United States.)[1] Unfortunately, little is known about how these relationships work when they are successful, since most information on the subject is just now emerging and not presently supported by sociological research. For the needs of both partners to be met, many challenges must be addressed.

This book is unique in presenting information gathered from a large number of spouses in an effort to shed light on these often misunderstood partnerships. The authors have interviewed and consulted with an estimated 100-plus individuals not on the autism spectrum (or NS, short for "non-spectrum") who live with and love someone with an ASD. We have tried to portray the reality of their relationships, noting the challenges and the gifts in their day-to-day lives. Also included are strategies used by NS partners to sustain and improve their relationships.

What this book doesn't include is ASD-ASD partnerships, same-sex partnerships and NS men living with ASD women, as these couples were not participants. There are other resources, notably the Global and Regional Asperger Syndrome Partnership (GRASP) (see Useful Resources section) that do address ASD-ASD relationships and their specific idiosyncrasies. Zosia Zaks is a woman with an

---

1   Studies of ASD prevalence in the United States during the 1990s have identified rates of 2.0–7.0 per 1,000 children, a greater than tenfold increase from rates of 0.1–0.4 per 1,000 children identified during the 1980s. Young Shin Kim of Yale Child Studies Center *et al.* have recently reported a prevalence rate (actual count of children aged 7 to 12 in Korea) of 1 in 38. However, this has yet to be replicated in the US.

ASD who has a successful same-sex marriage. She has written about her life and gives advice on the GRASP website, in articles and in her book, *Life and Love: Positive Strategies for Autistic Adults* (Zaks 2006). It is our hope that our book will encourage future works to address the needs of people in these other situations.

As authors, none of us claims to have a perfect marriage or to be a marriage counselor. However, we have relevant professional and personal experience. Marci Wheeler has a master's degree in social work and has worked in the disability field since 1978. She has been married to a man with high-functioning autism since 1983 and has raised three children with him. Susan Moreno has a master's degree in applied behavioral science with a strong counseling component, and has conducted numerous workshops for NS partners. She is the parent of a daughter with autism and in 1984 founded MAAP (More Advanced individuals with Autism, Asperger syndrome and PDD-NOS) Services for Autism and Asperger Syndrome, an organization that connects parents, professionals, extended family and individuals with ASDs and gives information and support. Kealah Parkinson is a communications coach whose specialty is in fostering clear communication in the cognitively challenged brain, including those clients with mental illness and developmental disorders. She married into a family with autism, and so has a personal investment in the success of ASD individuals.

We hope that by sharing the many experiences of NS spouses, we will give readers a better understanding of NS-ASD partnerships and what experiences NS partners have found to be helpful in better understanding themselves and their partners, and in enriching their relationships.

As in any other marriage, there is a divorce rate. This book is not expected to be a cure-all. Even within the group of spouses with whom we have interacted, there were instances of relationships changing or ending. We feel it's important for NS partners to use a wide variety of resources. One way to do that is to visit the OASIS (Online Asperger Syndrome Information and Support) website (www.aspergersyndrome.org) and use their forums. Also, see the Useful Resources section and the Bibliography in this book.

Notes to the reader

Except for rare examples, the pronoun "he" will be used when referring to the partner on the autism spectrum. This is because the overwhelming majority of NS partners who shared their experiences with us were females in relationships with a male partner. Perhaps this is because there are so many more men than women diagnosed on the autism spectrum. It may also be because women tend to want to discuss marital issues more openly than men.

Although we acknowledge and respect "people first" language, for ease of reading, the abbreviation "NS (non-spectrum) partner" will be used, instead of the often cumbersome "partner not on the autism spectrum" or other similar person-first phrases. For the same reason, the abbreviation "ASD partner" is generally substituted when referring to the partner with Asperger syndrome or with another diagnosis on the autism spectrum. (We prefer the terms "challenge" or "difference," rather than "disorder," and will use those terms also.)

In some of the examples shared in this book, the ASD individual has not been formally diagnosed. In such cases, another family member has usually been diagnosed and the characteristics of the diagnosed individual have led to an informal diagnosis (by the ASD individual and/or the NS partner). Further, in many cases at the start of marriage, the NS spouses did not know that they were in a relationship with a person with any form of exceptionality, although most realized that their partners were unconventional. This likely led to unique communication challenges and other barriers to success in the relationship—issues that may not be encountered in the same way by those who willingly and knowingly enter relationships with ASD partners who accept and disclose their diagnoses.

Chapter 1

Internal Issues for Non-Spectrum Partners

When an NS partner seeks support from a friend or professional, she may be highly emotional. Many spouses feel great relief and even validation when they discover that their partners are on the autism spectrum. For others, feelings of anger, anxiety and grief are typical and are usually the first to surface. It is important for NS partners to share their unique lives with someone who understands, as their emotional pain can otherwise seem unbearable. So, how do these relationships begin?

Courtship

Each ASD-NS courtship is as different as each couple involved in courting. However, in many cases—based both on our research and on that done by Tony Attwood and other experts—there is a distinctly common pattern that occurs.

Very frequently, these couples seek out partners who are in many ways their opposites. The ASD partners are looking for socially outgoing, creative and even verbally oriented mates, while their NS partners are seeking quiet and intelligent mates to complement them. Great differences in age and cultural background are often present as well. Often there is an initial attraction that's comfortable in many ways and highly flattering in others, because the ASD partner is in some ways a chameleon, adapting to social situations as best as possible without showing his true colors to avoid feeling vulnerable. For instance, he might go to parties to be closer to his new love, even though he finds it painful to socialize. The NS partner, without realizing it, has become a special interest to her significant other. (See Chapter 6 for more on special interests.) Another noted similarity was that the great majority of these couples married within a year after the beginning of dating.

Marci and Phil met while living at the same rooming house near the Indiana University (IU) campus in Bloomington, Indiana. Marci, an IU graduate, was working and planning to attend graduate school and Phil had returned to IU to complete his undergraduate degree. Marci was attracted to Phil's intellect and his commitment to his daughter from a first marriage. She also appreciated his views of the world, which were much more "radical" than those of most men from the Midwest that she had met. Initially they were friends who hung out and had fun and conversation on the front porch along with a group of others who lived in the rooming house. As Marci finalized plans for graduate school in a different city, they realized their strong feelings for each other.

Jane and Trevor met at the wedding of a mutual friend. Jane was attracted to Trevor's obvious intellect and humor, which put her instantly at ease. They felt as though they had always been friends. They ended up spending much of the weekend together. They dated for less than a year and quickly had their first child, bought a house in a suburb of Indianapolis and seemed to have a wonderful future ahead.

In the case of Pam and Jim, Pam liked his steady ways and his religious beliefs coincided with hers. Jim was also very smart and good looking.

In Kaye's case, her ASD partner Pete seemed like a real social butterfly. The two met at a networking function and quickly became close friends, moving into a romantic relationship after just a few months. Over the next year, Pete and Kaye went to parties, weddings, networking functions and concerts, and even went dancing at clubs. They frequently met up with friends (mostly Kaye's) and often stayed out late.

Kaye was drawn to Pete's innate shyness and supreme intelligence. As the oldest of several children born to young parents, she is nurturing, which Pete benefits from and enjoys. Both grew up in homes with depression and hostility from one or both parents, and so learned to draw into themselves emotionally in various ways.

They married after less than two years of dating. Kaye says that Pete's personality "completely changed" in a matter of a few weeks after marriage. She now goes alone or with friends to most social functions, counting on Pete only for family events.

Sheila was first attracted to Harry's great knowledge of history, his excellent manners and his excessive attention towards her. They would go to stores to browse. If she showed interest in something, he would often buy it when she was looking elsewhere and surprise her with it on the way home. He often arrived for dates with flowers or a nice wine. He picked up her dry cleaning for her and ran any errands she needed. He loved to dance and so did she. He seemed to have a great sense of fun. His friends from work regarded him highly and loved his sense of humor. They were married less than a year after meeting.

For a more detailed profile of these couples, as well as five others, please see Appendix III.

During the courtships of the couples we highlight in this book, intimacy was achieved at various levels. Intimacy must begin in order for courtship to progress to establishing a more solid relationship. However, intimacy is a common area that can abruptly change for couples where one partner is on the autism spectrum. This can happen in any number of ways. Some of the examples we heard included the sudden end to cuddling or foreplay. In extreme cases, sexual activity ceased altogether. A few partners reported that some improvement in sexual activity occurred when they were able to gradually shift their ASD husbands' routines during intimacy toward the NS wives' own preferences.

In almost every case in the interviews we conducted, NS spouses were surprised when their husbands suddenly and often permanently stopped attending social events with them or abruptly changed in some other way after marriage. In some cases, changes occurred after moving in together, becoming engaged or otherwise denoting the relationship as lasting and valuable.

Acknowledgment of ASD differences

When speaking with many NS partners in depth, we find that nearly half share that their partner has not been diagnosed with autism, Asperger syndrome or PDD-NOS. Further, among those non-diagnosed partnerships, over 50 percent of the NS partners have not disclosed their partner's challenges with family, friends, employers or even sometimes their partner! Some have only touched on the subject for fear that a discussion would traumatize or frighten the partner, damage the relationship or harm the partner's professional or social standing.

Why, then, do we include these women in our book? They and their life profiles are completely consistent with those women whose husbands *have* been formally diagnosed. Kealah Parkinson has been actively facilitating a spousal support group for NS partners both online and in person. Both Susan Moreno and Marci Wheeler have been working in the field of autism and Asperger syndrome for over 50 years combined, and through their personal and professional experiences, clearly recognize the behaviors and symptoms of an ASD in the relationships of those we interviewed for the book. We have, in fact, excluded some first-person accounts, because we don't believe the husband described by the spouse is on the spectrum. In one instance, a wife contacted Susan Moreno and said, "I'm certain my husband has autism because he never listens to me and refuses to pick up around the house!" There is a difference between an unhappy marriage between non-spectrum people and a different marriage of someone with an autism spectrum challenge and someone who is not on the spectrum. Not listening is not a criterion for diagnosis. If that were true, more than half of the world's marriages would be NS-ASD!

Some NS women who have contacted us have shared that after marriage and moving in together, they experience an uncomfortable change in their ASD mate. They feel something is "missing." Their ASD spouse does not seem to adapt well to interacting on a 24/7 basis. The ASD partner is described as either "ignoring" the NS partner and/or expecting the NS partner to act in a certain way. Perhaps a theory about the differences between male vs. female brains applies or possibly the explanation goes beyond these theories.

Simon Baron-Cohen, clinical psychologist, researcher and professor at Cambridge University, and director of the Autism Research Centre in the UK, has studied individuals with autism spectrum disorders for many years. He is credited with the theory that autism spectrum disorders are an extreme manifestation of the male brain. Baron-Cohen describes the male brain as tending toward being systematic, mechanical and logical in approaching the world of both objects and people. The result is a tendency to treat people as if they are logical systems or machines. The "extreme" male brain treats people as if they are machines with no feelings or thoughts of their own (Baron-Cohen 2004b).

This view has its controversy but provides an interesting and, some would say, helpful way to explain the interpersonal skills of someone on the autism spectrum vs. a "typical" male. Is this what the NS wives were noticing for the first time—an "extreme" male brain that was not as apparent before they were married?

In many cases, the NS partners say that their spouses have *traits* of ASD but not the full, classic set of characteristics, leading to speculation that the challenged partner likely has PDD-NOS. In other words, while some symptoms of ASD may be present, they don't seem to have all three of the essential areas of challenge that are required for an autism or Asperger syndrome diagnosis: communication anomalies, problems with reciprocal social interaction and insistence on sameness. Lacking one of the three criteria is part of the diagnosis of PDD-NOS.

The NS spouse often describes characteristics such as little interest in social relationships, inappropriate responses in social situations, literal interpretation of language and preoccupation with a hobby that takes an excessive amount of time and/or money. These concerns may seem to be an issue only at home but not in the community or at their job. In other cases, they permeate all aspects of life: family, community and job.

NS partners may be aware that people considered high on the autism spectrum can be very precocious and charming, especially when motivation is high and needed supports are in place. Some NS partners insist that their concerns remain highly confidential since the ASD partners may be in jeopardy of losing their jobs and status in the community. Several of these spouses hold high-paying jobs of high status within their community, including accountants, engineers, rabbis, ministers, physicians or various positions within the field of information technology. Specifically, NS partners fear that disclosure may mean loss of their partners' self-confidence, loss of a job or loss of prestige at work.

Are these successfully employed ASD partners "disabled," or are they people with strong traits associated with a disability? What is the definition of "disability," especially when discussing ASDs?

If the challenges a person faces in society perpetually impair his ability to (a) maintain long-term friendships (close friendships that last longer than one year and involve regular contact *on a voluntary basis* on the part of both parties), (b) safely navigate the community and (c) maintain long-term employment with compensation allowing him to live independently without further financial assistance, most would suggest this individual is at least partially disabled. Many NS partners note that their partner has a few characteristics of a disability on the autism spectrum but, at the same time, has great compensatory abilities. These compensatory abilities often serve to make the ASD partner's behavior even more perplexing to the NS partner.

Sheila told us:

> It is as though Harry can play the part of an affable guest at a party. When we were dating, all I saw was that act. But when we were married, I saw him *all* the time at *all* the parties. That is when I saw through his act. When going to a party or returning, he is sometimes a complete mess –

threatening not to go or saying, "never again." When this happens before a social event or when I suspect there will be an aftermath, the effort on my part to act as if all is well at the event is exhausting.

When Sheila first suspected that Harry might be on the spectrum, they had already been married for over 20 years. As the truth began to dawn on her, she wanted to confide in her NS son, who was away at college. She phoned him and said she needed to talk to him about something important. She confided that she thought Harry might have an ASD. Her son's reply was, "Well, DUH, Mom!" She asked why he said that, and he told her he'd realized it years before and was surprised that she hadn't. The true shock came when she told her ASD son, who by then was an adult. His reply was, "I was pretty sure, but I thought you knew."

While all NS-ASD relationships are unique and complex, the extent of the partner's traits and/or disability plays a major role.

One NS spouse told us:

I'm pretty sure that Jack is on the spectrum, as he has most of the characteristics of our ASD son. But he is funny, reliable and kind. I don't feel the need to confront him with my suspicions or insist on a diagnosis. I just know that he isn't ever going to have spontaneous fun or deep conversations with me.

Receiving a diagnosis and getting information about autism spectrum disorders can be a great relief for both the NS and ASD partners. There may still be frustration, but now there is a reason for what was once seen as "illogical behavior" and some possible strategies to make changes and cope.

Once the NS partner understands that the ASD person feels that he *can't* change a comforting routine or deal with applying for jobs, she can begin making constructive plans to help her partner. And for his part, the ASD partner can begin to feel that he is not weird" and that there are others like him in the world who share a life experience similar to his.

It is most helpful when both partners acknowledge the characteristics of ASD and how they manifest in the partner, whether or not there is a formal diagnosis. NS partners feel less stress when there is acknowledgment and interest by the ASD partner in understanding ASDs and how the characteristics affect him. Having others to talk with who understand is extremely important to the majority of the NS spouses we heard from. This helps relieve the feeling of isolation, as does having activities with others. It is important to be socially connected with others. This often means finding others to share activities with and excusing the ASD partner from frequent social expectations. When both partners are committed to work *together*, there are strategies mentioned throughout that can help make social events easier and sometimes enjoyable for the ASD partner.

Not disclosing the partner's challenges can lead to a very lonely journey for the NS partners. The rest of this chapter describes the most common issues of concern and distress NS partners consistently and continually share with us: isolation, frustration and grief.

Isolation

A sense of isolation in an NS-ASD relationship is common. Sometimes the isolation is self-imposed, stemming from a desire to avoid a display of the ASD partner's lack of social skills to family and friends. Not knowing anyone who understands or who will continue to listen to the NS partner's ongoing concerns results in further isolation. After all, it is hard for others to understand why one puts up with stomping around, slamming of doors or unkind remarks when dinner is not ready at exactly 6 o'clock every night, whenever a new recipe is served or when something else unexpected happens.

Outsiders can judge someone with these behaviors as very demanding and controlling and feel uncomfortable witnessing a display of "rude" behavior. Other outsiders often feel the need to give advice, suggesting that the NS spouse leave the relationship if the spouse cannot control himself. Over time, these people may no longer accept or offer invitations to the NS-ASD couple. As we will see in Chapter 9 in the discussion of Cassandra syndrome, some outsiders often judge the NS spouse as a shrew who nags at her sweet spouse.

> NS Sara shared how her ASD husband, Josh, ruined a small informal dinner party she had by commenting in a loud angry voice that they could not serve the pumpkin pie that guests brought because they had brought flavored whipped cream. He then went on to ask why they hadn't brought the "regular whipped cream." After a few more of these incidents, it wasn't long before Sara gave up on inviting other couples to their home.

Most of the NS partners interviewed shared feelings of dread and exhaustion when contemplating and/or preparing for social occasions involving their ASD partner. This was especially true when the event was to take place at home. It seems that the need for routine and control that many on the autism spectrum have makes hosting visitors more of a problem than when they socialize outside the house. The ASD partner feels that home is the only refuge he has, and it is very hard to let others invade this refuge and the routines that comfort him. Several spouses gave accounts of their ASD husband ignoring guests or "hurrying" them out as quickly as possible.

> NS Sheila said:
>
> > You can't imagine how terrified I can feel when I'm with family or others important to me and I know that Harry no longer is in control of his behavior. Sometimes I try to end the social event. Other times, I know that if I just leave, he won't be able to abuse me verbally in front of people who would then think badly of him.

NS Sara explained that most family gatherings for someone's birthday, or other special occasion, are difficult. Occasionally her husband Josh falls asleep on the couch and does not participate at all. Once, at her sister's house for her niece's birthday, he was very rude when he was served chocolate cake instead of white cake, yelling at Sara, "Can't you remember that I don't like chocolate?" She decided to leave because she knew from past experience that Josh, already agitated, would continue to yell a "script" of negative things at her until he calmed down.

Many NS spouses related how lonely and isolated they feel because they have no one (until they started meeting and networking with other NS spouses) with whom they can talk who understands.

One woman who has been married to a man with PDD-NOS for nearly ten years said:

> My girlfriends are always saying how lucky I am to have a spouse who is so good to me. They think I'm spoiled. What they don't know is how hard I work to make him always look good…to avoid letting them see him in one of his PDD-NOS moods.

Alternatively the NS partner may feel responsible for the problems and/or protective of the ASD partner, considering sharing with others as destructive or disloyal, and therefore choosing to confide in no one. A few NS spouses informed us that because there was a communication issue due to their ASD husbands' native language or culture, they felt it was up to them to accept and respect the differences in their husbands.

Since choosing to confide in no one also leads to isolation, it is important to talk with someone who understands. One way to do this is to get connected to other spouses with similar partners. This and other strategies will be discussed later. We'll sum up our discussion of isolation with a profound quote by an NS spouse: "Sometimes, you just cry alone in the dark."

The ASD partner often needs routines to help him through the day.

NS Sheila explained that every morning her husband Harry had to take a shower first thing upon rising, no matter what. This included a situation when he overslept and knew he would be late for a board of directors meeting at work. Before dressing and rushing off to the meeting, Harry insisted on taking his usual lengthy shower.

In addition to strict daily and perhaps weekly routines, such as mowing the lawn or shopping, there are often routines for traveling or attending recreational events and other activities that happen on a more limited basis.

NS Bonnie learned early in her marriage that ASD Brad has the same routine every Sunday morning. He eats eggs (the other items may vary somewhat), then he reads the paper and goes through the week's mail. When invited to spend the weekend at a lake cottage with another couple, Bonnie was eager to accept the invitation. They had spent the day with the couple at this cottage a couple of times before they were married, and Bonnie was excited at the opportunity to spend an entire weekend. She asked Brad, "Would you like to spend the weekend at Joe and Paula's lake cottage?" Brad exploded: "NO! Are you trying to ruin everything?" Bonnie had no idea what the problem was. She reluctantly turned down the invitation and asked Brad many questions. Brad finally answered, "You know I have to be here to look at the mail on Sunday mornings."

Many NS spouses relate that it is hard to accept invitations, because the ASD partner is not able to plan ahead and make a commitment to go. This causes many NS partners to decline invitations to avoid the possibility of their partners' last-minute changes in mood or behavior. This is likely due to the unpredictability of social events and their having a hard time adding a change to their routines.

ı says that Josh is often not able to commit to dinner at a
ıurant with another couple. One factor is the restaurant
chosen:

> He likes two familiar restaurants where he will agree to eat.
> When the restaurant chosen is not one of these two, it is
> hard for him to commit. He will have to wait until the last
> minute to decide. He says he just does not know how he will
> feel until about one or two hours before we are supposed to
> meet up with the others.

Often, Sara is frustrated because she enjoys spending time
with other couples and Josh typically provides only a vague
explanation: "I just don't feel like going out," or "I can't be
around people right now."

A significant number of NS spouses had similar stories. Rarely do
NS partners confide this hard-to-explain phenomenon to others,
which furthers their isolation.

> One NS partner told us she used the excuse of her partner
> getting a last-minute headache to avoid a social invitation
> if her ASD partner was angry or impatient. She used the
> excuse so many times that her friends began to wonder if her
> husband had an undiagnosed illness.

> NS Molly shared with the group that she is very careful to
> prepare Sam before social events, even making sure that he
> eats in advance in case there is no food he might tolerate.
> She explained that if Sam gets hungry and cannot eat
> something at a particular event (he is a very "picky" eater), he
> gets irritable and may say something inappropriate. Because
> he wants to be a good provider, sometimes Sam offers to
> get Molly's plate. However, he will select what *he* likes,
> seemingly oblivious to what Molly wants. To observers at
> the event who are unaware of the details of Sam and Molly's
> relationship, Sam seems very devoted to Molly, while she can

appear unappreciative when she goads him about his foo‹ choices for her.

Other spouses thought that because their ASD husbands were very intelligent, there was more they could do as wives to give them the benefit of the doubt with some of the problems. In some cases, friends and family blame the wives for the problems in the relationship. The husband can't be that bad, they reason, dismissing certain behaviors as a case of "boys will be boys." In other cases, the NS partner may stop confiding in others because she is told to stop talking about her problems or just to leave her ASD partner.

Some ASD partners who are obsessed with their NS spouses seem to outsiders to be the ideal husband. They see the ASD partner as very diligent and concerned for the NS partner's finances or health, or for the upkeep of her car, for example. They may hear of the frequent purchases of music or personal items such as perfume. As a result, the NS partner is repeatedly told how lucky she is. In reality, however, the NS spouse often feels smothered, controlled, trapped and unsupported emotionally. She would rather choose her own music or perfume or go together, as a couple, to make the selection.

It is hard to explain the ASD partner's obsession with a particular perfume or musical performer. All too frequently, the ASD spouse is choosing items because he wants only certain smells or sounds (this extends to other sensory preferences or obsessions, such as textures, styles and colors). What looks to others as a caring gesture (indeed the ASD partner himself may believe it is a caring way to look after his partner) may be very upsetting or seem false to the NS spouse.

A positive focus on the NS spouse can be a reflection of the ASD spouse's obsession or exaggerated concern for the "preservation" of the NS spouse in a state that will never change or to preserve the sensory environment of the home as determined by him. The NS spouse feels she has no one to talk to about this without making her husband look bad or making them both look crazy. This can further isolate the NS spouse.

In addition, the ASD partner frequently has obsessions that might, on the surface, look like a "typical" hobby, but are extreme and all-consuming. We have heard of a variety of these obsessions that tend to take extreme amounts of time and often money. Computers, army gear and reenactments, electronics, musical instruments, movies, chemistry and books on a particular topic were some of the hobbies described by the NS partners. When just about all the ASD partner's time and money are focused on a particular obsession of choice, there is not much time or money left for the couple to do other things together, such as socialize with others or dine out as a couple. This tends to be a pattern that plagues the majority of the NS spouses we heard from. This can also further isolate the NS partner from others.

When the obsession takes over all available time outside of work, it can be the last straw in an NS-ASD relationship.

> An NS spouse with whom we've had regular contact has told us about her husband's obsession with computer fantasy worlds. His obsession is science fiction. He dresses up in his *Star Trek* costume and locks himself in his room all night. She feels that his fantasy has become his reality. He has gone as long as three months without speaking a single word to her.

> Sheila says Harry is obsessed with germs and often spends time and energy cleaning and recleaning certain areas to make them germ-free. One afternoon, the couple's minister came to visit. During casual conversation, the minister leaned on the kitchen counter, to which Harry snapped, "Get the hell off of my clean counter!" Harry was so angry that he refused to join the minister in prayer at the end of his visit. Sheila was deeply embarrassed, but didn't know how to explain her husband's eccentricities.

Frustration

Early in the relationship, as newlyweds perhaps, partners feel a strong need to please each other. Routines and expectations get started, but seem impossible for the ASD partner to change. A frequent problem in an NS-ASD relationship is when the NS partner feels the need to change a routine and/or ask for more help from the ASD partner and meets extreme resistance. This can range from changing how a household chore is shared to joining a new social group at a place of worship or in the community.

> NS spouse Bonnie was frustrated when her ASD husband, Brad, did not want her to attend a women's Bible Study at their place of worship on Thursday nights, which was their movie date night together. This just seemed illogical to Bonnie. After all, the Bible Study was offered only one night a week, but the movie could be seen on other nights and at other times. Even though Bonnie pointed out these facts, Brad would not agree.

> Another NS partner, Sally, was frustrated with David because he would go bowling on Wednesday nights regardless of any other commitments that Sally felt were important. Once, a friend needed a ride to the hospital to visit his terminally ill brother, but David could not alter his plans to go bowling. Sally explained, "One night the bowling alley was closed due to a power outage, but David insisted in going over and sitting in the parking lot in case the power came on and they opened up for business."

Frustration mounts, and the NS partner gets anxious because there does not seem to be a logical explanation for the ASD partner's behavior. At the same time, the ASD partner often appears not to care or to be oblivious to his partner's distress. Often he retreats to be by himself or becomes more focused on his interests and/or routines as the tension escalates (an ASD coping mechanism the NS partner may not recognize). A vicious cycle continues; the rollercoaster pattern of the relationship takes off again in a negative direction.

Many NS partners shared a common frustration that their partners had lost or quit a job and appeared not to be trying very hard to find work. There were many excuses that the ASD spouses used for not looking for a job. These do not seem reasonable to the NS spouses and add to the feelings of frustration. For example, an ASD spouse may say that his medications make him so sleepy that he needs to sleep until 10 a.m. each day. Since that makes employment in a "standard" office situation impossible, he just refuses to look for any kind of an office job. Others say that it is a waste of time to apply for jobs because they never get the job anyway because they are not sure they have the skills, when in fact they are overqualified for the job. Still others refuse to interview for anything that they see as "educationally beneath" them, or as anything less than their ideal job—even if their idea of an ideal job is something unrealistic like being the manager of a garage or an orchestra conductor although they have no previous experience or skills in those areas.

Receiving a diagnosis and getting information about autism spectrum disorders can be a great relief for both the NS and ASD partners. There may still be frustration, but now there is a reason for the "illogical behavior" and some possible strategies to make changes and cope.

Once the NS partners understand that the ASD person feels that he *can't* change a comforting routine or deal with applying for jobs, they can begin making constructive plans to help their partner. And for his part, the ASD partner can begin to feel that he is not "weird" and that there are others like him in the world who share a life experience similar to his. Feeling these stressors, many NS spouses feel frustrated over appearing to those outside of the marriage as ungrateful and/or shrewish.

Grief

Many NS partners feel an overwhelming responsibility for the problems of communication, social life and generally "running interference" for their partner in their relationship and finding solutions to problems that seem never-ending. Feeling unable to change things, or at least not knowing how, can turn from frustration to grief. The NS partner may be grieving the loss of simple things like spontaneity in the relationship, or more serious issues like self-esteem, self-identity, emotional support—even hope.

As more and more unforeseen daily challenges appear, and it becomes evident that they will never stop coming, the NS spouse grieves for the relationship that she thought they were building that never will be. In other cases, the ASD partner becomes deeply depressed over economic and employment failures, both partners feeling frustrated and powerless to break the cycle. Sometimes wives report a feeling of grief over many "wasted years" spent trying to fix the relationship. They grieve that they cannot retrieve those years, especially if they are choosing to separate or divorce.

Lessons learned

- Find a professional who is knowledgeable about ASDs and can help with coping strategies for both spouses.

- Sometimes medical intervention for depression for one or both partners is needed. About three-fourths of the NS spouses informed us that they were being treated for depression or had been at some point in their marriage.

- Encourage your ASD spouse to seek a diagnosis if you think it will help him and you.

Chapter 2

Communication Differences

Communication is a core challenge for ASDs and one of the criteria for receiving a diagnosis. The overwhelming majority of NS spouses we interviewed shared that communication is the most serious problem in their relationships. A serious deficit of meaningful communication between any two individuals spells trouble for a marriage. Not surprisingly, anger is often expressed by the NS partner because she feels the harder she tries to communicate with her spouse, the more problems seem to emerge.

Sometimes an NS spouse will try to translate internally what she believes her husband is saying—or even what she believes he is hearing when someone else speaks. If she makes an assumption that her husband interprets language in the same way as a non-spectrum person, this is certain to create further friction. The need to listen without assuming is very important for NS spouses if they are to resolve common communication problems in their relationships.

NS interpretation

Making the decision not to "unscramble" something our spouse tells us can be a hit and miss experience. Sometimes they mean exactly what they say. Other times, they are communicating "around" something. In other words, what they say is just a concise version of a deeper feeling or need that they may not be able to express. Also, they sometimes say things in anger that they don't really mean, just to vent.

Author Marci has experienced this kind of communication problem with her husband Phil, especially before his diagnosis:

I attributed the communication difference to differences between men and women or the fact that my husband was too busy to "listen" while he was going to school, working, and trying to be a good father and spouse. All the while, though, something did not feel right. After about four years of marriage, I began wondering if I were crazy.

Phil only conversed about a short list of topics, and those were of interest only to him. At times he tried to or did listen to me, but we were not having a true conversation, just sharing information.

When we had been married for six years and had two children together, an event convinced me that I was sane and that my husband did have challenges. One morning, as he was leaving for work, Phil said something along the lines of, "I can't take it any more. I have to quit my job." I interpreted his words to mean that he was frustrated and wanted something at work to change, reasoning that most people occasionally make similar extreme expressions in frustration without literally meaning to follow through. However, in this case and many others with my husband, my conclusion was wrong.

That day, he quit his job! With a growing family (his daughter from his first marriage had come to live with us, too, bringing the total to three kids), I considered his behavior totally irresponsible. What was his plan now? Because of Phil's inability to communicate his thoughts effectively, I tried to ask questions. Slowly, in response to carefully chosen questions, he shared piece by piece what he was thinking and how his way of thinking had led to what had appeared to be an inexplicable action.

Phil could not deal with a promotion at work and the added responsibilities it would bring, and was unable to discuss this with anyone (his wife, his boss, his co-workers, a friend, etc.). Unbeknownst to Marci, this had been a pattern with him in earlier jobs: do a good job, get promoted, then as responsibilities change, feel overwhelmed and quit. This time, his inability to communicate with his employer affected not only him, but also his family. Marci wonders now what might have happened then if she had asked him: "Are you really going to quit? What is your plan?"

ASD interpretation

Individuals with an ASD often interpret words in a very narrow, somewhat idiosyncratic fashion through a filter that is reflective of their unique perspectives on the world. As a result, they may jump to unwarranted conclusions. Many individuals on the autism spectrum process both oral and written communication very literally, and process verbal input more slowly than their NS peers. Further, they seem to have a hard time staying focused on the entire verbal message, seeming to hear only part of what is being said.

In her 1980 paper "The near-normal autistic adolescent," Margaret Dewey quotes a young man with autism as saying:

> "Now I have good hearing and I think I listen well. But sometimes I latch onto the wrong words as most important and shut out the ones the other person thought were important. It is not a question of hearing the words, but of knowing what is important in the situation and what the other person assumes I already know." (Dewey 1980)

Although this man misinterpreted the question, "Do you listen well?", he spoke eloquently about his interpretive and expressive differences.

> In discussing her husband's communication interpretation problems, one NS spouse shared:

> We have a lot of problems with communication! This is one of the most difficult areas for us. I have a hard time when he doesn't seem to know something [like the meaning of a word or phrase] that most people learned in preschool. It makes me crazy because he is so intelligent; it doesn't make sense that he wouldn't know [a word or phrase that's] so simple. The Asperger syndrome makes it like we are speaking foreign languages to each other. Also I process

rapidly, and he processes slowly. This is another aspect that trips us up quite often. In many ways it is like being married to a child.

A common assumption often made by the NS partner is that a general question such as "What do you want to do tonight?" means the same to the ASD partner as it does to her. Many NS wives say that this vague question usually gets a reply like, "I don't know," or "Whatever you want to do." Similar responses will also arise from, "Where do you want to eat on the way to Mom's?" and "Where shall we go for our summer vacation?" Again this communication challenge is intertwined with executive functioning skills. More examples of these various issues in NS-ASD verbal exchanges are shared throughout this chapter.

> The NS-ASD couple Sheila and Harry were on their way to a party. "How do I look?" asked Sheila. "Fine," replied Harry. When they arrived at the party, the hostess hurried across the room and pulled two large, red curlers from the back of Sheila's hair. "Didn't you check your hair before leaving?" she asked. "I'd have thought that Harry would have at least told you." Later, Sheila asked Harry, "Why didn't you tell me about the curlers when I asked how I looked?" "Your dress was very pretty, and I thought you knew about the curlers," he replied.

Interpretation differences of individuals on the autism spectrum can change the meaning of a message and neither party may realize a message was misunderstood. In the case of Sheila and Harry, she might have asked, "Does anything look out of place on me?" to elicit some specific feedback from Harry. In fact, relying on a mirror and her own judgment was her best bet.

Communication about domestic tasks

Time and time again, NS partners relate how difficult it is to discuss the happenings of the day with their ASD partners. They mention the difficulties discussing family issues, like household purchases and planning for future events.

Often the effort to communicate about domestic tasks becomes an argument. In many instances this relates to difficulty with executive functioning skills on the part of the ASD spouse.

> NS Sheila often asks Harry to organize the papers he keeps in their house. Despite once being a clerical supervisor, Harry tucks away bills, checks, bank statements and other important papers in everything from the CD cabinet to his sock drawer. Sheila complains to Harry each time she finds yet another household drawer suddenly invaded by Harry's papers. When Sheila makes these requests, Harry usually replies by saying that when Sheila can keep the items that are readily visible in the house in order, he will worry about organizing his papers. Harry is visually organized and Sheila is non-visually organized.

Other NS spouses relate requesting that their ASD partners start or complete painting the house or cleaning the garage and are met with positive assurances that never evolve. In other cases, the ASD partner will physically or verbally withdraw from the conversation or change the direction of that conversation.

In families with children, NS spouses shared frustrations with discussing responsibilities involving the children. Some feel that their ASD spouses don't play and interact enough with the children. Others feel their husbands are too rigid in their disciplinary rules. Still others feel that their ASD spouses seem to be more like playmates to the children than parents, because these fathers will play computer games or play make-believe, but won't help with homework or transportation.

This frustration in discussing household management and parenting responsibility is likely a result of not only the communication issues but also theory of mind and executive functioning issues, both of which are discussed in Chapters 3 and 5.

As Marci and Phil's example illustrated, when communicating with someone on the autism spectrum, it's important not to structure the message using "common-sense" assumptions based on presumably shared knowledge. The perspectives and assumptions between the NS and ASD people in the partnership are often vastly different. Often the processing issue is trivial and may result in just a slight annoyance.

Author and lecturer Kristi Sakai talks about how she used to ask her husband to pick up items at the store for her. She might say, "Bring home some milk." Even if the family always drinks white skim milk, he might bring home a gallon of chocolate milk. She finally made it her standard procedure to write him a list and include brand names, sizes, etc., to make clear what she needed. She sometimes even attached labels of the requested items to the list.

An example of differences in processing the meaning of a message is shown in an incident with Dennis and Sam:

Dennis is NS and his friend Sam is on the autism spectrum. Dennis was amused by a conversational exchange with Sam and shared it with Sam's NS wife, Molly. Dennis and Sam commute to work together. Sam loves to go fishing on the weekends and often has fishing foremost in his thoughts. On the way home from work, Dennis would occasionally ask Sam, "Do you want to catch some dinner on the way home?" "It would take too long," was Sam's standard reply. Finally one day, Dennis realized that Sam wasn't refusing to eat with Dennis. Instead he had interpreted Dennis's question as a suggestion that they stop and fish so that they could bring home fish for dinner. They would literally "catch their dinner." The word "catch" can mean either "capture" or "partake of." Dennis meant one and Sam meant the other.

Many NS spouses share examples of literal interpretations and literal definitions of words by their ASD partners.

"Are you done yet?" was a problem for ASD Sam, because "done" to him was a word that applied only to cooking, meaning the food was ready. When his NS wife Molly or one of their children asked, "Are you done yet?" for a variety of actions such as using the bathroom, this caused frustrations for all.

Often, NS spouses find that the common meaning of the phrase, "Can you do _____?" is not productive to use with their ASD mates.

Asking Josh, "Can you get the milk out?", for example, did not get the intended results for NS Sara when she was trying to get dinner on the table. Josh would undoubtedly say, "Yes," and sit down at the table without the milk. Josh had answered the question literally without realizing the intent of the question. He was being asked to get the milk from the refrigerator. Sara has since learned to be more specific with phrases such as, "Please get the milk from the refrigerator."

General processing differences

Individuals with an ASD often process communication quite differently from their non-spectrum counterparts. They often latch onto different information as the most important and/or interpret the conversation in a more literal fashion. In some cases, the processing issue can become a major source of conflict in the marriage.

One NS wife spent many years trying to adhere to her husband's rigid rules about grocery shopping, many of which were contradictory. For example, soda pop could be bought only at a certain store that sold it at discount prices, even when the store closest to home was honoring competitors' coupons. It wasn't until this woman shared her husband's "rules" with a friend that she finally realized, as she says, "It wasn't me! Other people told me they were confused by his rules, too," and wouldn't be able to follow them successfully. Before then, she'd thought she was a bad wife or was dim-witted for "not getting it." After she finally gave herself permission to do the shopping on her own without "reporting" to him, the weekly arguing over this subject ceased.

Eye contact and communication

Many people with an ASD have a hard time listening to someone and looking at them at the same time. Many articulate individuals on the autism spectrum, when asked directly, will say that really to "hear" and process the meaning of someone's words and conversation, they need to turn away from the speaker. They describe having to look at someone when they are talking as "painful" or "confusing."

Research on the brain is constantly changing. Neurological research supports that those on the autism spectrum commonly have differences in the amygdala (an almond-sized area in the brain), including but not limited to its role in facial gazing. This research seems so relevant here, since lesions on the amygdala were shown to eliminate eye contact (Spezio *et al.* 2007).

Several of the NS spouses described how they have learned that sitting side by side results in better communication than sitting across from each other. Also many of the NS partners shared how having discussions in a "romantic setting" often results in better communication. (See "Lessons learned" at the end of this chapter.)

With the lights down low, soft music and candles, Jane and Trevor feel more relaxed and able to communicate. It wasn't until years after they began this practice that Jane realized how a "romantic setting" helped her and Trevor in different ways. Jane felt pampered and special, and Trevor felt relieved that it was quiet and that he could focus on the flame of the candles while they talked. Trevor explained to Jane that he was much better able to "hear" and understand her when there were no distractions to his attention.

Nonverbal communication

Many seemingly simple communication differences make up each day in an ASD-NS relationship, such as more in-depth conversations and nonverbal communication. People with ASD have difficulty interpreting gestures and other nonverbal communication. Facial expressions, hand gestures and other body movements are frequently misinterpreted by someone on the autism spectrum. In fact, this form of communication can easily overwhelm an ASD partner who is not naturally wired to understand nonverbal messages. Several of the NS partners realized that their "animated" hand gestures— whether used in frustration or when happy—made their ASD partner "anxious." The ASD partner might begin to pace, leave the room or start talking loudly and, as a result, the opportunity to communicate would end.

Processing of emotional communication

As we have seen, the ASD person likely finds it difficult or impossible to process large streams of verbal information that is shared by the NS person during a typical conversation or even a brief verbal exchange. This becomes even more complicated if the message is on an emotional level. This may be processed by her ASD husband as merely sounds with little meaning.

This becomes even more complicated if the message is an emotional one. Even if he is able to hear all the words being spoken, the ASD person may not know what the NS speaker sees as important, so that he can understand the intended message.

Many spouses have shared with us that positive emotions can become overwhelming for their ASD husbands, too.

NS Kaye, for example, says that her husband Pete, who is on the autism spectrum, sometimes shouts at her in anger when she excitedly points out a rainbow in the sky. Kaye explains: "He can't tell the difference between when I shout for joy versus when I shout from anger."

Molly, an NS spouse of an ASD partner, Sam, shared that on days when she went to see her mother, she would be emotional before she left in anticipation of her monthly visit. Her mother is in a distant assisted-living facility, and it is hard for Molly to witness her continuing deterioration each month. Other factors had also upset Molly, such as the disappearance of her mother's personal items.

Once, Molly asked Sam before she left for one such trip to "please keep the kitchen clean," so she could return and easily fix dinner without a hassle. She was somewhat tearful and on edge before leaving and was very expressive with her hands when asking Sam to keep the kitchen clean.

When she returned, Sam met her at the door. Initially she felt this was a gesture of comfort and empathy on his part, but this thought was quickly shattered. As soon as Sam had said he was glad to see her, he blurted out, "I'm starved." Sam had not eaten all day. He had assumed that Molly did not want him in the kitchen while she was gone. He took her body language and words, "Keep the kitchen clean," to mean he was not to go in there. This made for a rough evening for both of them.

Literalness

In an example of miscommunication over literalness, NS spouse Molly explained that she can ask what she thinks is a simple request of her husband Sam—such as, "While you are in the bathroom, please draw the water for my bath." Sam interprets this to mean Molly wants a picture of the bathtub as they had been discussing remodeling. He decides that a digital picture would be better than anything he could draw and starts looking for the camera. Molly is left clueless as to what happened. Sam has gone to another part of the house and has not turned on the water in the bathtub.

An occasional incident such as this might be humorous to most couples. But such scenarios between ASD and NS spouses can seem much less humorous for the NS partner, who views her husband as being deliberately annoying and/or choosing to disregard her wishes. This is especially true when such exchanges occur frequently and the husband reacts with displeasure or a blank look.

We have spoken with couples who are not aware of the ASD diagnosis, who have not accepted the diagnosis and/or who have little understanding of Asperger syndrome and often are caught up in negative beliefs that do not give them hope for change. Some knowledge, understanding and acceptance of the autism spectrum disorder and its effect on communication between the partners will go a long way to finding solutions that prevent further negativity between the couple.

> NS wife Jane gave us another instance of literal communication. She asked her ASD husband, Trevor, if he could find the hammer so she could hang a picture. He said, "Sure." So Jane stood in place, holding the picture, waiting for Trevor to bring the hammer. When he had not appeared after a while, she called out, "Where are you?" To which he replied, "In the kitchen." She asked, "Are you coming with the hammer?" and he replied, "You never asked me to bring the hammer." Trevor needed a direct, literal command, such as, "Please bring me the hammer," because he lacks the ability to interpret meaning.

At first, adjusting to this method of direct and thorough conversation can be a challenge for NS spouses, as it requires a shift in thinking. However, many wives reported that, after some practice, they were able to adjust and to speak their husband's style of communication. To clarify how words and phrases can have more than one meaning, we note that it can help NS spouses to find a book of idioms and metaphors to look through and discuss examples together with their ASD husbands. The elementary school Amelia Bedelia books by Peggy Parish or Herman Parish are fun to read for many couples, as they discuss the literal interpretations that the lead character Amelia makes. (There are currently over 20 books available in the series; see, for example, Parish 2002, 2003.)

If possible, before a conversation, the NS partner should explain the purpose of the conversation and what the ASD partner can do to respond. For example, telling the ASD partner, "I had a hard day today, and I'd like you just to listen without interruptions and without advice right now," works well for some wives. We suggest that NS spouses directly ask for a hug too, if needed.

Communication gaps

NS spouse Bonnie shared that she and her ASD husband, Brad, a professor at a small college, were both very frustrated with their conversations. After a long day with students, Brad needs time to be by himself in his den, whereas Bonnie looks forward to seeing Brad and discussing their days. In the past, any attempt by Bonnie to talk with Brad before his "den time" ended with Brad's not answering her or responding with something rude.

Bonnie learned that she should not disturb him while he is in his den, taking a talking and listening break, so she waits until Brad comes to the dinner table and then tries to share. Even so, Brad seems uninterested, and if he does say anything, it doesn't connect with what Bonnie considers helpful or pertinent. Brad is not able to listen and empathize with Bonnie's feelings when he's already in the middle of decompressing his own. After Bonnie starts talking, he starts giving her advice or asks why she is upset if nothing can be done. In this way, NS-ASD couples are similar to other gender-different couples who are not on the spectrum.

Frequently, when Bonnie asks Brad about his day before "den time," he responds, "It was okay," or he might mumble a statement such as, "The incompetence of students these days is inexcusable," without elaborating further. Should Bonnie ask him what happened with the students, he becomes more upset. Bonnie often feels as if Brad wants to distance himself from her. In all likelihood, however, Brad has no clue that

Bonnie doesn't already know what is happening day by day with his students. Brad assumes she has this knowledge and sees no reason to discuss the issue. He wants to talk about a new project he wants to research and talks on about this for the rest of the meal.

This anecdote also illustrates the challenge surrounding theory of mind, discussed in detail in Chapter 3.

In really vital communications, NS partners shared that it was very helpful to ask their ASD spouses questions to find out if they understood what was conveyed. It seems it is not just about the husband's challenge in the area of processing and participating in conversation; it is also about the NS partner's challenges in the ability to speak "autism spectrumese." His method of communication is not *wrong*; it is different.

We recommend the following exercise: One partner may start with the statement, "This is what I heard you say," and restate what was heard. Then the statement, "This is what it means to me..." should be made. Finally, asking questions like, "Was this the question you were asking?" or "Was this the statement you were making?" and most importantly, "Was this what it meant to you?" will help explain some of the communication gaps in ASD-NS interpretation. The ASD partner may seem irritated at being questioned, but with patience on both sides, asking for clarification will prevent many misunderstandings and help each member of the couple learn more about each other.

Communication at work

Many NS spouses are concerned that if their ASD spouses are such poor communicators at home, they are bound to have problems at work because of their literal interpretation of language, slow processing of verbal exchanges and misinterpretations of a speaker's intended message. Unfortunately, if there are communication issues at work, NS spouses may not learn of them until they are serious. Indeed the ASD husband often has no clue a problem exists, or perhaps if he realizes there is a problem, he has no idea what to do about it, as illustrated in the following somewhat darkly humorous example.

A crisis had arisen at work. David's boss told everyone in the office, "If you don't attend Thursday morning's meeting, you might as well clean out your desk." David, who has ASD, had promised to drive his wife, Sally, to the hospital for minor surgery on Thursday and had already cleared it with his boss. As a result, he missed the Thursday morning meeting.

In the afternoon, after David returned, an irritated boss approached David's desk. Seeing stacks of papers, pencils and other debris piled in stacks on the desk, he asked, "What are you doing? I expected you in my office as soon as you got here."

"Cleaning out my desk like you asked," replied David.

Retaining and retrieving verbal information

In addition to the processing difficulties that hinder good communication (such as literal interpretations and timing of conversations), NS spouses often report problems with ASD partners' abilities to retain and retrieve relevant information, use appropriate language and follow the general rules of conversation. While most people on the spectrum tend to retain factual information, they often retain only parts of interpersonal communication or retain it in a context different from what was intended. This can lead to their retrieving the information at inappropriate times. Also, when under extreme anxiety or stress, they may fail to retrieve pertinent information at all—or they may go to the other extreme, spewing out an unending stream of information, possibly alienating people around them.

NS spouse Molly is often embarrassed when her husband Sam asks questions or makes statements that come to his mind when it is not the proper time or place to discuss the subject matter. One time, while attending a cookout with several other couples, Sam announced from across the yard: "Molly, I'll let you get your drink. It looks like they have the kind of drink that gives you hives, so you'd better pick something else." He then added to someone standing closer: "I don't know why she forgets to take her medicine or bring it with her, so she won't be up all night getting sick and rubbing cream on her bottom."

Another NS spouse, Sara, shared that her husband Josh cannot be trusted with private information. He does not remember a caution to be discreet or a warning not to tell anyone. Once information is in his head, it comes out regardless of propriety.

One time Sara told him that a friend was planning a surprise party for her husband's fiftieth birthday and that it was to be kept secret. The next time Josh saw this couple, it triggered a thought, and the information just rolled off his tongue: "Hey, I didn't know you were going to be 50 this year. Are you going to take the day off and play some golf or do you need to rest before the big birthday bash your wife has planned?"

Some spouses have told us they explain the appropriate time and place for specific information. They use statements such as, "This financial information will be helpful to you in doing our taxes or for you and me to discuss in budgeting for the future," or "This would be good information to share if you are ever in trouble with the police," and so on.

Social "rehearsals" can help in some situations. For instance, the NS partner may say, "When my parents are here tomorrow, don't tell them that I said I was mad at my sister." Instead of telling him what not to do, we note that it might be more helpful to tell him what he could and should say, and then rehearse it—such as, "It has been too long since we have gotten together. Sorry we missed the visit at Aunt Helen's."

Another frustration related by many of the NS partners is the inability of their ASD partners to engage in a give-and-take discussion. The rules of polite conversation, such as taking turns without interruption and providing an appropriate amount of information on the topic, seem forgotten or unimportant to the ASD partner. This often makes for a one-sided conversation.

> Marci's ASD husband Phil explains that he has to say what is on his mind or he will forget. If he starts and stops as in a typical conversation, he will lose his train of thought. When interruptions occur, it is extremely difficult for him to pick up where he left off; he may have to start back at the beginning or drop his piece of the conversation. In such situations, it is hard for him to remember who said what and what was actually said, which easily leads to misinterpretation and misunderstanding. It may seem ironic to non-spectrum people that someone so brilliant as Phil fears forgetting to relate what is on his mind in a social conversation.

Many on the autism spectrum express pride in being experts on specific topics, and are puzzled as to why people wouldn't want to hear all the important information they have to share. If the topic of the discussion is not familiar to the spouse with an ASD or is about the NS partner's feelings (something that seems totally foreign to individuals on the autism spectrum), he may shut down and not contribute at all to the exchange. In the meantime, since he has shut down, or his mind is "stuck" on his thoughts, he does not hear the information that his NS partner is sharing.

Despite many having incredible powers of memory for facts and figures, ASD partners frequently have great difficulty retrieving names, even those of people they see daily.

> One NS partner reported that her partner worked with four people on a place of worship committee that met weekly to prepare communion. After five years, he did not know the name of a single person on that committee.

_xpressive language: making appropriate subject choices

The frequent, often seemingly tactless, honesty of people with ASD can get them in a lot of trouble, both at home and in the community. Their ability to express their feelings is not tempered by diplomacy, which can make them seem intentionally rude or insensitive. Additionally, many of them have problems regulating the volume of their voices and/or the rate of their speech. NS partners had many stories to share with us about being so embarrassed that they had taken to limiting their social activities.

> NS Sara anecdotally noted that her ASD husband Josh's expressive language abilities seem to fluctuate depending on his anxiety level and the time of year. During the period from November through February, it appears to be more problematic for her husband to express himself appropriately than at other times of the year (possibly because of changes in his brain chemistry caused by low levels of sunlight then; it's interesting to note that this phenomenon is not experienced solely by people with an ASD). Often someone will ask her a question and her ASD husband will blurt out an answer. He may realize the question was meant for her but, in the anxiety of the moment, seems compelled to respond. When Sara tries to clarify the answer (after all, the question was directed at her), this usually brings on an argument.
>
> In another example, a friend asks NS Sally: "How was your day at the spa?" Sally's husband, David, immediately replies: "The place was hard to find, so the session was cut short." Ready to answer the question for herself, Sally says: "It was fabulous. I would recommend this place to anyone." David seems to get hostile and adds: "I don't know why she wants to spend the time and money on something like this. She could just work out and get the same benefits and lose weight at the same time."
>
> David's attempt to participate in the conversation is seemingly a disaster, frustrating Sally and making her friend

uncomfortable. David, for his part, feels he is being truthful in this scenario, and has no idea why Sally is frustrated. Like many people with Asperger syndrome, David does not understand the subtle nuances of social graces.

Expressive language difficulties often create barriers to the intimate exchanges that are usually a cherished part of a good relationship. In an effort to clarify the communication of an ASD partner, some NS partners have used their creativity.

Kaye and Pete receive help from their marriage counselor, who specializes in working with people on the spectrum. The counselor encourages creativity and emphasizes the use of visuals. But it is an invisible, imaginary tool that ultimately has given ASD Pete the ability to show empathy to his wife. At the therapist's direction, the couple employ the use of a "meter" that Pete visualizes to "read" NS Kaye's emotions when he doesn't understand her reaction. Sometimes he uses the meter on himself as well. All of this takes the pressure off Kaye to be the primary communication translator, thereby benefiting the marriage.

Communication is a core difference of autism spectrum disorders and interaction can be very stressful for both partners. These communication differences will always be there to some extent.

Conversational exchanges

Social use of language involves three reciprocal areas of communication, known by experts as expressive, receptive and evaluative skills. The back-and-forth, give-and-take nature in each of these aspects of dialogue is often confusing to people on the autism spectrum.

Certain facets of social chitchat, including asking about another person's day or plans for an upcoming event, often seem of no significance to the ASD partner. For the NS person, on the other hand, hearing about others' experiences and opinions is often an important step in bonding and feeling closer to other people. If their ASD partners don't give or ask for this type of expressive information, NS partners often feel rejected. Sometimes they try harder to promote these dialogues, but this may lead to the ASD partners' withdrawing more to escape from what they feel is an onslaught of emotion and overload to the senses. The result is that both partners are left feeling bewildered.

One spouse says she has learned to keep a diary instead of trying to talk to her husband about her day. A few NS spouses mentioned stopping by a store to chat about their days with, for example, a cashier they know is often there when they get off work. This occurs whether they need to purchase anything or not. They need that friendly face and someone who looks interested in some details of their days.

Sometimes the problem is not what is being said, but how is it said. Because of the total honesty common among individuals on the autism spectrum, they can appear very critical or impolite when they express themselves.

> Sara has certain dishes she makes for the holidays, but Josh always seems to make statements such as, "Is that green bean casserole ready yet? I'd like to see how much we have left over this year. Is it really worth fixing?"

For change in this area to be effective, it's important to be sure that both partners wish to change. Often in social situations, the ASD person does not see there is a problem or understand the consequences. However, if he recognizes that there is a problem, and that he is contributing to it, there are some strategies for change. Rehearsal is a key strategy. In the next section, we take a look at the receptive and evaluative issues in conversations.

Following the rules of conversation

Taking turns in a conversation, paying attention to the speaker and not interrupting are examples of rules of conversation that are accepted parts of speaking with others. Those on the autism spectrum need to be taught and/or learn strategies to follow these social rules of conversation. Although books on the subject may be helpful, no amount of hearing or reading rules of etiquette and polite conversation is sufficient to prepare ASD partners to function well in society. Because of the way their brains are wired, they need many opportunities to practice appropriate conversational skills.

For example, an NS spouse may explain to her ASD husband that it is really important to precede a request for something with the word "please," and that after someone replies, it is proper to say, "Thank you."

> NS Molly did just this, resulting in the following situation: At a family dinner, Molly's husband Sam requested a second glass of wine from his mother-in-law. She replied, "Absolutely not! I think you are becoming a drunk." Sam then replied, "Thank you." Not surprisingly, Sam's response in such moments is interpreted as sarcasm, even though he is trying to be polite by following the rule Molly taught him. Sam's inability to subjectify the appropriate times to use the phrase often works against him.

As people on the spectrum practice effective, appropriate and/or polite communication in a variety of supportive environments, they gain not only experience and fluency, but also confidence. Beyond the skills already discussed, an important part of their need to learn pragmatics is to learn to show speakers they are paying attention, to ask questions, make compliments and politely exit a conversation. Learning "exit lines" helps ASD spouses go a long way to appear polite and get out of distressing or overwhelming situations.

> NS partner Sheila told us that it took her four years of reasoning, arguing, pleading and negotiating to get Harry to agree to learn and use effective exit lines. She wrote:
>
> > I still feel proud of him each time he says, "May I speak with you privately?" instead of yelling at me in front of others. It took many years of honest feedback from me and close

friends for him to realize that others felt his snapping at me in public was rude. I had to learn about his needs, too. When he shows me that a situation is becoming distressful to him, I've learned not to delay exiting. I use an excuse of an appointment or being tired or something along those lines.

This kind of practice and rehearsal can take place just between the two partners via rehearsal techniques, with each playing the part of each other or someone else.

Writing and talking about the "rules" of polite public conversation—such as saying something nice to a host about the food that's being served—will reinforce the ASD partner's ability to understand and use them. If this is a big problem for the NS-ASD couple, it may be helpful to them to write rules for specific situations, such as workplace, place of worship and family gatherings. However, it's important not to expect to achieve perfection. Taking reasonable, small steps is the appropriate path to lessen awkwardness gradually. It can also help both partners to remember that everyone makes a social faux pas now and then.

We offer the following advice: In private situations, NS partners should not expect deep or romantic thoughts to flow off their partners' tongues or pens. Even for intimate exchanges, however, words can be written down and practiced. Initially, this may seem insincere and phony, but most partners we have spoken with think that over time, it feels genuine, especially when the ASD partner realizes (perhaps through the appreciation shown by the NS partner) that these kinds of words are extremely important to his partner's happiness.

When discussing information that the ASD partner will need to apply to another situation, NS partners note that writing down the information and presenting it to him is quite helpful. Imagine the following scenario: A wife found out via a school visit that her son's teacher does not like to be reached by phone and would prefer an email or note. To assist her ASD husband, this woman may put that information on a card, show it to her ASD partner and tape it by the phone as an easy visual reminder.

For best results, NS wives can be encouraging, practice with their partners and then rehearse, rehearse, rehearse! Involving others who are discreet and sensitive and who truly care to help with these rehearsals is often helpful. When teaching social information, it may help to write the information down or draw stick figures engaged in making compliments, asking questions and using exit lines. The technique of videoing the ASD spouse using the various exit lines can also be an effective way of practicing.

The 3 Rs of Marriage©

Author Kealah recommends a concise conversational script, called The 3 Rs of Marriage.© She originally developed this questionnaire with her own husband, and has since shared it with her communications coaching clients. Many have found it successful—including those on the autism spectrum—because it is brief and easy to follow. It involves the couple asking each other the following questions:

1. What is one thing I did that REALLY made you feel loved today?

2. What is one thing you did in an effort to RETURN the love?

3. What is a REQUEST you would like to make for one way that I can show you love tomorrow?

A fourth "bonus" question is, "How have you shown love to yourself today?"

To keep things simple, NS-ASD couples can follow these directions:

At any point in the day or evening that is most convenient for you and your spouse, take time for a 5- to 15-minute conversation. Take turns asking each other and answering these questions. This activity reveals that little things often mean a lot. For example, when the wife does the laundry, she may be trying to show that she loves her husband; or the husband is telling his wife that he loves her when he takes the car to be detailed. The activity also reveals the spouse's internal thought processes. (Parkinson 2009)

Some of Kealah's clients say it helps build intimacy and reminds the couple of their love all over again, because they learn to appreciate lovingly intended gestures they might otherwise have taken for granted.

ASD spouses may sometimes come across as rude, overbearing or uncaring, as we have seen in examples from this chapter. However, when given the opportunity to express themselves in an atmosphere and timeframe that works for them, ASD partners can surprise their NS spouses by revealing a deep caring capacity.

Lessons learned

- Be concise in your communications and point out what you think is the most important part of what you are saying. Leave out unnecessary information.

- Ask specific questions, and be aware of the literal meaning of your words, choosing words carefully so your message is clear.

- Listen without assuming.

- Ask (if you are uncertain) how your spouse has interpreted a communication.

- Speak at a slower pace and allow more time for an answer.

- Consider carefully what information to share with your ASD partner if he has a history of blurting out confidential or embarrassing information.

- Use visual cues and other tools to help your spouse read emotions.

- Rehearse social conversations, especially exit lines and strategies.

- Write down important information and keep it visually handy.

- Use scripts that are short and concise to help both of you process emotions as calmly, clearly and consistently as possible.

Chapter 3

Social Skills Differences

Communication, the subject of Chapter 2, is not the only social interaction that can cause confusion for ASD spouses and their NS wives. Even in the most advanced individuals with PDD-NOS, social awkwardness and occasional obvious social differences are evident. Difficult reciprocal social interactions can range from wanting a quiet life of routine to occasional social gaffes.

Several NS spouses informed us that, looking back, they realized that they had fallen quickly in love and that, early on, they overlooked the social problems or concerns they had about their ASD spouses. In many relationships described to us, in the dating phase, the NS partners did the planning of social activities, and the ASD partners went along. It was only much later, after they were committed to each other and living together, that the NS partners realized the lack of social skills and planning abilities in their ASD partners.

Initially, social interaction difficulties seen in the ASD partner may not appear problematic, possibly as a result of misinterpretation and/or assumptions made by the NS partner. For example, the "shy" demeanor in public may be dismissed as coming from a particular type of background, such as being raised in another culture or in an abusive household.

Having only simple dates at home, watching movies, studying or sharing a meal during the courtship may be just fine to the NS partner, who may well assume that limited time or finances prevent their going elsewhere or doing things with other couples. Or maybe such a pattern is overlooked because the routine of staying in together is cherished by the NS partner, because of all the focused attention she receives from the ASD partner.

Many of our NS-ASD couples have age, cultural or religious differences. However, they met due to shared interests or organizations. In her book, *Alone Together*, Katrin Bentley (2007) relates that her husband loves to watch movies. This was fine with her until their honeymoon. They were at a lovely beach cottage, but instead of enjoying romantic walks on the beach, her ASD spouse just wanted to sit and watch rented movies by the hour. Before their marriage, Katrin had attributed many of his differences from other men she had dated to his being Australian, while she came from Switzerland. But she quickly learned that a majority of his quirks were a part of his expression of Asperger syndrome.

Another common scenario during the dating period that may mask social differences is when an imposed structure with somewhat defined roles dictates "expected" behavior in a particular setting: at work, school, recreation or worship. When there is structure, routine and defined roles, the ASD partner's social uneasiness and lack of social knowledge may not be evident.

NS Sally said that she and ASD David met in their college choir:

> We walked to and from practice together. We didn't make dates, so to speak, because we saw our choir time as our "together time." When we did have meals together or rode together on the bus to concerts, we discussed the music and what we did or didn't like about it. I found his looks, his voice and his musical knowledge fascinating. It was a quick engagement and then marriage at the end of college. But with the end of choir and school, things changed fast. We moved into our first apartment. Without the structure and clear social expectations of our choir regimen, our relationship grew strained and awkward. David still just wanted to talk about music—no "How was your day?" language.

In another example of blindness to poor social skills, when Harry and Sheila were dating, Sheila and her three roommates held a party at their apartment. ASD Harry graciously contributed food and wine to the event, but when politics were discussed and the guests didn't agree with him, he asked everyone to leave. He said, "All you've done is criticize our country. If you don't like the country, why don't you just get out! As a matter of fact, why don't you just leave this apartment!" His "get out" speech seemed quite patriotic to Sheila, as he was defending the government. However, her roommates informed her that the next time her boyfriend ended a party in that manner, he would no longer be welcome. Since the relationship was relatively new and she was infatuated, Sheila didn't realize that Harry had found a way to end a situation that made him uncomfortable: too many people chatting away and other men talking to his girlfriend!

The first few times an NS partner is aware of inappropriate ASD-related behavior in social situations, she may be confused and frustrated, even convinced that her ASD partner knows exactly what he is doing and can control his behavior. She may think the partner knows he is rude and wants to be rude. It is often a trying process that painstakingly and gradually educates the NS spouse about her husband's true social naivety, something that is made even harder to see because it is based on her husband's intellectual brilliance.

A few NS spouses informed us that it is this kind of misunderstanding over repeated rude social behaviors that leads to crises in relationships.

Kaye and Pete's honeymoon was a mixture of Kaye's overlooking future problems and feeling overwhelmed and confused by the issues at hand that she did not comprehend as being AS-related. (Pete was not diagnosed until they had been married for over a year.) At the wedding ceremony, some of Kaye's non-spectrum friends engaged in "typical" social behavior: They decorated the newlyweds' car with tin cans and signs that read "Just Married" and "Honk if You're Happy for Us." The day after the ceremony, Pete appeared furious with Kaye, stating that he was not going anywhere in the car until Kaye took everything off it. He said her friends were out of line for "pulling a prank" and "messing with the car" without their permission.

Kaye chalked this up to their having grown up in different parts of the United States, in addition to Pete's innate shyness, which made her protective of him. However, when this same "shyness" led Pete to insist they tell no one at their hotel that they were honeymooning, Kaye was deeply disappointed. She felt robbed of some of the traditional fun attention bestowed upon a new bride. There were other benefits that were missing from this "secret honeymoon," too, such as gift baskets, room upgrades, and perhaps a special table at a choice restaurant.

Some of our respondents searched the internet for answers, unable to understand how such an intelligent person who appeared sociable before marriage—or at least cordial with people—would now avoid people or behave rudely or aggressively with them. These NS spouses describe how they were upset when their ASD husbands would not want to interact with others at a place of worship, the neighborhood cookout or when people came over to their house.

Frequently, when Molly and her ASD husband Sam stayed after their worship service to socialize, Sam would get very agitated and tell her (and many others within earshot) that it was "Time to go NOW!" He would then stand with his arms crossed staring at everyone until Molly said her goodbyes and started for the door. Sam was likely reaching a point of sensory overload, brought on by the strain of navigating social rules (see Chapter 2). However, Molly did not understand this at the time, and did not know how to respond to it without offense.

Long before author Susan began to delve into the subject of NS-ASD marriages, she knew a woman who told of what a great father and husband her spouse was. However, whenever this couple had dinner guests, he just left the table when he was finished eating without further addressing the company and went off to another room to watch TV and read the paper. This woman argued, cajoled and pleaded with her husband to stop this kind of behavior. In response, he said that he could not see what was wrong with it, as that was what he always did after dinner. In retrospect, Susan wondered if that man was on the spectrum. His behavior was certainly that of someone whose lack of social skills could fit the evaluation for Asperger syndrome.

Appearing rude and disregarding others' thoughts and feelings are common complaints.

ASD Brad mentioned to the host and several others at a gathering that it would be nice if the food had been cooked "properly" so that it could have tasted "the way it should." Brad is known to be the family cook and he takes great pride in serving home-cooked meals that are carefully planned and cooked to his specifications. He thought that he was being "helpful" in pointing out the cooking "error." Needless to say, his comments made everyone uncomfortable. His NS partner Bonnie was mortified and tried to apologize, saying Brad seemed to have forgotten there is more than one "good" recipe for Hungarian goulash.

Such lack of social understanding and ability often becomes a major factor and barrier to socializing for the couple. While less socializing may be welcomed by the ASD partner, the NS partner may feel alone and isolated. In the rest of this chapter we will describe, in more detail, the common social skills differences that our NS wives and partners discussed.

Social "rules"

Society functions via unwritten rules of behavior and appearance. This set of "social rules" is something that a great majority of non-spectrum people pick up by observing others in their environment.

However, ASD individuals have to be specifically taught not all of these social rules. A great source of these rules of l hygiene, polite conversation, introductions and proper Brenda Smith Myles' book and calendar series titled *The rttaaen Curriculum* (see Myles, Trautman and Schelvan 2004; Endow 2010, 2011).

Some ASD partners have strict lists of social rules, while others seem to know none of these so-called rules at all. We heard stories that covered every end of this spectrum—from men who become incensed at perceived violations of such rules to men who pass gas in public, mutter rude things loudly in a group, or yell, "Don't touch my hands!" when someone meeting them tries to shake hands with them. The NS spouses we spoke to who were able to communicate verbally with their husbands effectively (see Chapter 2) were most successful at mitigating scenes like these.

Many NS partners say that their ASD spouses "disappear" when visitors come to their homes. Others describe ASD partners who go about their regular routines, rituals or rigid rules without acknowledging the visitors at all.

NS Sheila reports that her ASD husband is very uptight about the fairness of turn-taking. This boils over into many daily situations: "When we are disembarking from an airplane, Harry insists on us leaving before the people in seats in back of us," she told us.

> Even though we are not on a tight connection schedule or other time constraint, Harry insists we have our proper turn to leave. Forget a family with a crying child, it is *not* their turn! This can carry over for leaving church in the proper succession, signing in to wait for a table at a restaurant—just about anything that adheres to "place in line" etiquette.
>
> Once we were in line to pay our condolences at a funeral of one of my relatives. Although we lived in neighboring towns, I hadn't seen much of them in recent years. However, I saw them several times a month as a child. I took the time to tell my relative's widow how much my time with them used to mean, but Harry kept poking me in the back.

Finally, I asked him if there was a problem, and he said, "You are making others wait in the line too long." He had no idea that this was my one time to tell her this in person.

This was an attempt by Harry to observe the social rules of turn-taking.

NS wife Sally shared one example of her own such learning experiences with us. She was married to a bank clerk, David, who had ASD. David loved his routines. This made life pretty lonely and boring for Sally, as he liked to come home from work and read the paper before dinner, eat dinner quickly and then spend the rest of the evening watching TV in their basement recreation room.

Shortly after moving into a new neighborhood, Sally asked David if it would be okay to invite a few (six, to be exact) neighbors over for a drink and a simple dinner. David protested, but finally agreed. Sally neglected to state that this would require a different routine for the evening. This was an unfortunate omission.

The neighbors arrived just after David came home from work. When they entered, he was reading the paper. Sally said, "David, I want you to meet our new neighbors." David continued to read and replied, "That's nice." Realizing that an uncomfortable situation was arising, she continued on by saying, "Everyone, this is my husband David," then introducing them individually by name. David never looked up, but did say hello, and then returned to his reading. Sally then explained: "I hope you'll forgive David. He has to wind down after a long day at work." The guests nodded in confused agreement and rushed into the kitchen to chat with and help Sally.

When dinner was served, David joined them and asked for a reintroduction. He was polite but didn't initiate conversation. However, when dinner was finished, while others helped clear the table and spoke of the good meal, David went directly downstairs and began watching TV as always. The neighbors helped with the dishes and then quickly made excuses and left.

Sally was both embarrassed and angry with David, yet she realized eventually that she had not discussed and rehearsed the situation to prepare him properly. She tried again with just two neighbors about a month later. This time, she and David discussed the situation ahead of time, and Sally suggested specific things he could do in place of reading the paper before dinner—like helping to set the table and asking to take the guests' coats—and ways he could participate after dinner instead of watching TV.

David tried valiantly and held a rather one-sided conversation with the two dinner guests about his work and how much he hated it. After dinner, he retreated once again to watching TV. In Sally's mind, the dinner was another failure. But David felt he had done a great job and told Sally that he had endured enough and that was why he had retreated after dinner. Sally made one more attempt. After that, she stopped entertaining in her home, but she always volunteered to co-host with others for larger events, explaining that David was too tired to attend.

To David's credit, his weathering this party was a step forward. He had also shown empathy in trying to understand the importance of socializing to Sally. In our research, we've found that it's highly common for those with Asperger syndrome to feel intruded upon during large—or even small—gatherings in their homes, and that it is also common for NS wives to feel isolated when they try to honor their husbands' wishes. Looking for a compromise, such as Sally did, can help both partners.

If the problem is an almost total lack of understanding about social rules, we've found that NS-ASD couples who want to teach or learn these rules can start with the worst infractions (only one or two to start) and then brainstorm about a new way to act or speak in those situations. For instance, if the ASD spouse has been yelling, "It's my turn!" at people who get called into the doctor's office before him, his NS wife may volunteer to write down the rules of who goes in first. (This can be a situation that occurs when more than one doctor shares the same office. Dr. X may be running on time, so several of his patients get called in before the next patient of Dr. Y, who is running late.) It may help if the ASD partner is given a card by the reception desk that says, "My doctor has ___ patients before me. I will wait to hear the name of the patient in front of me. Then, I know that I will be my doctor's next patient."

Perceiving and understanding social cues

As mentioned in Chapter 2, individuals with ASD have difficulty monitoring and interpreting nonverbal communication. Some of these areas of nonverbal communication are interpreting body language, reading facial expressions and establishing and maintaining eye contact. When NS individuals become bored with listening to somebody, they give social cues such as looking at their watch, clearing their throat loudly, sighing, tapping their foot or fingers, crossing their arms, etc. ASD partners often do not pick up on those nonverbal communication signs. Instead, they may drone on and on about a favorite topic, or repeat a joke everyone has already heard without noticing the looks of embarrassment on the faces of their audience. At a gathering, if a person with ASD is managing to have a really good time, he may fail to notice that the majority of the guests are leaving and the hosts are getting tired. This can result in staying past the point of welcome.

The ability to read body language in the form of social cues varies according to the intensity of focus or distractibility of the ASD partner. In some cases, he has to use a huge amount of his powers of attention to process the verbal communication being presented, especially in stressful situations. Therefore, he has no energy or patience left to try to attend to the tone of someone's voice or loud sighs conveying irritation. However, practicing and gaining proficiency in the ability to read body language or social cues can help.

We recommend the following exercise for ASD-NS couples who want to practice reading body language:

Start with four or five basic social cues to which the ASD partner doesn't respond. Be specific about the cues. Create a visual cue card where the NS partner can perform the cues for the ASD partner to practice noticing. In the beginning, the cues should be exaggerated.

They may include toe-tapping, sighing, looking at one's watch, crossing the arms while letting out an exasperated sigh or pacing. Discuss the "hidden message" behind these common social cues.

Adding game-like fun and humor by exaggerating the cues at first or ringing a bell right before each cue or wearing a funny hat during each cue can take the chore out of this exercise. Ultimately, couples can expand the repertoire by watching for these cues in other environments.

Make social situations less overwhelming by giving the ASD partner a role to perform. Within the role he is given, such as taking care of the children, handing out drinks or preparing a specific dish, it is much easier to follow a "script" and "rules" for interacting. This will help to alleviate the need to retreat. Assigning "brief escape" moments may also work. Perhaps the need to walk the dog can excuse the ASD partner for a brief break.

Using social autopsies can also help teach successful social skills. Well known in the autism spectrum therapy world, the term "social autopsy" refers to dissecting what's going on in a social scenario, either through cartoons and videos that can be read or viewed and paused for discussion, or through reenacting and discussing a situation that has already occurred. This last option is best for negative social consequences. The NS and ASD partners can switch roles, each taking a turn being the ASD person at the social event. It may help to be humorous and intentionally overact the skit. In this type of reenactment, the partners are to express what they remember as their thoughts when the situation occurred. This allows the couple to explore not only the negative situation that occurred, but also each spouse's reaction to the situation, if both were present. Many of the NS spouses we spoke with used this technique, both formally and informally, to help improve their partners' understanding and navigation of social rules.

We recommend the series *Manners for the Real World* by Coulter Videos to help teach social manners, rules and cues (Coulter 2008). In addition, some wives (particularly those who were also mothers to ASD children) told us that the British TV show *Mr Bean* and the Canadian show *Just for Laughs* were very helpful in discussing both social blunders and facial expressions.

Reading facial expressions

Facial expressions are another form of nonverbal communication that is difficult for people on the autism spectrum to read. Sometimes this can create big problems for NS-ASD couples. Not knowing the difference between a frightened expression and one of shock can be disastrous in raising children, for example, and failing to recognize a look of anger can ruin a work situation.

> One very creative NS partner took a series of snapshots of herself in every mood she could imagine, made two copies of each and labeled one set. Then she had a discussion with her partner in which she said that she didn't think he always understood what emotions her face was showing in various situations. Rather than "blaming" him, she was careful to point out that it could simply be because her face conveyed unusual expressions. She then went on to explain that, due to her theory, she had photographed her face in ways that showed different feelings and suggested that they label one set of the photos together.
>
> At first, pointing at the corresponding photo, she just said things like, "I'm feeling really sad today. You can see that my sad face in this photo and my calm face look alike, right?" Then they would rehearse, with her making an expression and him looking at the cards, trying to guess which emotion it was. As a next step, they rehearsed with the ASD partner trying to identify emotions by looking at the unlabeled photos. And finally, they practiced identifying the emotions by looking at her face and not the photos.

Another form of rehearsal can involve watching a movie together (preferably a favorite movie of the ASD partner) and pausing it to study the facial expressions of the actors. Other versions may include looking at family photo albums and guessing the mood of family members by their expressions or looking at the expressions of models in magazine photos and ads. Many videos are available to teach people with ASDs how to identify facial expressions, but most are aimed at teens and younger children. A notable example is

The Transporters by Simon Baron-Cohen and his team at Cambridge University (see the Useful Resources section). Simon Baron-Cohen also developed a computer program called *Mind Reading* with over 400 different video and audio expressions of emotion (Baron-Cohen 2004a).

Eye contact

Establishing and maintaining eye contact is one of the best known ASD challenges. It often causes misunderstanding, as the NS population perceives the person with ASD as cold, aloof or totally uninterested. This can lead to an ASD spouse's losing a job or experiencing trouble and confusion in various social situations. For example, if an employer is having a serious discussion about missing items in the workplace and the ASD employee is gazing away and seeming to avert his eyes, the employer may begin to suspect that he is the one taking items.

> NS spouse Sara shared that while ASD Josh and she were dating, Josh had a very intimidating experience when the business where he worked was burglarized. There was money and merchandise missing from this small electronics shop. It appeared the incident happened during Josh's shift. The police were called, and they interviewed the employees who were present. Later that night, the police came to Josh's apartment with a search warrant. They felt there was probable cause to search, because Josh had appeared unusually nervous and "shifty eyed." Nothing was found in Josh's apartment, and the police pursued other leads until the case was solved.

In many intimate situations, lack of eye contact typically denotes lack of interest. However, this may not be true at all for the ASD spouses. Many NS spouses share that it can be very upsetting when their spouses don't look at them or their bodies during sex. Some NS spouses report that their ASD mates cannot stand to be looked at during sex and can become quite upset over this.

Eye rolling is another expression of social communication. Using and detecting it in others can be challenging or impossible for ASD individuals. This is partly because ASD people very seldom look into the eyes of others. For NS individuals, eye rolling often indicates disbelief or a "Wow! Is this person irritating or what?" type of reaction. It is usually expressed between two people who are listening to a third person speaking. It can also be used by someone who is listening to another speak and doesn't believe what's just been said. Also it can indicate "Enough already!" In cases of sexual or kissing contact, for NS people, it can also indicate extreme arousal as in a positive "Wow!" reaction.

Eye sweeps can be used to indicate a request to look or move in a specific direction.

> ASD Harry was beginning to come to his wife Sheila's work and linger a bit too long while engaging in banter that sometimes became repetitive. Sheila didn't want to embarrass Harry by saying, "Why don't you leave now?" in front of her colleagues. She began looking at Harry with her back to the others and using an exaggerated eye sweep toward the door to indicate it was time for him to leave. Luckily, Harry learned to take that cue after only one or two brief discussions about it.

In *The Self-Help Guide for Special Kids and Their Parents,* James Williams suggests that people with an ASD practice looking at others' ears when they are supposed to look them in the eye (Matthews and Williams 2000). This can give the appearance of eye contact if the person truly cannot establish eye contact. Author Kealah similarly coaches her clients on the spectrum to look in the center of the forehead. Several NS spouses we interviewed learned many years into their relationships that their partners were using a strategy such as these to avoid true, "classic" eye contact.

It's important to remember that people with an ASD do not get the same information from eye contact that NS people do. Many ASD partners say that they are concentrating on the sounds coming from the speaker's mouth (language), so looking at the speaker's eyes is too confusing. Even when they are able to maintain eye contact, it is so uncomfortable for many that they are not able to glean any information from others' eyes.

Emotional regulation

The vast majority of individuals with an ASD have great difficulty controlling their emotions. This may include what emotions are expressed, how they are expressed and when they are expressed. Further, many find it difficult to recognize when their emotions are rising in intensity. Some scientists attribute this area of challenge to differences in the amygdala, the structure in the inner area of the brain's limbic system that we know contributes to the ability to regulate and express emotions (Spezio *et al.* 2007). It is also known that individuals on the spectrum have different levels of certain neurotransmitter chemicals than those who are not on the spectrum. This can also lead to challenges in regulating emotions. Regardless of the cause, this area of difference is very marked in many individuals with Asperger syndrome.

A big, muscular partner can suddenly cry like a baby when getting a paper cut, being bumped lightly or even touched on the head, or when experiencing some other form of minor injury usually not worthy of comment by adults. Some ASD partners seem to make no effort to disguise a bad mood and, for example, they may answer the phone on a bad day by screaming "HELLO!" into the receiver. Others may be in a very happy or giddy mood and be unable to suppress that mood even when news of a death in the family or some other serious event occurs. To the unsuspecting, such behavior can be puzzling and off-putting. Difficulty with emotional regulation can lead to unsuccessful interactions with the public in jobs like grocery bagger, bank teller or store clerk. Certainly, family members might be upset if someone with an ASD were smiling and giggling at a funeral because he was recalling a very funny movie he had watched the night before. In fact, most situations in which anyone expresses unexpected emotions are potentially negative.

NS Sara explained that she and her husband Josh were planning to buy a house. They were working with a real-estate agent to look at options when they were informed that the dream home they had picked out for their family was no longer available. Josh broke into uncontrollable laughter. The agent was confused, but Sara was angry. This was not funny. They were under a deadline, and not just any house would do since they needed an extra bedroom and space for Sara's mother who was staying with them for an indefinite period of time.

It took much time and patience on Sara's part to accept that her husband was as distressed as she was and did not think it was funny at all. In fact, Sara was initially convinced that Josh's laughter was directed at his mother-in-law and the fact that she might not be able to move in with them, after all, if they didn't have enough space. Josh, on the other hand, thought Sara should understand his true feelings despite the outburst of laughter, which he could not explain well. It was only later that the two came to an understanding of each other's perspective over the situation. One night, Sara sat down to write a note to Josh. She had plans to spend the weekend at her sister's and thought writing down her feelings in a note would help her get the house-buying incident off her mind, so she could enjoy her weekend.

She explained in her note that Josh's laughter at losing the house made her feel that he was not committed to her and the plans they made as a couple, including helping out with her mother. After Josh read the note he was able to explain calmly to Sara that the laughter was his reaction to feelings of failure and not knowing what to do next.

Many times in this book, we have emphasized that neither spouse is "right or wrong"; they are just different in which of their ways are accepted by society in general.

As a good example of this point, NS Sheila told us she has an odd nervous habit of laughing when someone she loves and depends on gets hurt or is ill. Therefore, when she began dating and then married her ASD partner Harry, she completely confused and irritated him when she would laugh if he was injured. She had to explain her "quirk." It was Harry who had to learn a new interpretation of Sheila's behavior. It was Sheila's behavior that was odd by society's standards, not Harry's reaction to it.

The same is true of any of the behaviors and differences we have described in the ASD partners whose stories were shared with us.

A significant number of NS partners and spouses informed us that their ASD significant others seemed stuck in one emotion most of the time. This can be very difficult for the NS spouses to live with and can cause many misunderstandings.

Bonnie related how her ASD husband, Brad, seems to be in a contented state with a soft grin on his face most of the time. Bonnie was drawn to Brad in part because of his seemingly positive outlook and contentment with life. She did not realize until after they were married and faced serious household matters that there were many things that Brad could not deal with. Though she still tries to appreciate his contented smile, she sometimes wishes she had a partner who could help her comfort the dog and get him to the vet when hit by a car or relate to the pain she felt when she broke her arm in a fall. In both situations, Brad just smiled softly as usual and did not appear concerned at all.

Many NS spouses described their ASD partners as being in a state of continual anxiety. This probably stems from the many things that can be almost terrifying to them, such as changes in routine, expectations in social situations, sensory overload, being interrupted while focused on something or encountering events or verbal comments that are unexpected. In some cases, sensory sensitivities cause almost constant anxiety. Moving next door to a barking dog, being exposed to a screaming child, experiencing strong scents at home or in the workplace, having to use fluorescent lighting at work and many other sensory stressors can create nearly unbearable anxiety. This can result in panic attacks.

NS spouses frequently report that their ASD partners cannot function without anti-anxiety medications or use of natural relaxation techniques—including meditation, massage and even cannabis.

NS spouse Kaye told us that her husband Pete sometimes wakes up in the middle of the night with an anxiety attack. He uses an anti-anxiety medication or mild stimming behaviors (rubbing his own neck or moving his head from side to side) to relieve the attacks. When Kaye suggests using breathing exercises instead of the medication, he often says, "No. I'll take Dr. Zachary's [his doctor who prescribes the medication] form of relief." Often Kaye helps to soothe Pete by gently rubbing or lightly scratching his back. Pete calls this his "scratchies" and often requests it of Kaye when he senses he is growing anxious.

Still others said that anger was a common state for their ASD spouses in many unexpected life situations.

In the example of Pete's anxiety above, NS Kaye told us that she is alert to her husband's potential for anger on the heels of his anxiety and is motivated to help him soothe partly by her own fear of his angry outbursts. "When I see him rub the back of his neck, I start to be on guard [for other signs or ways to help him]. If he does this a second time, I know he's about to blow," she told us.

NS spouse Sheila told us that early in her marriage, if her husband Harry was in an agitated mood from a long work day or just generally having a "grouchy day," he would become very angry if he heard her laughing with others, likely due to sensory overload compounded by his existing anxiety. (See Chapter 4 for more information on sensory processing differences, and Chapter 6 for information on coping with stress.) She would notice him beginning to pace or make hand gestures behind those who were laughing. Sometimes she would try to defuse the situation by saying something serious to stop the laughter. Other times, she suggested the person or people go elsewhere with her. However, she knew that many times this attempt would not defuse the situation and that Harry would only stop his escalation once he was able to abuse her verbally. He might say, "It would be a lot funnier if you could actually clean your house once in a while" or "Why don't you start dinner instead of sitting there laughing with your friends" or even "You are so stupid, Sheila!" These scenes were painfully uncomfortable to Sheila, as well as to her friends.

Other NS spouses reported that their husbands say they would like to hit them or make other verbal expressions of wanting to commit violence. A few actually experienced physical violence. In situations of actual or threatened violence, we advise spouses to remove themselves from the immediate situation if they do not feel safe. The NS spouse then needs to set boundaries for behavior and inform the ASD spouse of these expectations. Ideally, there should be access to counselors and/or other professional supports available to both partners. It is likely that both need to learn ways to deal with emotions in themselves and their partners. *A spouse with a challenge does not make physical violence allowable and does not make verbal abuse excusable.*

Author Marci shared examples of an agitated state that her husband, Phil, displayed early in their marriage. Often it seemed more like a fretful state where Phil would pace, yell and perseverate on an opinion with which he thought Marci should agree. When first married and living in a tiny one-bedroom apartment, Marci would occasionally leave and walk around when Phil displayed this intense agitation. Putting some space between them helped Phil to move beyond his agitation and helped Marci to get away from what felt to her like an attack.

On several occasions, when the weather was bad, Marci went into the closet and sat there to get away from the situation. Phil might still continue to perseverate verbally, but would soon walk into the other room after asking Marci why she was in the closet and hearing the response, "To get away from you." Years later, while in counseling, Phil made the statement, "I still don't know why my wife used to hide in the closet," to the counselor.

Emotions are even more difficult for people on the autism spectrum to regulate when they feel pressure from social occasions. A significant number of NS spouses shared that their ASD partners become overly stressed when they have company. Sometimes an ASD spouse will go to the garage or into the yard when others are visiting. Some go about the house ignoring the company. Still others stay in the room with the guests, but do not interact, or do so very minimally and in a very uninterested or angry fashion.

Difficulty with social events can reach into everything from company parties at work to communal picnics to dances at the country club.

Sheila told us that it used to be that if her husband Harry got too upset, he would stand behind their guests and make wild gestures toward the door and mouth things she often could not understand, usually in an effort to "wish" the guests away. Although he was sometimes merely one or two feet behind the guests, he was unaware that they often could tell he was flailing his arms and sometimes could even hear the words he was "mouthing." When the guests would leave (in many instances, never to return), he would be shocked that Sheila was angry with him. After years and years of enduring this behavior, Sheila (who didn't realize until recently that her husband had an ASD) has negotiated with Harry that when he is tired of the company, it is okay for him to excuse himself by saying he must make a pre-scheduled call or that he is tired and must rest for a while.

See Chapter 6 on coping with stress for detailed illustrations of this behavior.

For strategies to help ASD partners learn emotional regulation skills, Elisa Gagnon offers *Power Cards* (Gagnon 2001). *Power Cards* (usually the size of an index card or a business card) are used to remember an important rule or self-command. For instance, a card saying, "Answer in a friendly voice," can be placed on the telephone receiver. Or the NS spouse may give her ASD partner a card saying, "Use your 'poker face,'" before heading to a somber ceremony like a funeral.

Personal space

A significant number of individuals with an ASD seem either to underestimate, overestimate or not be able to gauge personal space boundaries at all. Getting too close to people can be interpreted as simply strange or, more seriously, as threatening. Neither is good and can lead to charges of sexual harassment or cause others to fear physical harm when the ASD person is angry. At the other extreme, standing too far away can give the impression of being uninterested or rude.

Improper observance of personal space is a frequent source of complaints about ASD partners who are in the fields of medicine, teaching or the clergy. The consequences in these cases can be a loss of a job or a career.

Earlier in this book, we mentioned an ASD person who would scream, "Don't touch my hands!" when someone was being introduced to him. Others on the spectrum misjudge how close to stand to someone with whom they are engaged in conversation. In an elevator, some ASD people will stand immediately next to the only other person on the elevator or stand facing that person with only a space of two or three inches between their faces. In those cases, they may think they should speak to the person in an effort to be friendly. People not on the autism spectrum know that is *not* how such an action would be interpreted.

NS Bonnie was embarrassed when her ASD husband Brad stood shoulder to shoulder with others at church during the social hour. It might have been okay to lean in when saying hello, but then to continue in this stance even as others would back away was unnerving to many of their fellow churchgoers. Bonnie would try to pry her husband away quickly and explain to him how uncomfortable this was for others. It took Brad many months of practice finally to keep an appropriate distance.

A good "rule" for personal distance is to be an arm's length away from another person when standing, and an elbow's length away when talking to someone who is sitting. It is okay to lean down toward someone who is sitting when you are standing, or crouch next to them at eye level, if you plan to speak to them or if they are speaking to you. However, the elbow length distance keeps the other person comfortable. The exception is if someone wants to whisper to you. Then it is okay to go closer, but to turn your ear toward the person's mouth, which has you looking away from them. Again, rehearsal can help with this.

Facial recognition

Prosopagnosia, also referred to as face blindness, is an impairment in the ability to recognize other people by their faces, which can clearly impact social interaction. This appears to be a relatively common problem for individuals on the autism spectrum.

Several NS partners mentioned feeling embarrassed when their ASD spouses were unable to recognize familiar people such as neighbors or people from church whom they saw on a regular basis. In extreme cases, people with face blindness are unable to recognize their own children, especially after an absence.

ASD Pete works as a freelancer and often meets new employers and co-workers on each job site. He has no problem recognizing such people in context (although even then, he may forget their names). However, if he runs into them outside of the workplace, he's usually embarrassed at not knowing who they are when they suddenly introduce him to their own spouses and children. Outwardly, he will act courteous and even say the appropriate social greetings: "It was good to see you—and nice to meet you [to their families]. You all have a good day."

To help him in situations like this, Pete and his wife Kaye have come up with a system. If she is with him, she'll jump in and introduce herself with her hand outstretched for a handshake, saying, "Hi! I'm Kaye, Pete's wife." In most situations, the other person will automatically introduce himself or herself, stating something like, "I worked with Pete on the _____ job last spring." Pete will then pretend that it has simply slipped his mind to make the introductions and apologize, laughing. Many times when they are out together, Pete will pull Kaye aside and say, "That guy over there in the red shirt looks familiar. If he comes over and says, 'Hello,' introduce yourself, will you? I'm not sure how I know him or even if I know him."

NS Kaye is happy to help Pete out this way now. However, early in their marriage, she didn't understand his face blindness and was often offended when he'd hold entire conversations with people without introducing or even looking at her. It seemed implausible to her when Pete would tell her, "Obviously, I worked with that guy [based on the conversation I've just had], but I don't remember him."

Theory of mind

Theory of mind (ToM) is a term used to describe the ability to have insight into the thoughts, feelings, intentions, desires and beliefs of others. ToM is necessary to be able to interpret, predict and anticipate others' behavior. The terms "mind blindness" or "lack of mind reading" are also used to label this phenomenon.

Theory of mind also refers to the ability to attribute mental states to oneself. It is still unclear how ToM develops, to a limited extent, for some and not others on the autism spectrum. ToM does seem to be selectively impaired in many adults with ASDs. It is often felt that if ASD individuals are able to have a ToM, it is not intuitive or instantaneously developed.

Most ASD individuals do not have a fully operational ToM, and thus do not realize the different beliefs, thoughts, feelings, wishes and knowledge of others around them. As a result, they often appear rude, rigid, paranoid and anxious. At times, it is hard or impossible for them to empathize with others. They have difficulty trusting others, because they cannot predict their behavior and find it hard to make sense of it. Simon Baron-Cohen is known for his work on ToM and autism spectrum disorders (Baron-Cohen 1995; Baron-Cohen, Tager-Flusberg and Cohen 2007).

The ability to understand what others know, think and feel has been learned by some people in an academic fashion, using intellect and rote memory. Dr. Marcel Just, a psychologist, and his colleagues at Carnegie Mellon University and the University of Pittsburgh, have published a study that suggests that, in ASD individuals, there is an underconnectivity between the frontal and posterior areas of the brain during tasks that require the understanding of the intentions of others. The researchers then suggest that many people with autism could be "trained" to infer the intentions of others (Kana et al. 2009).

A number of NS partners informed us that their ASD partners seemed to study their actions and learn to respond appropriately, but that they did not understand their NS wives' thoughts, feelings or motivations. A few NS spouses informed us that their ASD husbands have learned to "listen" to their explanations of their thoughts and feelings and respond accordingly (though still not understanding why). This may not seem much different than "typical males" just trying to understand the opposite sex, but it does appear that much more effort is needed by the ASD spouse to understand his NS wife's thoughts and intentions.

NS Molly shared that early in their marriage her ASD husband of five years, Sam, used to think that the reason Molly would run to the bedroom crying after company left was that some of the guests had been rude and stayed too long. This was how he was feeling, not Molly. He attributed his own feelings (the guests' staying too long) to Molly to explain her behavior, not realizing that Molly was upset because of something he had done.

Molly related that one evening when neighbors were over for a cookout, Sam was not appropriately emotionally responsive when a neighbor was discussing that her dog was missing. Sam's comment was, "A good steak will help you take your mind off your dog." After a few scenarios like this Molly realized Sam was clueless and not being rude on purpose. She since has decided to make some attempts to explain people's thoughts and feelings to Sam, especially her own.

Since rewarding relationships are dependent on being able to recognize others' mental states, realizing that they may be different from one's own and responding appropriately, deficiencies in this area can cause problems in marriages and other intimate relationships.

An excellent example of this difference in sensitivity associated with an inability to see the perspective of others is a Christmas experience that one NS partner shared. At the time, the ASD husband had not been diagnosed. If he had, it can be speculated that the confusion and hurt of the NS spouse and her sister might have been avoided. Instead, the following incident caused a lot of bad feelings for the two sisters (as well as the ASD spouse, who was convinced the incident happened because his interests were completely ignored).

A sister of the NS partner was visiting for the holidays. She had taken great thought and care in choosing a gift for her brother-in-law, picking out a shirt that resembled the flannel-patterned shirts that he always wore. Upon opening the gift, the yet-to-be-diagnosed ASD husband exhibited a rude, thoughtless and over-the-top reaction, yelling that this gift was not for him because only a thoughtless idiot would have bought a gift in the wrong size—the shirt was a large instead of a medium.

His meltdown disrupted the rest of the day. He kept focusing on "idiots" who cannot give a gift that is even the correct size, and eventually left the room and refused to participate in the rest of the gift exchange. His own beliefs, needs and intentions were the only ones that existed for him. He was not able to see his wife's sister's wishes to please in choosing the gift she bought for him. Even the fact that the shirt could be exchanged was not able to calm him.

ASD Harry worked hard at trying to be subtle when he was upset because guests visited the home. He had been chided by Sheila, his very social NS wife, many times for being rude to guests. Therefore, he worked independently on strategies that might alleviate this problem. (Sheila did not realize Harry was on the spectrum until 25 years into their marriage, despite their having an ASD son and having studied ASD extensively.) This probably illustrates two important points: that all individuals on the autism spectrum are different even within the same family and that, in this case, Sheila was so focused and busy with their son that it did not occur to her that her husband's quirks and challenges were also related to having an ASD.

One day, a couple of friends stopped in to Harry and Sheila's to say hello. They had moved across the country but happened to be in town for a conference. A very relaxed and sociable couple, they arrived unannounced, which immediately presented a problem for ASD Harry. They stayed for over an hour, laughing quite a bit. Harry, who often had trouble with the sound of a lot of laughter—especially if he didn't see the humor in a discussion—soon began to pace. Then he stood directly behind the couple (about two feet away), wildly gesturing to his wife toward the door and mouthing, "Get them out!"

Sensing what was going on in the background, the couple nervously said they had better go. As Sheila escorted them out, she profusely apologized for her husband's behavior, saying, "He gets in these very uptight moods and can't seem to calm down. I just don't know what the cause is." (She was still unaware at the time of his ASD.) The couple simply replied, "We had no idea he didn't like us. We won't bother you again." In relating this scene, Sheila simply said, "[That was] another important friendship for me that was totally ruined."

When an ASD has been diagnosed, of course, there are many alternative methods to approaching such scenarios. Dr. Thomas H. Powell states in many of his lectures that when his teenage sons had visitors over to his house and his older ASD brother was there and would act in a decidedly unusual fashion, they would jokingly say to their friends, "He's okay. It's just that he is from France."

Other challenges: inappropriate social touch

In a series of gripping communications with one NS partner, we learned how tragically things can turn out when a person's challenges are not recognized or disclosed. In this case, neither the ASD partner nor the NS spouse was aware of the inappropriate social touch issues—nor even that the ASD spouse was on the spectrum—until a series of devastating incidents occurred.

The ASD partner was a highly respected scientist who studied childhood cancer. He was trusted by his colleagues as someone who related well to kids and who won their trust quickly by playing and kidding around with them when they showed up for an examination. Most kids facing cancer are frightened and cringe at the thought of painful procedures that may have to occur. To help diminish their fear, this professional playfully interacted with the children, sometimes wrestling with the boys who were patients. On two occasions, in which the boys were in their early teens, they decided, upon later reflection, that one of this man's "wrestling moves" was sexually provocative. It is unclear whether these allegations were accurate. After facing the suffering of chemo, incidents associated with early parts of the diagnosis and treatment can look very different upon reflection. In addition, this man had no idea of what was or wasn't appropriate in many aspects of life. His naivety led to charges against him of improper sexual conduct with a minor. He is prohibited from ever resuming his work and is in prison.

In the months preceding his trial, this man received an ASD diagnosis. The judge in the case was convinced that the alleged offender's lack of awareness of real dangers and the nature of his offense put him at great risk during his imprisonment and, therefore, placed him in solitary confinement. Even there, he was teased and mentally abused by the guards. To cope, he retreated into an intense interest in studying the law, which became an obsession, so that even when his loyal and loving partner and family visited him, all he could talk about was some aspect or other of law. The love and concern of his NS partner are commendable. However, she blames herself for not seeing that her spouse's odd behaviors were possibly more than just eccentricity and naivety. This couple's story is still unfolding. As with any relationship, not every outcome is positive. Though the man and his partner are still very much in love with each other, they have a lot to work out.

Several other stories shared by NS spouses about their ASD partners involved incidents of innocent physical touch that caused problems. Many were in the context of a teacher-student relationship. In some incidents, a supportive pat on the back or an excited spontaneous squeeze of the hand or shoulders to acknowledge a student's achievement have led to immediate job loss. The students in such cases reported feeling uncomfortable and/or being touched inappropriately. In each case reported, the ASD partner had no understanding of the student's negative thoughts or feelings. It took a lot of discussion to explain to the accused ASD men why the students and employers felt and reacted the way they did.

One such individual was a rabbi who had a completely limp handshake, which was interpreted by his congregation as an aversion to greeting them. His problem with hand-touching combined with many inappropriate comments to people ended badly for him. The temple later asked for his resignation.

When to intervene

How can those in relationships with ASD partners anticipate problems before it is too late? Too often, the NS partners know nothing of the problem until it is too late to help. This is an area where direct instruction is helpful to teach ASD individuals explicit boundaries and rules for proper interaction with others—especially when used at every opportunity. Also, NS wives can learn to gather information from sources other than their ASD husbands. This might be in the form of someone at his workplace who is also a friend. This is a delicate matter, as the NS spouse's inquiries can make her seem to be gossiping about her partner. Ideally, she can invite the workplace friend to share what is going on at work and make that part of their regular conversations, so that if something occurs or is building in the workplace, this person will feel comfortable in revealing the difficulty to her. It is important to find someone trustworthy who has the ASD husband's best interests at heart.

> Sheila established this kind of relationship with her husband Harry's secretary. She admitted that most of the people in his workplace resented Harry's comments and behaviors until they began to see that "He just has a really different sense of humor, but he really works hard and is fair with everyone. Also, he is very smart."

NS partners are able to consider any comment about work, places of worship and other organizations in which the ASD spouse participates for warning signs of serious miscommunication.

One spouse told us:

> Whenever my husband starts saying that someone is really stupid or is plotting against the group, I know that there may be a misunderstanding on his part about the

intent and content of his interactions with the person he is mentioning. Occasionally, he is correct, but many times he has misunderstood a joke or the way someone behaves. Sometimes, I or someone else he trusts can discuss his possible misapprehensions and he changes his attitude.

These cases speak to the need for disclosure of the diagnosis whenever it will not negatively affect the ASD husband. See the discussion on executive function in financial planning and management in Chapter 5 for a tragic example of what can happen when disclosure is withheld. However, the risks of disclosing any brain-related differences can be great (such as discrimination that could result in job loss or personal traumatizing), so public disclosure should be discussed by both partners, while ultimately remaining the sole decision of the partner with the ASD.

We would like to note that, privately, it is often important for the NS spouse to have a form of support by an individual—such as trusted family members or a close friend, a professional counselor or members of a support group. When disclosing sensitive personal information, however, the marriages that seem to have the most sustained "peace" are those where the NS spouse respectfully guards her ASD husband's right to disclose publicly on his own.

Sometimes spouse intervention can go too far.

One NS wife divorced her husband. Even after the divorce, however, her ASD ex-husband continued to ask her advice and complain to her about his lot in life. Even his mother called the now ex-wife repeatedly and asked, "Who is supposed to take care of him now?" This was hard for the NS woman to hear, as her ASD spouse had been unfaithful to her and also had a very lucrative job. Even more bizarrely, when this man remarried, his new wife would call and ask the NS woman for advice, too. "I finally had to cut the cord, and informed them all that I was no longer available as a sounding post," she said.

Lessons learned

- If your partner has strict, overly rigid social rules, demonstrate ways he may cope when others violate those rules, such as excusing himself and leaving the situation if the violation really upsets him.

- Teach some tactful conversational or written ways for your ASD spouse to tell people that their social gaffes have offended him—for instance, stating, "I don't know if you are aware that you have more than 15 items in your shopping cart, and this is the fast lane."

- Rehearse "reading" the different types of social, nonverbal communication with your ASD partner. Make it into a game through role reversal and other gimmicks.

- Watch or create your own videos to help learn to identify facial expressions.

- Avoid using eye contact and eye gaze or movement to give social information unless you are sure your partner has acquired the skills to interpret this.

- Develop and practice your own cues to give social information in advance of social functions.

- Prioritize and decide which social gatherings are important to host in your home.

- Give your ASD partner a specific role or roles for social events to alleviate some of the stress: greeting guests, parking people's cars, being the bartender, doing the grilling or running to the store for last-minute items.

- Review the sequence of events ahead of time before hosting or attending social events, as such priming alleviates stress caused by uncertainty of what will happen.

- If there is a lot of social chitchat as the focus for a gathering, give the ASD partner an excuse and opportunity to "escape" the situation for a while.

- Bargain with your spouse to make social events worth his while: "If you stay at the card game for a complete set tonight, I'll go to the electronics store with you on Saturday."

- If appropriate, confide in some of the visitors upfront and explain that your partner may be uncomfortable and as a result may not be joining you, etc.

- Work with your ASD spouse to find a variety of relaxing activities, such as retreating to a quiet spot, listening to music, rocking (or other repetitive movement) or perhaps reading or doing another short intellectual activity of interest.

- Use concrete physical estimates of proper personal space.

- Consider disclosure of the diagnosis carefully. If the ASD partner is employed in a capacity that involves nurturing trust, it may be better to disclose his challenge, rather than risk a misunderstanding that could lead to serious job consequences.

- Realize that this is a neurological condition and some assistance and coping strategies are needed.

- Do not rely on your ASD partner to notice changes pertaining to your face and hair even when asked directly about it.

- Find creative mnemonics to help him recall names and faces: "Red-headed Rita," for example.

- Use social autopsies to help teach successful social skills.

- Remember, being the NS person in an NS-ASD relationship does not make you automatically correct. Sometimes you are the one who has misjudged a person's intentions or the appropriateness of a situation.

Chapter 4

Sensory Processing Differences

A great majority of individuals with an ASD process sensory information differently than non-spectrum individuals. Though sensory sensitivity is not currently a diagnostic criterion for a diagnosis of an autism spectrum disorder, research attests to an unusual pattern of sensory perception and response (Attwood 2006; Carley 2008; Grandin 2008). Not surprisingly, then, according to the vast majority of NS spouses interviewed, sensory sensitivities of vision, touch, smell, sound and taste have caused a lot of challenges for their ASD spouses and have seriously impacted parts of their relationships with each other.

Sensory processing refers to how the brain registers, organizes, filters, integrates, understands and then responds to sensory input. This can affect each of the five senses of hearing, sight, touch, taste and smell, as well as the less well-known vestibular (movement) and proprioceptive (awareness of muscles, joints and body position) senses. Someone with sensory processing differences can be oversensitive or undersensitive to sensory inputs or can be a combination of both. For example, the person might be highly distressed by bright lights, but almost totally unaware of pain stimuli.

Sensory processing differences are seen across the autism spectrum. The senses involved and the degree of sensitivity vary from person to person. While often viewed as a challenge, under certain circumstances the unique sensory processing abilities of a person on the autism spectrum can be an asset.

ASD Pete exhibited this during a family barbecue. His wife Kaye told us that when an oil lamp suddenly caught fire, she and the other family members panicked. But Pete stayed very outwardly calm and reacted with cat-like reflexes: first, running to the garage for a fire extinguisher; then, when the extinguisher malfunctioned, quickly using it to knock the lamp (now a ball of fire) to the ground and stomp it out. He was later confused as to why no one else had reacted so clear-headedly. Kaye explained that just the sight of the fire was enough to paralyze her and everyone else at the gathering.

In her work as a communications coach, author Kealah has seen this ability to react well under pressure in others who aren't on the autism spectrum when the "fight-or-flight" reaction occurs in their brains, changing their brain chemistry and allowing them to make critical snap judgments. In each case, a strong fear component (such as the presence of phobia or past traumas) is always absent from that particular fight-or-flight moment. This allows the judgment and reaction to happen unimpeded.

For those on the autism spectrum, however, the centers of their brains that control this response (the locus coeruleus-noradrenergic (LC-NA) systems) are inherently different (ScienceDaily 2009). Therefore, they are statistically prone to being over-reactive in what seem to be non-emergency situations and vice versa. Many of the NS wives we interviewed shared similar stories about their husbands behaving in what one of them called "superhero" fashion.

Auditory issues (hearing)

People on the autism spectrum often experience sound distortions and sensitivities. Some hear sounds around them in waves of echo. Others experience an abnormal variation in volume level, almost like turning the volume on a radio up and down.

For many, sound frequencies can range from mildly irritating to downright excruciating.

In the case of author Susan's daughter, who has an ASD, the sound of whistling almost always incites her to extreme agitation, sometimes to the point of an emotional meltdown.

She also has a hard time tolerating a relative who loves music and sings loudly and very off-key most of the time.

The hum of fluorescent lighting, the sound of fireworks, the "scratchy" sound of plastic bags being moved around, certain types of music: All these everyday sounds can be upsetting to individuals with ASDs.

In a marriage, a lot of give-and-take is expected in all areas of life. For many ASD-NS couples, sound sensitivity needs to be considered frequently. Often the sound level at parties, sporting events and other large social gatherings can be so distressing that the ASD partner either refuses to attend or becomes upset and leaves. Most public gatherings are filled with simultaneous conversations. Although few of the conversations are directed to the ASD person, he has problems filtering them out in an effort to attend to comments that are directed to him. This is a cause of stress and can impair social interactions.

Some ASD partners become very agitated at the sound of children crying, tantruming or even screeching with glee. In fact, the typical sounds of children have led to shutdowns for ASD partners in several of the relationships recounted here. Many NS partners shared that it was difficult for them to leave their children with partners on the spectrum due to the ASD partners' inability to cope with the noise of their children. In some cases, upon arriving home, NS wives found that their husbands had escaped into a different room or activity (such as watching TV) to focus, stay calm and drown out the sounds of the children. This behavior seemed irresponsible to the wives and, in fact, could have potentially put the children at risk.

However, by identifying sounds that upset the ASD partners and finding accommodations that help them handle the noise better, couples can facilitate healthy compromises in this area. Some find ear plugs or sound-blocking headphones helpful for everyday use. This is just like using sunglasses on bright days or nose plugs for swimming. It also allows the ASD father to observe visually his children and their safety, even as he tends to his own sensory needs.

Visual processing (sight)

In this chapter, the term "visual processing" refers to, in its general sense, how the brain interprets information taken in through the eyes. This includes depth perception, peripheral vision, direction of gaze and even visual distortion as opposed to the ability to see clearly. Black-and-white checked floor tiles, "busy" carpeting and wallpaper with multiple patterns are all examples of things that can cause confusion, anxiety and even mobility problems in someone with an ASD.

We have observed at autism conferences the distress caused by the busy patterns of hotel carpeting that individuals with an ASD experience. Many freeze on such carpets, unable to walk or keep their balance. Some place notebooks in their lower line of vision to avoid becoming dizzy or distracted.

Certain colors, light intensities, light pulsations and visual configurations can distort the sight of people on the spectrum. In some cases, this can trigger seizures.

> An NS partner wrote, "My husband is easily over-stimulated by excess action, such as people moving in varied directions, crowds, etc."

Sensitivity to bright colors can overwhelm some ASD partners.

> One NS spouse who loves to wear bright red was asked by her ASD husband to stop wearing this color because it nauseated him. He was not able to look at her when she wore red; it overwhelmed him so much that he had to close his eyes. Another NS partner mentioned that certain shades of yellow or orange gave her ASD partner a headache and sometimes led to aggressive behavior on his part because he perceived the bright colors as a threat.

> One ASD husband was terrified by specific motions he detected in his peripheral vision. Every time he saw a truck approaching when walking on the sidewalk, he would yell, "Look out!" and shove his wife against a building or fence,

trying to get her as far away from the truck as possible. He was certain they would be hit by the truck.

Visual processing can be a strength for people on the autism spectrum.

Marci's husband Phil is known by their friends, family and neighbors for his ability to open up the hood of a car and instantly notice if a wire, hose or anything else is not attached properly or is dirty, out of place or is otherwise not in working order. He has also used his amazing visual processing skills to help with building walls, fences, decks and other structures. He is able to see if something is out of place and needs to be moved—often down to less than a quarter of an inch.

In another example of using strong visual abilities and visual processing abilities, many of the NS partners explained that written communication such as notes, letters and emails were often a better way to communicate with their ASD partners than verbal communication, as the ASD partners could focus visually and not become as easily distracted. At such times, the ASD partners were better able to recall the information read, rather than when the same information was given verbally. This visual information can be referred to over and over again as needed.

The good news is that there are many ways to cushion visual sensitivities. Irlen Lenses (http://irlen.com) produces a variety of specialized glasses overlays that can help people with color, pattern, reading and other sight distortion and distress issues. Also, some forms of prism lenses and visual therapies, also supplied by Irlen, can help. Visual therapy, done with the aid of a specialist, can range from training a person to tolerate visual challenges with less anxiety to simply training individuals to wear sunglasses whenever exposed to all but low levels of light. Wearing a hat can help block out bright light even in stores and at home.

NS Kaye has taken to buying cheap sunglasses in bulk and storing them in various places, so that if she is with her ASD husband Pete and he begins irritably complaining of the light in his eyes, she can quickly hand him a pair. Pete has recently begun taking a cue from his wife on this, and now stores one to three pairs in his vehicle at all times.

Olfactory processing (smell)

Everything from perfume, deodorant, hairspray and hand lotion, to animals, foods, dyes and/or fabrics can produce a negative reaction in individuals with an ASD who have odor sensitivities. In one extreme case we heard of, one ASD partner was odor-sensitive to his own child!

David and NS Sally had adopted a child internationally. Something in the baby's diet made him have an odor similar to French fries, according to David. This smell distressed ASD David so much that Sally had to shampoo their new son's hair with lavender-scented shampoo several times a day for the first month he was with them to alleviate the smell. Finally, the smell went away and David was relieved and more interactive with their son. Sally resented the fact that her husband was avoiding the baby in those important bonding experiences of the first few weeks of his time with them. She expected that David would love the baby so much that he would subject himself to the unpleasant (for him) smell, rather than staying away from their new son. In some ways, this was akin to expecting a partner who is allergic to strawberries to eat them and, therefore, not a very reasonable expectation.

NS Sara had an interesting example of sensitivity to smells that she shared. When she and ASD Josh were first married, Josh was a heavy smoker. Josh had expressed, however, that he wanted to quit and had tried on several occasions. He felt that, with Sara's support and the motivation of his father's recent diagnosis of lung cancer, he could quit for good. He did, in fact, quit smoking, going "cold turkey" and stopping instantaneously one morning. About three weeks after quitting, Josh called Sara while she was at work very concerned that something in the refrigerator had gone bad. He complained of the horrible smells, and insisted she had to clean out the refrigerator when she came home from work. It turned out that Josh's very sensitive sense of smell was returning. This was just one example of many to come that illustrated Josh's highly perceptive nose. From this point on, Josh had to relearn about his strong sense of smell that he had "lost" and forgotten while he was smoking. He began to recall and share with Sara more examples of his keen sense of smell even from his childhood. For example, he could not sit in the same room with his favorite aunt if she had used a particular hairspray.

Many NS spouses explained to us that they were unable to wear perfume around their husbands, or that if they did wear perfume, it had always to be the same brand.

Somatosensory processing (touch)

Some people with an ASD cannot stand to be touched in any way. In extreme cases, unwanted touch can bring a feeling of pain. Others can tolerate touch only when properly notified ahead of time and after giving special permission. In general, a firm touch to the arms or legs is better tolerated, whereas a touch that is perceived as lighter may bring on a feeling of pain, panic or general discomfort. For some, any touch around the head or midsection may bring a feeling of pain or panic.

Intimate touch

Not surprisingly, for many ASD partners, romantic touch can be extremely stressing and sometimes just about impossible. Specific acts are often taboo, ranging from intercourse to massage and kissing, even to hand-holding, depending on the couple.

NS spouse Sheila told us that her ASD spouse Harry cannot stand to have his hand stroked, as one may do to soothe someone. Also, he "jumps out of his skin" if she forgets and scratches his back.

To create some marital peace around this issue, the NS partner may need to lower expectations for touch and sexual intimacy. The ASD partner may attempt to slowly desensitize himself or perhaps pursue sensory integration therapy, as this type of therapy can train his mind and body to react differently and to cope better with distorted sensory information. Counseling can help with issues of past abuse, if these are a part of the sensory problem. This therapy helps people think differently about distressing issues and to learn new ways of coping with difficult situations.

In other therapeutic examples, some people benefit from working through the tactile sensitivities by experiencing touch in the dark, as at least one other sense (sight) is blocked for them. It may also help to muffle sound or eliminate or reduce some other sense to prevent it from adding to the touch sensitivities.

For couples who wish to create their own desensitization plans, we recommend that they make sure to anticipate a slow pace, using a plan for slow exposure that increases over time (using a lot of love). In rare cases, this issue has persisted to the point that a couple decides it is okay for the NS partner to have a sexual partner who respects the rest of the relationship that the couple wants to maintain. While unorthodox, this seems to work for a few partners with whom we spoke.

Fascination with touch

In some cases, if an ASD person *likes* some of these sensations, he may become obsessed with touch or with sex. If he is not able to reduce this obsession to private situations, he can be arrested. Sadly, this has been the case in some situations.

A young ASD teen was becoming very interested in the difference in female anatomy versus his own. One of his fixations was the female breast. One day in a store, the young man was waiting in line to purchase an item. He repeatedly stared at the breasts of the woman behind him in the line. Curious about how those breasts might feel, he reached out and touched one of them. He was charged with and convicted of sexual battery. Now he must live his life under the constraints of a sexual offender. This impacts his ability to live in supervised disability housing and his ability to be a teacher's aide.

It is important to note that obsession with sex is relatively rare in married ASD individuals, according to statistics that correlate with our research (Hénault 2006). The vast majority of ASD-NS couples fall in the former category. Sex poses difficulties for most of these couples in some form.

Texture touch

Sensitivity to touch can involve problems with certain textures. Temple Grandin (1986) writes that she can only stand to wear one style of clothing, mostly made out of the same fabrics: western-style shirts with blue jeans and boots.

> NS Kaye's husband Pete is similar: he wears polo-style shirts with short sleeves and often stretches out the arms and waistbands, so the light rubbing of the elastic or fabric on his skin doesn't bother him when he walks. He is so emphatic about his clothing preferences that he wore a short-sleeved dress shirt to their wedding, with no jacket or tie.

Texture is involved in foods, also. Authors Susan and Marci each have an adult child on the spectrum who gags on certain textures of food—one on anything that is the consistency of pudding, the other on drinks of a pulpy consistency.

Pressure touch

A significant number of ASD individuals are helped by deep pressure, finding it calming and relaxing, whether through therapeutic massage, weighted vests and blankets or other similar methods, such as Temple Grandin's "squeeze machine" (Grandin 1986), a contraption she created that puts padded pressure on both the front and back sides of her prone body when she lies down in it. Many individuals known to us have various ways to provide a certain amount of pressure to points on their bodies throughout the day. Tightened belts, shoes, armbands and hats are some examples that have been shared with us.

Pain

Individuals with an autism diagnosis may experience more or less pain than NS people. This means that simple touch incurred in daily life, such as a handshake or a pat on the back, may be painful to them. In the case of hypo-sensitivity to pain, where an ASD individual has a heightened pain threshold, such a person may not realize he has a broken bone or other serious injury.

A few of the NS spouses we spoke to mentioned serious medical conditions that were not detected and addressed in a timely manner, because of their husbands' extremely high pain thresholds. These conditions included heart attacks, appendicitis and gall bladder attacks. In less dramatic cases, hypo-sensitivity may cause an ASD person to shake hands too firmly or to hit someone when he means only to gently pat someone.

Different sensitivity levels, like many other aspects of Asperger syndrome, can be a gift in many circumstances.

Sheila reported that her ASD husband Harry once demonstrated incredible ability to concentrate and ignore physical pain. While driving home from work, Harry was stopped at an intersection when his car was struck from behind by a drunk driver. The driver was so intoxicated that he had not even decreased his speed before impact. The back of Harry's car was imploded into the rear seat of the vehicle, piercing the fuel tank of Harry's car. Harry told Sheila that, as he emerged from his car, he could see the pavement was covered with gasoline from his now destroyed gas tank. The drunken driver was staggering toward Harry, mumbling apologies, with a cigarette dangling from his mouth. Harry reached out and grabbed the lit cigarette from the drunk man's mouth and smothered it in the palm of his hand to extinguish it. Only later did he notice the burn in his palm from extinguishing the cigarette.

Seeing touch

A rare but interesting strength in the somato-sensory system that is experienced by a small number of individuals on the spectrum is synesthesia. This neurological phenomenon involves one sense stimulating another. In the case of touch, a few individuals on the spectrum can detect an object's color by touch.

> Author Susan remembers the brief time during which her daughter, Beth, was discovered to have synesthesia. She was able to detect an item's color by touch. This phenomenon lasted about eight weeks from the time it was detected by her occupational therapist. It seemed that the more social skills Beth gained, the less she showed extraordinary savant skills.

Temperature

Some individuals on the spectrum experience an extreme sensitivity or lack of sensitivity to temperature and climate. They may not be aware of heat or cold to the point of danger. In other cases, a change in temperature can be very distressing to them, or they may be sensitive only to cold temperatures or only to hot temperatures. Some eat cold foods exclusively; others strictly adhere to tepid or warm food and liquids. Several NS spouses informed us that their

ASD husbands seem to have a very narrow temperature comfort zone, which is hard to maintain constantly. A couple of the NS spouses informed us that they needed to sleep in separate rooms at times, due to the wide variation of temperature needs between them and their husbands.

Proprioception

Proprioception is another piece of the somato-sensory system. It refers to one's awareness of one's body's position in space. This can lead to an odd gait, looking rather unusual when dancing (stiffness in the shoulders or a lack of rhythm) and awkwardness during sex. Sometimes individuals with poor proprioception have an odd posture, which affects their social acceptance.

When stressed or excited, some individuals with an ASD will draw up their arms to about waist height with their hands down-turned and their elbows against their bodies. Others will rock back and forth while hugging themselves (as one might do when cold). Still others will flick their fingers (usually using the middle finger against the thumb). It's important to note that many individuals with an ASD are very physically graceful and don't have these issues. Those who do have proprioception issues will experience them in different ways. One man we heard of had regular difficulty maneuvering his body into a vehicle.

Kristi Sakai does a wonderful presentation entitled "Sanctuary" (Sakai 2007). This describes making a sensory-secure and comfortable environment for ASD partners and children within the home. Respecting the sensory sensitivities of the partner and/or children's special challenges can make home a true refuge. Read her book, *Finding Our Way* (Sakai 2006), to learn more about accomplishing this goal.

Lessons learned

- Identify sounds that upset your partner and find accommodations that help him handle the noise better.

- When appropriate, use visual accommodations and therapies to alleviate the intensity of sensory reactions.

- If these therapies are explored and don't work, or if you cannot afford to try these therapies, negotiate with your ASD partner to find out which situations are the most distressing and then avoid them when possible.

- When possible, work out accommodations for smell sensitivities such as keeping a scented handkerchief that has a smell the ASD person likes, so that he can smell the "good" scent rather than the distressing one.

- Avoid "smelly" situations. Remember, if something gave you a headache, which is what usually happens when somebody has a sensitivity to certain smells, you probably would not want your partner to expose you repeatedly to it.

- Be sure *both* partners pursue adaptations. Consider sex therapy that is sensitive to the needs of someone with an ASD.

- Be aware of lack of sensitivity to temperature to the extent of going outside with no coat on when it is below zero or not wearing light clothes when it is dangerously hot. Sometimes the only successful accommodations in such situations are teaching the person to watch, listen or read the weather conditions and forecast then establish a list of appropriate dress for certain temperature ranges. For individuals who must have a cold room or must have a really warm room, NS spouses may have to accommodate by adapting their mode of dress to the situation.

Chapter 5

Executive Function Skills
and Challenges

The term "executive function" refers to a set of mental processes that are performed when we plan, organize and sequence the steps of a task, manage time or use past knowledge to carry out an action or activity. It also affects the mental strategies we use to memorize things and retrieve information from memory, as well as the ability to reflect, evaluate work and monitor progress toward a goal.

Planning, organizing and executing a task or project to its completion are areas where some on the autism spectrum seem very skilled, likely because it applies to a "special interest" or obsession. However, most ASD people are challenged in at least some aspects of planning and organizational skills. Their planning may be entirely inflexible, because they are not able to "shift gears" to incorporate new information and problem-solve an alternative solution. This then looks to others like an obsession that they feel the need to control.

Even individuals who insist upon order and may, therefore, seem to be proficient in executive functioning may not be able to execute home improvement tasks, projects at work or craft projects. It is not always that they don't start these tasks, though setting priorities to get started is a common problem. It is more that they seem unable to complete those tasks. Developing timelines, making outlines of the steps to a task, even following video instructions for how to complete a certain task, may not be sufficient to help ASD individuals begin, go through the required steps and complete even basic projects.

A few spouses describe fluctuating executive functioning abilities in their ASD partner. Sometimes something as simple as making a sandwich can appear to be overwhelming for the ASD partner, especially when he's depressed, stressed or especially anxious (emotions that are not uncommon for many on the autism spectrum).

Consider the steps that are involved: (a) deciding what to put on the sandwich; (b) gathering the ingredients, including a plate and utensils (and maybe a pan and appliance if making a grilled cheese sandwich, for example); (c) sequentially putting the ingredients together; (d) washing and/or putting the ingredients and utensils away (and possibly dealing with appliances).

Think of the many possibilities to execute a variety of seemingly simple tasks that can cause friction in a relationship unless there is understanding and extra allowance made for these executive function deficits. Paying bills on time, keeping up the exterior and interior of a house or apartment, cleaning out the garage and many other "regular" tasks of daily living for a married person can be so daunting to an individual with an ASD that he may not even begin the effort.

On the other hand, planning and organizing activities or events can be so compulsive for some ASD partners that everything must be executed according to the plan they have in mind or else they are distraught. Still others can plan, but never support the NS partner in helping with chores and carrying out the efforts they've planned.

One NS wife told us that her husband would agree to hosting dinner parties with her. However, the joy of entertaining was smothered by his absolute need for control during these events. He would plan one half-hour for cocktails and then, regardless of the mood of the guests or a late arrival, cocktails would be removed (sometimes even pulled out of the hands of someone who hadn't taken a sip) and all present would be ordered to sit down to dinner. The courses of the dinner would proceed in like fashion, with half-eaten salads or barely tasted soups taken away according to the serving schedule.

In this chapter, we review some of the areas of married life that are most gravely affected by this difference in executive function, such as work skills, domestic chores and vacations.

Vacations

Many NS spouses shared that taking a family or couples' vacation was very frustrating. Many a spouse has told us that her ASD partner has a great time planning vacations or local trips, but absolutely does not enjoy the actual event. Usually, they will start a trip, but as soon as delays or diversions occur, the ASD partner becomes upset or refuses to comply with the safety aspects of slowing down a "timed" plan. Thus, road detours, flight cancellations or delays, children or partners needing to stop to eat or use the bathroom, all can lead to a meltdown by the ASD spouse or his use of excessive emotional or physical force in reaction to these delays. Some ASD partners openly weep or yell. Others stop talking to anyone. Yet others might swear at a police officer during a traffic stop or road block. One ASD spouse hit the steering wheel of an older car with such force that it cracked.

Many of the NS spouses we have interviewed have said that their husbands take them on car trips in which they stop the car only for gas. All eating and bathroom stops must take place at that time and only for the time it takes to fill up the car with gas and pay.

> ASD Pete explained to his wife in a therapy session that he often forgets to think of her needs on long car trips, because he is so caught up in the "map and timeline matrix" he's busy envisioning in his head.

Men like Pete often do this to their own detriment, as well, forgetting that they themselves need meal and restroom breaks and thereby pushing their bodies beyond healthy physical bounds. This is when executive function skills are shown, and exhibited dysfunctionally in overdrive.

One woman threatened to call the police on her ASD partner using her car phone if he didn't exit the expressway, so their child could eat. She said she would charge him with child abuse. The ASD partner never questioned how she would know the police number (this was before the common use of 911 for emergencies) or even how to describe their location. He simply complied with the request and stopped. This was an extreme but effective mechanism for altering her husband's rigid schedule.

In one meeting of a group of spouses, NS Sheila said:

> I would compare our vacations to the movie *National Lampoon's Vacation*, except there is nothing funny about our vacations. My husband hates to travel. He hates the unpredictability of it and the need to talk to strangers. He also hates unknown foods, using public bathrooms and sometimes even seeing new sights. He spends most of our vacation time after arrival doing errands for others, such as going to the store, because he knows how to do that and doesn't have to socialize to do it. I now spend most of my vacations with friends or alone. It is easier for both of us.

Continuing, Sheila pointed to another benefit of this arrangement for her husband:

> When I trot off on one of my trips, many of our friends think I'm an awful wife and partner. However, this works out well for my husband, as they include him in dinner parties and things while I am gone. He doesn't always go, but he appreciates being included. These are our friends who think his different behavior and naivety are due to his great intelligence.

Household projects: an executive function dilemma

Some wives report that their engineer husbands start home improvement projects but never complete them. Others report that their accountant husbands never do their taxes or pay their bills on time. Several spouses whose husbands had high-paying and high-responsibility financial planning jobs noted that these successful businessmen made no future financial provisions for their own families. Such circumstances present unique quandaries for the NS wives, who often feel it is improper to reach out for help in their husbands' fields of expertise.

These executive functioning dilemmas seem to be a very common high-stress issue for NS spouses. NS partners who are most successful in coping either negotiate the use of an outside contractor, accountant, financial planner, etc., or take over a given task. When financial resources are limited due to low income, the NS partners said they tend to resent having to take on yet another responsibility. However, some find a successful compromise by helping with a piece of the task or by prompting their spouses with reminders. Sometimes visual reminders can be put on calendars that are very specific for daily review. Some NS-ASD couples use management software, such as QuickBooks® or Microsoft Money,® and computer calendars that "remind" the user about important appointments and/or deadline dates.

In one tragic case, an ASD partner had risen to the post of chief financial officer of a large company. He had helped the company's accounting reporting system keep up with incredible company growth and was, therefore, highly regarded by his employer. Eventually, he split the records of the corporation into two divisions: the "everyday" records and those that covered the income and expenses of executive staff. The day-to-day recording was done by his staff. However, due to privacy concerns, he kept the executive records himself. His procedures were sloppy and depended on his incredible memory and retention of facts. He felt this proved his intelligence and how needed he was. He also felt it kept the records cryptic to anyone from outside the company who might look at them. These records always passed audits because he was there to provide the information needed to make sense of the records.

When new management took over, they became suspicious of these practices. They started taking over his areas of authority and inadvertently shredded the records that backed up the books related to the executive accounts, because of confusion over his unusual filing system. When the ASD man was questioned about book entries and didn't have the data to back them up, he was forced to resign, losing all of his company-related benefits in the process.

His NS partner told us:

> I knew how things had appeared and urged him to explain himself to the new management. However, he felt they had set him up to save themselves from paying the benefits due to him. I could never convince him otherwise, and I knew that if I approached them and tried to explain, it would look like I was making excuses for a crook. I had only learned of my husband's ASD a few years previous to his dismissal and had not revealed even to him that I was reasonably sure he had an ASD. I knew they would think I was making up his "disability."

In a later conversation, this same NS partner said, "Even if I'd known sooner about his ASD, I probably wouldn't have disclosed it to his employer [then], as it might have jeopardized his job."

Individuals like this man are externally (visually) organized, but internally disorganized. This can affect many areas of home life, too. Some ASD partners must have certain surface areas (kitchen counters, table tops, dresser tops) immaculately clean, orderly and completely clutter free. Yet those same partners may have drawers, closets, cubby holes, etc., that are completely devoid of organization, classification or any form of cleanliness. We heard many stories about copies of wills being stored in sock drawers or screwdriver sets mixed into the silverware drawer.

When the NS spouses try to help by organizing the disorganized materials, such as bank statements thrown into a sock drawer, by putting them somewhere logical and putting them in order, the ASD partners often melt down or verbally abuse their NS partners.

NS spouse Sheila says:

> It is hard to believe that someone so intelligent could lose really, really important items almost on a daily basis. Harry loses his wallet (in the house) once or twice weekly. This can result in missing or being late for appointments, airline flights and other important events.

Sheila has now installed a file cabinet that is just for Harry's papers in their home. So far, Harry has attempted to use it, but still stashes papers about the house.

Financial planning and management

Like the ASD partner in the anecdote above, many people with Asperger syndrome struggle to plan and manage their own household budgets, even if they have (as most do) above-average math skills. It seems their lack of theory of mind (see Chapter 3), or their inability to use forethought to project into the future, added to their poor executive function skills, can really trip them up in these areas.

> NS Joy always trusted ASD Frank, as he was a highly educated business professional. He did excellent financial planning for others. Therefore, when she would ask that they start a joint savings account and Frank would say he had company-related savings that were more lucrative, she demurred to his wisdom. She did, however, save for their children. She noticed that Frank was spending lavishly on her and the kids, but she thought it must be in proportion to his income. If she protested, he always chided, "When you make as much money as I, you can tell me how much to spend and how much to save." Later in life, Joy greatly regretted not insisting on receiving a portion of their income for a joint savings account, because there was only her small personal savings to fall back on when Frank's company ultimately went bankrupt.

(See Chapter 7 for more examples of financial planning issues in NS-ASD relationships, especially where children are involved.)

In some cases where financial goals and directives are very concrete, ASD executive functioning skills can be quite a boon.

Pam and Jim said that his ASD traits have always worked in their household's favor when it comes to budgeting and bill-paying. NS Pam shared that Jim's "system" involves a visual calendar and one designated desk drawer for all money-related items. This allows her access to budget information that not all NS spouses receive, and lets her supply Jim with additional points—like setting aside extra money for gifts around holidays and family birthdays—that his lack of theory of mind (see Chapter 3) may prohibit him from considering. In this way, they have been successful in both managing their money and saving for the future.

Activities of daily living

Day-to-day life activities can also be a challenge for ASD partners. Attempting to process new information that differs from routine "input information" (as one ASD spouse calls it) is not as easy as simply reprogramming a computer, as this man's allegory would imply. Instead, it can often take several requests from NS partners—plus reminder tools like written notes taped to walls, alarm reminders programmed into cell phones and personal computers, or even strategically placed photos—and a lot of time, practice and repetition to make a lasting change in daily routine. One NS spouse shared that it took her seven months of repeated requests before her ASD husband began regularly to put his shoes on the shoe mat in their foyer instead of dropping them in front of the doorway. Enduring this lengthy change period requires much patience on the part of both partners. However, once such changes are made, they are then, like all other ASD routines, difficult to break.

Because executive function involves decision-making, this can cause a number of issues regarding daily activities.

Brad is more than happy to go to the store for Bonnie. However, he often comes back without several items on the list. When Bonnie asks, "Where are the _____?" Brad will say that the brand they use wasn't there. Despite having a cell phone, Brad doesn't call to ask about a reasonable substitute; he just doesn't purchase a similar item.

Another NS partner told us that when they vacation at her parents' mountain cabin, her husband invents reasons to go to the store to buy *anything* mentioned as a need by *anyone* present:

> I think he doesn't know how to use the leisure and social time the rest of us enjoy at the cabin. We hunt and fish, and he hates both activities. He will chat amicably for a short time, but then retreat to the store or to doing dishes, burning the trash, etc. He seems to need to bring his daily household routine with him. The change of pace is not fun for him.

A change in assignments for daily or weekly chores between partners can be very difficult.

> NS Sheila travels frequently in her work. When she is leaving, she asks Harry to water their four plants twice a week. But this has presented an ongoing executive function challenge to Harry. When they began losing plants during her absences, Sheila asked that he water the plants every three days. When this, too, didn't work, she tried phoning home on the appropriate day and asking Harry to water the plants as she waited on the phone. So far, she reports, this hasn't worked either.
>
> "I can't ask a neighbor to come in when he is there to water the plants. That would embarrass him," she laments. "It seems that if it is usually my job, then he just can't do it."
>
> Another weekly chore of Sheila's is cleaning out spoiled food from the refrigerator.

One time, I was gone for several weeks. When I returned, Harry opened the refrigerator and scolded me for all of the spoiled items within. He seemed to feel no responsibility in this. Another time, he just threw out everything except condiments in the refrigerator.

Sheila is now trying to have Harry help her with these chores when she is in town, instead of when she is gone. Her hope is that he will begin to see them as shared chores and will learn how to do them effectively. Her reasoning, she told us, is that if he can't do a chore when she is home, he will likely not be able to do it when she is away. She is hoping he can begin to see it as a "shared responsibility."

The concept of sharing is often elusive or at best confusing for people with ASDs. This is partly an executive function challenge, because of the many hidden rules surrounding taking turns and "pitching in," and because of the multiple variables in play when determining how to "share the load" of any task.

Pete and Kaye have agreed to share the responsibilities of pet care for their cat. ASD Pete knows the feeding schedule and is diligent about cleaning up "kitty messes," such as hairballs and overturned planters. However, he leaves all dealings with their vet's office up to his NS wife Kaye. And he sees the litter box as a household chore that is not his main duty, Kaye told us.

Although Pete has agreed to "pitch in" and scoop the cat box from time to time, Kaye says that he will frequently forget actually to do so if his attention is drawn elsewhere. She has learned to post notes in key locations to remind him or to phone home and say, "You should probably do this now before you forget." Otherwise, she says, "I know if I ask him to take care of it as I'm on my way out the door for the day, I'm pretty much going to return home to a dirty litter box."

Author Marci has had success with a calendar to post appointments and important chores for her husband Phil. It took many months before checking the calendar became part of Phil's daily routine. It started with posting important appointments for all family members. After many months, it became a habit for Phil to check the calendar every day. Then two important chores were added to the calendar: taking out the trash and watering the plants. It took patience to start the pattern of using the calendar, but now both Marci and Phil enjoy how well this has worked. Even when Marci is away from home, Phil can now use this visual aid to remind himself, rather than relying on Marci, to participate in household daily chores.

When it comes to instructions for complex routine chores, many wives who are NS shared that they have learned to provide specific parameters—such as taping a note in the laundry room that says:

- Step 1: Sort out all of the all-white clothes from the rest of the clothes in the laundry hamper.

- Step 2: Put the washer settings on delicate cycle and cold water.

- Step 3: Turn on the washer.

- Step 4: Add one tablespoon of bleach into the water as it fills.

- Step 5: Load the white clothes into the water up to the "full load" line.

- Step 6: Close the lid on the washing machine.

They told us that they cannot assume any step is a given, because that often is just not the case for their ASD mates. Visual cues, such as the use of different colored or shaped laundry baskets, can also aid the often-confusing process of laundry in particular. For example, Marci and Phil use round baskets to designate dirty laundry and rectangular for clean clothes.

Another NS spouse reported that her two children were in elementary school when she began attending grad school for work-related certification. Her ASD spouse encouraged the kids to complain when she "deserted them" on Monday and Tuesday nights for classes. However, neither the spouse nor the kids ever complained when she left for her Thursday night classes. Then one Thursday, as she was leaving, one of their kids said, "Oh boy! This is chips and dip night!" Suddenly, the woman realized why Thursday nights were different: her ASD spouse liked to snack on potato chips and flavored dipping sauce every Thursday night as he watched his favorite sitcom, often eating until he was too full for supper. It seemed that he thought he could stick to his usual Thursday night routine, feeding the children what he liked to eat (instead of a nutritionally balanced supper) and still be doing a good job as a father.

Many NS spouses shared similar stories of executive function challenges in parenting where their ASD mates had difficulty processing new ideas when home routines were disrupted in some way. In some cases, the wives actually had a hard time trusting their husbands to parent alone because of this, and only left their children in the care of other trusted family members or babysitters, rather than with the children's own ASD fathers. However, some felt comfortable rehearsing scenarios with their partners (for example, "What will you feed the children tonight while I'm gone?" or "Who will you call if one of the kids gets hurt?") or leaving detailed instructions and/or ready-made suppers.

One of the most extreme episodes of executive function we heard of was the following:

An ASD man asked his wife to phone the water company to check on a bill's status. Although it was not an unusual request (she made all phone calls to utility companies, since her husband did not like to communicate via telephone), his timing was indeed strange: She was going into labor with their son! It took several conversations after this for the NS woman to explain to her husband exactly why it was poor timing on his part to make the request at that time.

Lessons learned

- Help your partner recognize his organizational strengths and weaknesses. Compliment him on strengths (packing the car or loading the dishwasher to optimum capacity, for example).

- Point out one area that needs improvement at a time, so that he can focus to change it and adopt the change as a new habit or routine.

- Share specific guidance with tasks that rely on judgment, for example, "When you clean out your office, please throw out any papers that are dated two years ago or more."

- Provide specific parameters for household chores: "Step 1: Sort out all of the all-white clothes from the rest of the clothes in the laundry hamper. Step 2: Put the washer settings on delicate cycle and cold water," etc.

- Use pictures or demonstrated actions to provide visual images that aid his memory.

- Consider taking separate vacations.

- Gain some time to eat or go to the restroom on shared vacations or long car trips by pointing out other car maintenance needs, like, "You probably ought to clean the bugs off the windshield while we're stopped." (Knowing your ASD husband well will dictate the wisdom of using this stalling tactic sparingly.)

- Write a vacation schedule that includes meals and other stops.

- Use outside help and resources as needed to meet household goals, even if this means reaching out to an expert in your husband's own professional field.

- Role play: Act as if you are a client who has come to your partner for advice or services.

- Don't be afraid to share your opinion as needed—often done best by explaining that you want to assist him and to work as a team.

- When assisting him with a task, be sure to follow his procedures, adding to them in areas he may not have thought of on his own (for example, pointing out that extra money is needed in the "Gifts" fund of your budget during the months of May and June).

- Know that ASD spouses are more likely to adapt via calm and consistent directives.

- Be patient: Change on his part will likely be slow and may come and go before it finally maintains.

Chapter 6

Coping with Stress

Stress is a normal part of life for everyone, even sometimes in happy, exciting life events. There are many proven coping techniques. Whether on the autism spectrum or not, different coping techniques work for different people. For the most part, NS partners are within the normal range in terms of using effective coping strategies, as judged by the ability to produce behaviors, actions and mannerisms considered to be "normal." This, of course, is not always the case. ASD partners commonly have what is considered to be "different" coping techniques. For example, crying at a funeral is considered normal behavior: It helps the person crying to let out some of the tension of grieving. However, crying out loud and hard when one gets a paper cut or crying when losing at a trivia game is not considered normal adult coping behavior. And yet these are some of the ways we've seen ASD adults behave.

Individuals with autism spectrum disorders often describe everyday coping experiences as extremely challenging. This can range from dealing with confrontations with a bill collector or unexpected company, to tasks of daily living like going to the store or putting gas in the car. Many successful adults on the autism spectrum have developed routines to cope with starting off their days or their daily activities like going to work.

This sounds not unlike the behavior of NS individuals who enjoy a certain routine when getting up each day. The difference is the extreme to which the ASD individual needs these routines in order to function. While many NS people may shower before going to work, ASD individuals may need to take exactly the same length of shower each day and use a specific type of soap. Using a different type of soap or shortening the length of the shower may result in full-blown panic to this ASD person. The majority of NS spouses we heard from describe very rigid routines that their ASD spouses have to follow each day. If the ASD partner is not able to follow his set routine, for any reason, he is likely to have serious behavior problems like those described later in this chapter.

One spouse explained how important her husband's routines are for him:

> If someone interrupts his routines or he oversleeps, he cannot break the vicious hold that his rituals have on him. He could be late for an important work meeting, presentation or a flight, but he still needs an hour in the bathroom to shower and read, as well as time to "properly" iron his suit. If he is rushed, he becomes agitated and even physically ill.

Meltdowns

Many ASD partners respond to stressors in their lives in ways that appear odd or disturbing to NS observers. Some cope with tremendous stress hour by hour, minute by minute—stress that often is not apparent to others—until they reach a point of a sudden "meltdown." This can include anything from screaming (and often saying rude things to others), hitting (objects, themselves or others) or stomping around.

Not surprisingly, such behavior sometimes prompts calls to the police or security personnel. In some cases, police officers have thought the behavior of the ASD person was a result of being on illegal drugs and that he was a danger to himself or others and arrested him. Sometimes the person having the meltdown may resist arrest, which can lead to serious injury and/or further legal ramifications.

Although the onset of a meltdown can be unpredictable, once begun, it seems to follow a very predictable path. At first, irritation builds, followed by an explosion of yelling, swearing, foot-stamping, door-slamming or even physical aggression, such as pushing or hitting. Afterward, the person may go off by himself. Some ASD partners express great remorse after such an episode.

Others either pretend or truly believe that what they did wasn't really out of normal, acceptable boundaries of behavior. Still others may say they don't remember the incident and may express surprise or confusion over their spouses' anger at them.

It is important to note that, just like any other human being, people with Asperger syndrome can learn to recognize and change this inappropriate emotional behavior. It may well take a serious incident—something that really gets their attention, such as physically hurting a loved one in a visible way or the threat of divorce or arrest—but ASD partners can and do in some cases begin to change their automatic patterns of behavior. If their NS spouses and other household members are also willing to change their own behaviors in support, this can help to facilitate new, more positive patterns of dealing with emotions for the entire family.

Author Kealah has developed a course called "Speak Your Truth" that helps people both on and off the spectrum to identify emotions to improve the way they communicate under emotional overload. As of the writing of this book, the course's workbook is available in e-book format at her website (www.speak-with-kealah.com).

When a person is melting down, he cannot consciously choose the location where it will happen, so it can take place in public just as easily as in private. Public meltdowns can lead to misjudgment and public scorn—toward both the ASD spouse and his NS wife, who may be viewed as having triggered her husband's emotional reaction.

The spouse of someone who has occasional meltdowns in public often feels a need to apologize or explain on behalf of her partner. Further, partners begin to avoid situations in which meltdowns seem to occur frequently or where a meltdown would be especially humiliating. Similar stress and even fear can occur in the offspring of the ASD person when they are present during the meltdown of their parent.

The children of these couples often react to the meltdowns also.

In one case, the ASD husband was prone to sudden meltdowns involving his children. He was obsessed with using the only computer in the house. This computer was on 24/7, and he was on for hours at a time, doing "research" (he was unemployed, but very smart in engineering). If one of the kids would interrupt him during these times to request use of the computer, he sometimes just lashed out and pushed or slapped them without even taking his eyes off the computer. Those children were truly afraid of Dad. Eventually, the NS partner decided she had to separate from him to protect the children.

In the case of Harry and Sheila, one of their two sons was on the spectrum. When Harry would melt down, their ASD son would comment, "and you think *I'm* weird!" It was as though he could see the irony and humor that might be in the situation. Their NS son would sometimes go to Sheila and say, "Dad's acting weird again. Can you do something?" At other times the NS son would directly confront Harry and say, "Dad, go off by yourself until you are finished with your meltdown."

Couples who have the fewest issues with meltdowns are those who have been proactive both in recognizing trigger situations and in putting alternative solutions into place to ward off meltdowns—or at least to cope with them. The ASD men in these couples have found means of retreat and privacy that help them calm down when a meltdown is brewing. Their NS partners share that they were open to discussing situations and states of fatigue and stress that often lead to the ASD partners' meltdowns. Such conversations help both partners identify risky situations and plan accordingly.

One NS spouse explained that her son was very embarrassed, while in his teens, during his father's occasional meltdowns. He avoided having friends over to their house then. She explained that it was common, if a package did not arrive as expected, for her husband to get very anxious and start pacing and shouting about the problems he was having fixing his car or computer or whatever it was he was planning to fix with the item that was being delivered. It did disrupt those around when this over-the-top reaction occurred.

In the workplace, ASD people often require extra breaks and downtime in order to avoid having public meltdowns that result in reprimand and job loss. Many ASD spouses have learned to find ways to "sneak away" to get such downtime, so that they aren't perceived as lazy workers. We have heard the following examples used as techniques for this: creating a hideaway area under one's desk or in a utility closet or an unused space to "disappear"; taking extended bathroom breaks; excusing oneself for a restroom break while actually leaving the building for five or ten minutes; feigning an emergency personal call that must be taken in private. Such tricks seem to be most successful when they are varied and used in moderation only.

If understanding and accommodations are needed in the workplace, which is frequently the case, there needs to be serious consideration as to whether the diagnosis is disclosed. This is certainly each individual's decision. This issue is discussed briefly in Chapter 3 in the section "When to intervene." Stephen Shore's book *Ask and Tell* is a valuable resource in making this decision (Shore 2004). We encourage use of any resources available to help in the decision of whether to disclose an ASD diagnosis on the job.

The sad fact is that, because of the pressure to avoid public meltdowns as often as possible, ASD spouses will more frequently have such episodes in private, with their NS partners being on the receiving end. It is very important, because of this, for NS wives to seek outside resources, like therapy, to help maintain their own emotional stability. Again, when all members of the household work toward individual emotional health, the atmosphere is more comfortable for everyone and helps the ASD individual maintain his own emotional equilibrium with far fewer meltdowns.

The MAAP Services organization that author Susan founded has helped many families develop "meltdown cards." Such cards, designed to be carried by the NS and ASD partners, as well as family members, explain the behaviors of the ASD person and make it clear that he is experiencing a meltdown. This can be very helpful in law enforcement situations. MAAP Services for Autism and Asperger syndrome (www.aspgergersyndrome.org) sells pre-made cards that are the size of a typical business card. Each card says that what bystanders are witnessing is the meltdown of an individual with an autism spectrum disorder. It further explains that "People with AS challenges often have trouble explaining things when they are in stressful or unpredictable situations." Finally, it says the bystander can contact MAAP Services if they have more questions. Seeing such a card leads unfamiliar observers to believe that this type of situation has happened before and that the person accompanying the individual who is "melting down" is experienced and capable.

When the ASD partner demonstrates "odd" behaviors that are non-aggressive, the NS spouse can "lead by example." That is, if the spouse begins to rock or recite a monologue, the NS spouse should ideally try to be calm and matter-of-fact with observers. If it is possible to remove the ASD partner to a private place without much fuss, we recommend this tactic. If not, the NS spouse may just calmly state, "This is how Jim calms down." This can help others to accept the behavior as the partner's way of coping.

Different coping responses

When they are distressed or emotional, some people with ASD rock, pace, flap their arms or hands, recite facts or use repetitive verbal arguments or monologues. Many adults with an ASD say that these behaviors are a way of self-calming and are enjoyable and/or comforting to them. Often these are referred to as "self-stimulatory behaviors" or "self-stims." In the movie *Rain Man* (1988), Raymond (the person with autism) recites the comedy routine "Who's on First?", made famous by Abbott and Costello. A well-known entrepreneur who is believed by many to have an ASD is reported to rock or jump on a trampoline to relax and think. Where a middle or lower class ASD individual might lose his job or be labeled as "weird" for doing these things, those who are wealthy are often excused by co-workers or society as being merely "eccentric." After all, some may rationalize, if he makes all that money, how strange can he be? This leads us to conclude that although money can't buy happiness, it can provide excuses!

While these behaviors are not perceived as threatening to others, they can make others feel uncomfortable and can cause the NS spouse and children embarrassment, and can risk public ridicule or loss of job or status within the community. What some might find a source of amusement, others will find as grounds for estrangement.

It is important for each couple to come up with a plan that works for them. Some NS spouses informed us that, after years of marriage, they began to understand that their ASD husbands' condition was "in charge" and that helped them to cope and deal with the situation, sometimes even in a humorous fashion. One wife we interviewed shared with us, "I started to see that I'm not perfect. Why should I expect my husband to be? That's made it easier for me." The majority of NS spouses we interviewed, however, took these quirks to heart and had a difficult time with this behavior, even if their ASD spouses were working hard to minimize it.

NS wife Sheila shared with us ASD husband Harry's cleaning obsessions:

> All countertops in the kitchen and bathrooms must be completely empty. He washes them daily and becomes upset over or hides things like tissue containers, soap containers, even attractive decorations. When I'm cooking, he expects me to clean up the kitchen before we eat. If I don't do this, especially when we have company over for dinner, he will jump up immediately after eating and clean up the kitchen in a great huff. In the case of company, if they offer to help clean up…even just helping to clear the table…he is usually rude and snaps at them to stop. You can imagine that we don't entertain for dinner often!

Sheila also reports that Harry loves to use "super cleaners" that are too harsh for the areas he cleans. She says they have even had to replace chrome faucets because he used cleaners on them that specifically warn against using on chrome. "Don't even get me started on his cleaning inventions," Sheila said.

Obsessive-compulsive traits

When stress is building, some ASD partners begin a cleaning binge of their rooms, their offices, their entire houses, their yards or themselves. In other instances, ASD partners obsessively talk about their special interest or work on a hobby in a compulsive manner.

We have spoken to many NS spouses who have problems with their ASD partners' obsessive-compulsive behavior. Many stories involve the ASD partner spending hours—sometimes not sleeping for days—at the computer or in the garage or office to the exclusion of any activity with family members. Asking the ASD partner to come do something else is met with either no response, a promise to stop "soon" or a form of emotional meltdown.

> One spouse's husband would lock himself in his room for hours and days at a time, staying up all night and pursuing his obsessions on the internet. Another ASD partner played one specific computer game obsessively to the exclusion of all family activities. Both of the NS partners in these relationships made ultimatums of separation if the behavior did not lessen. One ASD partner ignored the ultimatum, and his wife stayed anyway, becoming unhappier. The other ASD partner agreed to get counseling and limit his game time. This couple is still together, with the wife reporting that she is much happier.

For some ASD spouses, events such as dinner parties spark expectations of military precision in both the preparation and the execution of the event.

> ASD Frank would remove guests' drinks and snacks from their hands when it was time for dinner. This caused embarrassment and anxiety for his NS wife Joy, despite the fact that the two of them "enjoyed" hosting friends and often did so together. On one particular occasion, a guest was invited to a dinner party hosted by Frank and Joy. It was scheduled to begin before the guest could return home from

work. Frank encouraged their guest to attend regardless and so the man arrived about 40 minutes after the other guests. Frank greeted this man as usual, asked what he would like to drink and then brought him the requested beverage. After only a few minutes—when the latecomer had taken just a couple of sips of his drink—Frank asked him to put down his glass and get to the table, "because cocktail hour has now passed."

Travel is another area that can set off obsessive-compulsive tendencies in ASD people.

> NS spouse Sheila said she dreads travel with her ASD husband Harry, who hates the loss of control during travel. He is also very personally fastidious. Therefore, he doesn't like having to use public bathrooms and is appalled at the possibility of using an airplane lavatory. Because of this, he will not eat after noon the day before travel and doesn't eat again until after the day of travel.
>
> Sheila says:
>
>> He will linger in the bathroom before leaving for the airport for such long periods of time that we often have come close to missing our flight. I began lying to him about the time of the plane departure [to fix this]. I would say the flight was an hour earlier than it really was. That way, we would get to the airport on time. He finally realized that I was fibbing about the flight time and would check it himself. Now, we are back to rushing for the plane!

Since obsessive-compulsive behavior is usually non-aggressive, it is often better tolerated by partners, friends and the community than the meltdowns. If it happens frequently or becomes harmful, the ASD partner may work with a knowledgeable professional to learn more appropriate routines for dealing with stress. A few of the NS spouses informed us that a close friend or family member was helpful in teaching alternative coping strategies to their ASD spouse through discussion and modeling other behaviors during times of lessened stress. We are not suggesting to "remake" ASD partners. Their eccentricities should be respected and tolerated unless they significantly interfere with the household.

ASD individuals may benefit from building in daily times when they can attend to a favorite activity to de-stress. The de-stress activity or timeframe chosen by the ASD partner may seem inappropriate to the NS partner, but the needs of the ASD partner for this alone time are essential. So, while there may be room for negotiation, we believe the needs of the ASD partner must be respected and protected.

> One couple developed a successful routine whereby the ASD partner played computer games or worked on a special interest or hobby at a predetermined time each day, or at least on days when he worked. Once he comes home, it is understood that he is left alone for 45 minutes or more with no interruptions—no exceptions.

Special interests

Many ASD partners have hobbies, participate in sports, collect things, and so on, just like their NS counterparts. However, in people with Asperger syndrome, such hobbies, collections and activities often can be categorized as obsessions. In the world of autism, this very common phenomenon is known as the ASD person's "special interest," because it is different from the norm in its intensity and exclusivity.

A hobbyist may spend evenings after work focused on his hobby (yet still be available to some of his family's disruptions) and may even belong to a social group dedicated to his hobby that meets on the weekends, thus drawing complaints from his wife. Meanwhile, an ASD husband will often go directly into his special interest activity as soon as he arrives home from work, perhaps not even greeting his wife, even though he is not angry with her or intentionally trying to avoid her (see Chapter 2 for some common examples). This sends a mixed message that confuses the NS spouse, as does the fact that her husband focuses so intently on his special interest that he may completely tune out the rest of the world around him for hours or days at a time, even missing meals.

Some partners we spoke with reported obsessive special interests that seem to evolve from collecting to hoarding. This can be a tremendous stressor for the NS partner, because of the money and storage space involved with a particular hobby or because the hoarding takes over certain areas of the home. There is also often a fear by the NS spouse that her partner will alienate others at social functions by talking at length about his area of interest.

Some ASD partners are experts on a topic or a given field, from entomology to the history of hatpins. While such passion is socially acceptable, some individuals seem only to be able to converse about those interests or subjects. For example, when a visitor says, "How are you?" the ASD partner might reply, "I'm happy because I just purchased my 341st model train caboose. Did you know that the caboose was first introduced to the railway system in…?" An otherwise typical conversation soon becomes a monologue. To try to make the exchange more interactive, the visitor might interrupt, "I had heard you had surgery." The ASD partner might reply, "Surgeons have seldom ridden in cabooses, but many rail employees and hobos…", again reverting to the special interest.

This is another scenario where *Power Cards* may be helpful (Gagnon 2001). The card may contain a few sentences that remind the person with ASD to recite some of the sentences he has memorized. For example: "Enough about my hobby; what is yours?" or "I do rattle on a bit about all of this." Some NS women noted that they and their partners had devised signals, either as code words or phrases or as subtle gestures (such as tapping on the man's lower back) to let the ASD partner know when he was dominating social conversations with his special interest as a subject. For ASD people who wish to practice dialogue without the help of an NS partner, it is important to create segues that are as "normal" as possible, such as using a timer on a watch or cell phone.

In a case of a minister with ASD, a parishioner made an appointment to talk to him about a terminally ill parent. The pastor's response was to comment that she was a redhead and that he loved redheads! It is no surprise to learn that this man lost his position with the church after a series of similar incidents made people think he was sexually harassing women. His wife often defended him, explaining his brilliance and that he was a better writer and public speaker than counselor, but it did not make a difference in the congregation's decision to let him go. One of his obsessions was hair color. Way too often, he interrupted serious conversations to comment on a woman's appearance.

Unless the ASD spouse can use his special interest to make money, as some individuals have, certain obsessions can be problematic.

Many NS spouses report their ASD partners spend excessive amounts of money on special interests. In families with more limited finances, the NS spouses reported that this put the household in financial jeopardy, sometimes not allowing basic bills to be paid or essential purchases to be made. Common special interests we heard about included the Civil War, computers, music (CDs or instruments), cars, books and science-related subjects like chemicals, electronics, math, star-gazing/outer space and games.

Shutdowns

Shutdown behavior can range from seeming unable to speak or respond to curling up in a ball and rocking to physically hiding to even entering a seemingly catatonic state. Shutdown is a form of coping behavior in reaction to stress or panic. It is upsetting to observe, and if it happens in response to an encounter with law enforcement, it may be judged as a drug reaction or intentional defiance.

The more passive forms of this behavior, such as going off and disappearing into the basement or a workshop or study, or simply becoming very quiet and unresponsive, can be more tolerable to NS partners. However, imagine a shutdown happening every time the

ASD partner is engaging in sexual activity with his spouse. Or what if it happens frequently at work?

> One NS spouse related several shutdowns by her ASD partner throughout their 20-year marriage that had led to the police being called by others in the community. These situations were a result of the ASD spouse being very anxious and unable to function. All shutdowns were related to money matters. Once, he went to pay a bill and was told it was overdue and there was a late fee. At that point, he was unable to deal with this unexpected information, in part because he did not have enough cash to cover the extra charge. He went outside the building and began pacing and waving his arms while muttering incoherently. Some people in the parking lot were frightened and called 911. The first responders who arrived realized he needed to be checked at the hospital and not taken to jail. Being taken to the stress unit of the local hospital did not appear to be a better choice than being taken to jail, however. It still ended up being very traumatic for both partners and did not lead to any positive help from the mental health authorities who were consulted there. Each time the staff on the stress unit kept him for overnight observation; they then would call his wife the next day to say there was nothing they could do to "help" him, and would then discharge him.

There are many ways to help avoid shutdowns, such as the couple's negotiating appropriate limits to time spent socializing. We recommend that ASD-NS couples write a budget (if needed) to explain visually and keep track of important household expenses, so that the needs of the household and each family member are taken into consideration in terms of food, clothing, medical attention, etc., in proportion to the time and money spent on special interests. Some of the techniques described in the sections in this chapter on obsessive-compulsive traits and meltdowns can also be used to stave off shutdowns.

Lessons learned

- Understand that the rituals and routines your partner has help him feel relaxed and able to cope with his day.

- Allow him a certain amount of time—perhaps predetermined and agreed upon by both of you—to de-stress each day or week in order to decompress from the strain of social navigation and sensory overload.

- Be proactive in helping your partner find means of retreat and privacy when a meltdown is brewing. You can discuss situations and states of fatigue and stress that often lead to meltdowns in order to help both you and him identify risky situations.

- Discuss meltdowns and shutdowns when both partners are calm in order proactively to avoid further recurrence.

- Explore and practice strategies for escape from stressful situations or for changing activities, such as feigning a personal call that can only be taken in private.

- Keep "meltdown cards" on-hand in the event of more extreme situations.

- Make a list of "socially leading sentences" for the ASD partner to use if he is getting "stuck" or perseverating on his special interest. Ideally, this type of scenario should be rehearsed.

- Because segues in conversations can be particularly tricky, you can help the ASD partner by saying, "Remember you have an appointment in 15 minutes. I'll remind you when we should be leaving."

- Negotiate appropriate limits to his special interests.

- Write a budget (if needed) to explain visually and keep track of important household expenses, so that the needs of the household are met in proportion to the time and money spent on his special interests.

- Consider cognitive behavioral therapy to alleviate the frequency and length of shutdowns.

- Help your ASD partner to learn how to recognize the precursors of a shutdown and engage in an activity or move to a safe space that will help him feel calmer, like putting on headphones and listening to music or relaxation techniques.

Chapter 7

Parenting

Is there a distinct parenting style for ASD fathers? It would seem not. To quote a currently popular phrase, "If you know one person with Asperger syndrome, you know *one* person with Asperger syndrome." In other words, it is important not to stereotype people with ASDs, and to remember that there are no exact rules or limitations that apply to mentoring or any other parenting issue concerning ASD spouses. However, there are trends that have been observed by NS mothers that we share here.

Of the NS spouses we have spoken with, nearly half have at least one child. Many of the couples with children have at least one child who is identified with or suspected of having an autism spectrum disorder. Certainly, children add another dimension to any relationship. Indeed, a significant number of NS spouses felt that their ASD spouses often behaved like one of the children, even to the point of "ganging up on them" to protest a denied request. We should note here that this behavior is not restricted solely to ASD husbands, but that it is somewhat more common and relatively frequent in NS-ASD marriages.

Many NS spouses describe a "mixed bag" of positive and negative parenting experiences for their ASD spouses. Certainly, the many day-to-day challenges of persons with ASD can impact their ability to parent, both positively and negatively. As described earlier, children significantly impact the many sensory challenges for someone on the autism spectrum with their various smells, noises and tactile needs. Age-appropriate communication and socialization can also pose challenges for the ASD parent. In this chapter, we address eight different parenting categories that seem to impact NS-ASD marriages. They include when a child has an ASD, and the areas of play, discipline, social mentoring, the finances of parenting, healthcare and wellness, blended families and emotional connections.

When a child has an ASD

According to NS spouses, it appears that when both parent and child have an autism spectrum diagnosis, it can be either a positive or a negative. We have heard stories of a more natural bonding of the ASD parent with his ASD child. This is especially true if they share a special interest, such as math or electronics. The ASD parent can be a very positive role model, particularly if he understands his own diagnosis along with his strengths and weaknesses. Conversely, an ASD parent who either is unaware of or is in denial of his diagnosis—or who for any reason feels negative about his own ASD traits—will frequently foster a negative relationship with his ASD child or children, even inadvertently. This can range from demanding a child to be more "normal" to shunning a child altogether.

> NS wife Joy said that her husband Frank seems to have far fewer issues with her and with their NS son than he does with their ASD daughter. Father and daughter appear to "push each other's buttons" when they each become agitated, Joy said.
>
> "She is just like him, but she upsets *his* applecart," Joy wrote to tell us. "[Our daughter] is unpredictable, very messy around the house, forgetful, prone to angry outbursts when things aren't going 'her way'—all of which are problems I've dealt with [concerning my husband Frank] for years. He definitely thinks she should be [more like NS people than even he can be.]"
>
> She went on to write that she believes their daughter reminds Frank of himself in a negative way: "I guess when you need to go on a diet, looking in a mirror is frustrating."

In cases where special interests are the same between father and child—or even in such cases where the special interests are different, but still intense—costs can mount up and adversely affect the family budget. For more on this, see the section entitled "The finances of parenting" in this chapter.

Play

In the area of play, ASD dads can be one extreme or another: either exceptionally talented or almost totally lacking in play skills. Many are somewhat socially immature and use children's standards and outlook to evaluate and be able to enjoy play. Find an ASD dad who is into Dungeons and Dragons and he may have a wonderful play experience with his children if they take to that interest. Others are tremendous in making up imaginative games or leading and mentoring hobbies. In other cases, if the ASD father's interests are obsessive, things may turn in another direction.

Author Susan observed an ASD dad who was obsessed with the computer actually strike his children if they came up to him and asked for time on the computer. In some cases the ASD parent may want to be a good parent to the children, but may have no idea how to accomplish this or may truly be uninterested in the task at hand.

Others may ignore play opportunities and even basic conversation if they are truly obsessed with another activity. Again, there are no hard and fast rules. ASD parent and counselor Tom Jacobs told us, "You cannot imagine the self-control it takes just to adapt to the noise level that children bring into your home." Play can be a very noisy proposition.

NS Sheila reported that her husband Harry would make up wonderful games and activities for their two boys. He would even make mealtimes into pretend games, making "G.I. Joe burgers" and "Pac Man pancakes" when he was in charge of preparing a meal. At the end of each meal, Harry would put a towel over his arm and pretend to be their waiter. Then he would present them with an imaginary bill. The non-challenged son would say, "I'm not paying anything for this meal. It wasn't that good." The ASD son would then laugh and agree. Sheila said that Harry was also extremely patient about reading bedtime stories and supervising play dates.

NS spouse Sara explained that her ASD husband Josh was very creative, patient and appropriately playful with their son with Asperger syndrome. However, as an ASD husband and father, he was much too overwhelmed when playing with their NS son. The NS son wanted and expected much more conversation and social interaction, which was very stressful for Josh. While Josh would need to take many "alone" breaks, the NS son would often ask his mother, "Why won't Dad play with me any more?" Though she gave him an age-appropriate explanation of Josh's ASD, it never seemed to be enough of an answer to satisfy their son's concern.

The fatigue and general inertia of depression that are often present in people with ASD can also have a great effect on the father's ability to be present and interact with his children. This can also be influenced by a general feeling of inadequacy that depression sometimes brings.

Discipline

The issue of disciplining children is often a source of conflict between any parents. Many NS couples never resolve differing views on the rules of discipline. Others find shared views and make house rules that stand equally, no matter which parent is disciplining. In NS-ASD marriages, we hear more consistent examples of the NS spouse being given the disciplinary role, either by the ASD partner's request or due to lack of motivation or interest on the part of the ASD spouse. Some loving ASD dads just can't bring themselves to say no or enforce consequences of house rule or behavioral rule violations by their children. Others seem dispassionate. Still others do enforce the rules, but sometimes go overboard or are too rigid in their enforcement.

NS partner Bonnie related a disturbing story about her husband Brad's having a meltdown himself while trying to handle her ASD son's meltdown. Bonnie's daughter (both the children were from her previous marriage) was going to have a part in a school play, and her son was jealous of his sister. In the school parking lot, the son suddenly refused to take another step toward the building. Brad panicked, thinking they would be late. As they both began to escalate in the dispute, Brad grabbed his stepson by the hair and began dragging him into the building. Bonnie was surprised when Brad refused to apologize for several days. Luckily, the family found a cognitive behavioral therapist, who helped them to address this issue. Part of the therapist's resolution was to prescribe medications for Brad that helped him control his behavior.

"I still worry when Brad is in charge of our son (when I am away). He hasn't lost control with our son since this happened over five years ago. However, I still know that he is capable of this destructive behavior."

NS Sheila reported that her boys received different disciplinary approaches by Harry at different times in their lives. One of their boys is on the autism spectrum and one is not. Harry would go through phases in which he felt that the NS child "should know better" than to upset his ASD brother. Sheila told us it was almost a negation of normal sibling rivalry. Other times, especially during the teenage years, he would punish the ASD child for his natural traits if they upset the NS son. "Mostly, he was gentle and loving," Sheila said. "However, a few times, he was truly unfair and even cruel to our ASD son. I finally had to get [Harry] counseling to handle our ASD son more calmly and fairly." Today, the boys are grown and Sheila reports that both adore Harry and think he is a great dad. Both sons often feel their father favors the other one. They do, however, see their father's ASD traits with a kind heart and true acceptance.

Social mentoring

ASD dads can be great mentors to their ASD children in that they have been in similar situations to these kids as they grow and develop. Brian King, MSW, is an excellent example of an ASD father who truly mentors and guides his three ASD sons through life's ups and downs. As a lecturer, peer mentor and counselor, he also has a lot of professional experience to help him socially mentor his boys as their parent.

In Brian King's presentations, he uses examples of the mentoring he has done for his sons. He also conducts webinars on parenting ASD offspring to answer questions by parents who are, themselves, both on and off the autism spectrum. (For more information, visit his website, www.spectrummentor.com/5-minute-mentor.) We interviewed Brian to find out what he has personally experienced as the most challenging aspect of parenting with an ASD.

> Brian said, "The toughest part for me is consistently modeling the values that I want my kids to internalize. There are no bigger hypocrites than parents. [Whether on the spectrum or not,] we all say things like, 'Do as I say, not as I do.' So many parents generally only teach when they're thinking about it." Brian continued, "[My wife] Kathy and I really emphasize being conscious at all times that our kids are watching. They're watching how we communicate, how we respond to someone who's getting hurt or angry, or when we're angry out of our own frustrations. By doing this, I now have some credibility with my kids."

Brian and Kathy both admitted to having some challenges with seeing things from their children's perspectives—not only as adults who may have forgotten the feelings of childhood, but also as parents with ASDs who therefore lack theory of mind (see Chapter 3). They shared one story in example:

> Two of their sons had been scuffling over a game in the room where they were playing. The younger son raced into the room where his father Brian was sitting, while "passionately describing the injustice done to him by his brother." Brian made a point of calling in his older son to ask for his side of the story. This step is one he's had to learn over the years, because his first instinct was often to "give in to the passionate pleas of the first one to show up" and base his discipline and judgment of the situation on that information alone. In this case, by listening to both sides objectively, he learned that the crux of the matter was the boys did not know how to

negotiate turn-picking during their game, so Brian helped them to agree upon a set of rules to do so.

Author and GRASP president Michael John Carley is married and has a son on the ASD spectrum. In his book *Asperger's from the Inside Out* (Carley 2008), Michael John shares how he mentored his son, who participates in baseball, just as he did as a boy. In fact, the entire premise of his book is mentoring for others on the spectrum.

NS spouse Sara shared examples of her ASD husband Josh's impatience with their son, who also has an ASD. When their son was five, Josh did not realize that their son was not able to spend more than ten minutes at a time learning how to throw and catch a baseball. Josh also tried to teach the little boy various aspects of the game, like running the bases. Josh wanted this to be a way they could spend time together and also an opportunity for his son to learn team skills and make friends. It was a rocky start and took a couple of years, but Josh did gain the patience to mentor his son more appropriately to play baseball, and this was transferred to other activities, too.

Another NS spouse, Joy, told a story about her ASD husband Frank wanting to share his knowledge about bicycle safety and upkeep with his children. When their daughter with autism was ten years old, Frank wanted to involve her from start to finish in the repair of her bicycle. This included taking her to the bike shop to purchase needed items. Joy explained to Frank that their daughter would be more successful if she was not taken to the store, but was shown and helped to do the repairs once Frank purchased the items and brought them home. Frank insisted that the child go to the store to learn "the whole process." Unfortunately, they both came back very agitated, not speaking, and without the needed items. Their daughter, in fact, was not ready with the social skills required to purchase bicycle parts and tools at the store. This is a clear example of unsuccessful mentoring, based on expectations.

In cases of NS children, ASD dads can also socially mentor, but the advice sometimes is askew. It is very difficult for anyone with social challenges to mentor someone without them. It is somewhat like asking a person with no eyesight to mentor his children about famous paintings and the nuances of their colors. He could be brilliant and better than anyone in teaching them appreciation of sculpture, but it would be hard for him to relate something totally visually based. Using that line of logic, an ASD dad will successfully socially mentor NS children in proportion to the extent of his social challenges. Some ASD dads may say, "I dealt with an NS world, now you deal with it!" Yet others may say, "I'll share whatever I can with you. I know manners and etiquette, and those I'll teach."

Brian King also shared with us his advice to NS-ASD couples who are planning to start new families together, stating that most adults will parent their children the way they were parented, for better or worse. He cautions that negative self-talk—in NS *or* ASD parents-to-be—is usually a leftover stronghold of punitive parenting styles. Practicing positive self-talk along with patience and forgiveness of one's own errors can go a long way toward healthy child-rearing.

The finances of parenting

A significant number of ASD spouses become the stay-at-home parent due to the difficulties many have in finding and keeping a job that offers a wage the family can live on. According to the spouses who shared with us, this arrangement has both positive and negative results.

On the positive side, some unemployed ASD partners were able to get further training and/or volunteer experience that led to a paying position that focused on their strengths. A few of the ASD spouses, while at home, were able to start their own businesses. Computer consulting and tutoring were two examples.

For the majority of couples, the negative side prevailed. The ASD men in these partnerships had a difficult time being responsible for the running of the household, for the reasons discussed previously. The running of a household does take good organizational and planning skills, along with the ability to take care of a variety of household chores with some flexibility—especially when there are children to look after and their schedules to manage. Most families, where the NS wife was the sole breadwinner, had a very difficult time financially. This can be a further emotional drain on the wife, who can feel like she's "doing everything."

Finally, ASD fathers often have a hard time recognizing the necessity of therapy costs for their special needs children, especially those on the autism spectrum. Depending on the father's own relationship to his personal diagnosis, he may reject the child's ASD outright or he may rationalize with statements like, "It doesn't really help our child," or "I never received therapy, and I grew up just fine!"

> One NS wife told us that financial responsibilities were actually areas of strength for her husband as an ASD dad. According to her, he is very diligent about money and even pays for medical costs on a schedule with all of their other bills. As their children are aging, he has begun to teach them about the importance of investing, as well.

We heard several stories of ASD spouses who are the breadwinners and have high-paying careers, but the downside for most of them is that they do very little—or sometimes absolutely nothing—with their children and often very little even with their wife. It seems that, for these men, work is a special interest in itself and also takes up all of their capacity for navigating social rules. Gauging from the experiences of the NS spouses interviewed, it is common for ASD individuals to focus only on one major "life role"—work or home life. This goes well beyond the stereotype of the male being the breadwinner who is gone a lot but still shares some parental responsibilities.

> One ASD spouse told his wife that his role choice in their family was to be "the behind-the-scenes structure," specifically meaning that he would pay the bills, buy the groceries and tidy up the house at the end of the day. However, he wanted little to no part in helping mediate the

children's emotional trials, play with or mentor them, or even attend neighborhood block parties or birthday parties and other family events.

Special interests are an area that can put a big strain on family finances. Sometimes this is because an ASD father and his ASD child or children share the same special interest, investing most of their time and the family budget into that area or activity. Sometimes, however, if multiple ASD family members are obsessed with different special interests for which each of them draws heavily from the family funds, this will also adversely affect monetary resources. Even only one special interest from one ASD family member (most frequently the father) can pose economic hardship for an NS-ASD couple and their family.

One ASD father was intensely interested in race cars. His hobby of collecting, repairing and racing cars, as well as traveling to far-off places to swap parts and participate in races, became a top priority for the family, replacing family vacations with trips to swap meets and racing events.

Healthcare and wellness

In two-parent households, mothers are traditionally the parent who is in charge of keeping and restoring the health of the children. We have been told by some NS spouses that this may be more challenging when their partners have an autism spectrum disorder. Frequently we heard from NS wives that their ASD husbands do not trust doctors, psychologists and other health-related professionals. These NS wives who shared with us speculated this is because their ASD spouse had experienced an incident when they were very unhappy with an encounter with a healthcare professional.

We have heard some NS spouses' concerns that their husbands do not trust or respect medical personnel. Many explained that their husband did not feel they were taken seriously or that they received inappropriate treatments. As a result of their bad experiences, they do not want their children to be seen by doctors or therapists. They may even refuse to pay for appointments with certain professionals, saying, "Why pay to talk with someone about your problems?"

> NS spouse Sara explained that her husband, Josh, was incorrectly medicated for anxiety when he was younger and fears that doctors are just pill pushers. Also, in his opinion, the therapy he received from a psychologist was irrational and caused him more anxiety. The therapist wanted him to talk about his parents and how they treated him. Josh did not see any benefits from these sessions. When their son was having difficulty in school, he was very upset when Sara suggested they have him tested by a private psychologist. Josh insisted it was the school's job to teach him. He felt that a psychologist would only make their son feel "broken" and ask about them as parents.

Other NS spouses shared that their ASD partners were very impatient at medical appointments because they did not like the waiting rooms themselves, as well as the fact that the actual wait time was so unpredictable. A couple of ASD partners refused to go to any medical appointments for themselves or their children because of these issues. Several NS spouses expressed their frustration in getting cooperation from their ASD husbands to give medications and follow through with the doctor's orders when their child was sick.

Katrin Bentley, in her book *Alone Together* (Bentley 2007), devotes a whole chapter to her husband's reactions when their son, Marc, was chronically ill for a time. She explained how difficult it was for her husband, Gavin, to understand their son's illness and to show understanding and compassion for what Marc was experiencing. Adding to Gavin's stress was the change in routine and his usual place for "alone time" that occurred due to Marc's health and the things Marc needed. Fortunately Marc recovered, and both Gavin and she learned a lot about themselves and each other and how to cope with stressful situations more successfully: Katrin explained that she was much stronger than she realized and could do a lot on her own; Gavin learned, she said, that he needed to surrender control of some things and learn other coping strategies.

Blended families

Stepfamilies, or blended families as they are often called, are very prevalent in North America today. According to the latest statistics available from the US Census Bureau and the Stepfamily Foundation, there are more stepfamilies than traditional nuclear families in the United States. There are several stepmothers represented among the NS spouses who told us their stories for this book. There are also a few NS wives who had a child or children of their own before marrying an ASD spouse.

Of those NS women, whether they became a stepparent or their ASD husbands became stepparents, all said that becoming an "instant family" was harder than they predicted. Many of their concerns may be shared by all blended families, but we feel there were some unique and more pronounced concerns expressed by the NS partners. Much later, years later in some cases, they realized that "instant" children meant, among other things, a change in routine, more social and communication expectations and added sensory stimulation in the home.

These women did expect there would be transition issues. They had talked about it with their ASD partners. However, because none of the women we interviewed were aware of their partners' ASD prior to their marriages, they did not realize how inflexible their husbands were about a change in routine and how long it would take to accomplish these changes. They also did not anticipate the increased time their ASD spouses would start spending engaged in their special interests, to the exclusion of family time, once their child or a stepchild was regularly part of the household. We realize that there are certainly more varied experiences among stepfamilies. We feel it is important, though, to share at least one example that represents what we heard from participants.

NS Joy explained that when they were dating, she saw ASD Frank with his son from a first marriage on a regular basis.

At first, Frank was very protective of his son, Drew, and did not introduce him to Joy. Joy understood that Frank did not want to introduce her until he knew that six-year-old Drew understood their relationship. Joy could tell the devotion and love Frank had for his son, and she admired and respected their close relationship. After regular visitation on weekends during the school year, Drew spent a month with them the summer after they were married. This experience did not go as expected or planned.

Joy explained that Frank retreated to his workshop, leaving her and Drew to play and hang out together. Joy had a friend with a son the same age. She talked with Frank and made plans for the families to get together. When the time would arrive for them to meet up with the other family, however, Frank said he could not go. Joy was very hurt and frustrated. It wasn't until they had their own daughter that she and Frank were able to discuss the difficulties that "full-time" children posed to Frank. For one thing, Joy realized that Frank had to learn slowly to structure these longer time periods with the children and that "breaks" for Frank had to be built into his parenting schedule. Frank also had to cope with the added noise and stimulation that children added to the household.

Emotional connections

Readers have been given examples of when NS partners do not feel emotionally connected to their ASD partners. This undoubtedly is true in reverse; the ASD partners often do not feel emotionally connected to their NS partners. Discussion of this second scenario is not within the scope of this book. We do, however, want to touch on the feelings of emotional connection that children from NS-ASD relationships might be experiencing with a parent who is on the autism spectrum. We have discussed examples of how communication and social skills, sensory sensitivities and difficulties understanding the thoughts and needs of others have caused problems in the marriages of those who shared their stories with us. These same difficulties can be experienced by the children of parents on the autism spectrum.

For most NS children, emotional connections are developed and strengthened through shared communication and social experiences and a feeling of being understood and accepted. An ASD parent most often tries to develop a relationship with his child through concrete gestures such as sharing in a special interest (which might not be age appropriate or an interest of the child) or being the good provider, so that there is money to buy whatever the child needs. However, as time passes, the change in the parent-child relationship dynamics can be a stumbling point for ASD parents.

> ASD Frank has a special interest in trains and enjoys, among other things, watching them as they pass at railroad crossings. When his children were little, he would often take them on car rides past certain train tracks, especially when he knew a train was en route. The kids loved this fun activity. But as they grew and shifted interests, Frank struggled to keep up with new ways to bond with them. Frequently, he would automatically resort to taking them out to sight trains in an effort to connect emotionally; this often backfired as the kids complained about "having to watch boring trains again with Dad."

Sensory sensitivities may make it more difficult for many ASD parents physically to touch and cuddle with their children. ASD parents often have conversations about factual information, but not about issues that are emotional and related to feelings. The ASD parent sees sharing this factual information as important and a loving show of affection. However, if the ASD parent does not also relate to the child on a level that shows some understanding of his or her thoughts, feelings and needs, it will be hard for him to develop an emotional connection that is meaningful to his child. The resources used to develop further and enhance the emotional connection between the ASD and NS partners could be adapted to help NS children and ASD parents to connect better emotionally.

ASD parents and ASD children may be able to connect better emotionally. We have heard from some NS women that the bond between their ASD partners and ASD children is very special and close. It seems in these relationships the ASD children and parents can understand and relate to each other very naturally. Unfortunately from the stories we heard, there is also the opposite extreme in that the ASD children and ASD parents seem to be total opposites and/or totally at odds with each other. We have heard of a couple of situations where an ASD child and ASD parent could not be left alone together for fear of neglect if the ASD parent would avoid the ASD child. This seems rare, but dangerous.

One NS spouse, Pam, spoke to us about a time when she had two teens and her husband all at odds with each other. We acknowledge that the teen years can be difficult even for those not on the autism spectrum, but Pam's story illustrates what we see as an example of this scenario when an ASD parent may be operating emotionally at the same level as the ASD teen. Before she found a knowledgeable counselor, there was a "war zone" in the house, according to Pam. Her ASD husband, Jim, functioned as if he were competing with his two ASD sons. All three men found it very difficult to connect and regulate their emotions when they were together. As of our latest discussions with Pam, their first ASD son seems to have matured (along with Jim), and both father and son have a wonderful relationship. Their second ASD son and Jim are still struggling to become better connected emotionally.

Lessons learned

- Be aware that there is no single distinct parenting style for ASD dads, but rather that each father parents individually.

- Find proactive solutions to the sensory overload that children bring to a household, such as keeping ear plugs handy for your husband.

- Allow him to take breaks or gain "alone time" as necessary, so that he can parent more patiently.

- Find support in the form of family, friends and professional caregivers who can help tend to and teach your children, so that you give yourself parenting "breaks" as needed.

- Read through the "Lessons learned" sections in the chapters on communication differences and sensory processing differences (Chapters 2 and 4) of this book to adapt those suggestions as means to facilitate emotional connection between your spouse and your children.

- Set up situations where a specific role and support is given to the ASD spouse to interact with the children, like playing catch or other simple games.

- Coach (or seek experts who can coach) your ASD spouse on appropriate interaction.

- Use parenting classes, books on effective parenting and other parent coaching resources. (See this book's Useful Resources section.)

- Trust your husband to share what he has learned about navigating NS society with your children.

- Know that his thinking style—whether positive or negative—will likely influence the way he communicates with them.

- Practice positive self-talk and forgiveness to model self-esteem and love to both your children and your ASD partner.

Chapter 8

ASD and Illegal Behaviors

During our time spent professionally with NS partners, we hear questions and concerns that we feel are important to share in these pages. Earlier we mentioned incidences of ASD partners having brushes with the law. This is an important topic to many NS partners. We want to highlight it here, as well as briefly discuss concerns related to the use of drugs by the ASD partner, which is a part of negative encounters with law enforcement.

Brushes with the law

The ASD population is not exempt from breaking the law. A number of NS spouses fear that their ASD partners' behaviors might be misinterpreted and lead to problems with the law. In fact, we have already described a very serious situation where an ASD partner, a respected professional, ended up with a maximum sentence in prison for what was described to us by his wife as a misinterpretation of a playful wrestling match with a young boy (see Chapter 3).

The fear of having a meltdown in public that leads to the police being called is a real one for many NS-ASD families. As discussed earlier, having the ASD spouse carry a card explaining he has an autism spectrum disorder can be helpful. In a couple of cases a medical alert bracelet was helpful in avoiding an incident with police, because it verified and explained the disability. In their work, authors Marci and Susan receive a significant number of phone calls from family members because a teen or young adult is in trouble with the law, usually due to misinterpretation of ASD behavior. This also happens with ASD spouses.

One story we heard of involved a young ASD woman who was traveling with a companion to a destination wedding. After boarding the plane, the flight was delayed by a couple of hours until eventually, the pilot asked everyone to de-board for further instructions. This young woman became excessively agitated. She began to make a scene and have a meltdown, insisting that the airline was trying to ruin her trip. The flight crew was phoning security when the young woman's escort finally convinced her to de-board the plane and get herself to a bathroom to calm down before her trip was completely cancelled.

Behaviors such as staring excessively at a clerk in the store, slamming down merchandise, getting overwhelmed at the mall or "body rocking" while chanting are a few behaviors mentioned by the NS spouses that can lead to suspicions by store employees and security guards. NS spouses also reported occasions out in public when their ASD spouses got anxious, overwhelmed and upset, leading to meltdowns in the form of yelling, frantic pacing and/or arm waving. This behavior can seem to come out of the blue and may be a reaction to someone's innocently asking a question. Some of these behaviors can be especially frightening to bystanders. Some NS partners reported being able to help their ASD partners out of the situation before it escalated, using soothing techniques, for example (see the "Coping with stress" section in Chapter 6). Some NS spouses are prepared to help their ASD partners realize when a situation becomes too overwhelming and simply leave and go to the car or a safe, quiet spot as quickly as possible. This takes the understanding and commitment of both spouses working together.

While public meltdowns are upsetting and embarrassing to the NS spouse, having to avert a confrontation with law enforcement can make things worse. If the responding officer listens to the NS spouse, stays calm and does not attempt to touch or confront the ASD spouse, this can defuse the situation.

The worst case scenarios are those where the NS spouse becomes worked up and argumentative with her husband and where no exit strategy to rectify the stressful situation is in place. When this happens, the scene can turn hostile and even violent. Here are two examples where the potential for violence was luckily defused.

NS spouse Bonnie learned the hard way about the importance of staying calm with her ASD husband when in a stressful situation. Bonnie and Brad were returning home after visiting out of town with friends for the day. When they were about halfway home, they had a flat tire. They called road service to come and help, but Brad did not want to wait for an hour in the car for someone to come to assist them. He was ready to go home. He decided to start walking, and got out of the car. Bonnie started yelling for him to come back. She did not want to wait alone in the dark. Brad just started walking faster, and Bonnie started running after him and continued to shout. At that point, a police car pulled up behind them. The officer asked them if that was their car on the side of the road. Brad began shouting at Bonnie, "Now see what you have done!" Brad yelled to the officer that he had to get home. The officer said he would be going to the police station with him if he did not calm down.

Luckily, Brad did calm down, and they both went back to their car to wait for road service. It was days later when Bonnie realized it had been a long stressful day socializing for Brad, even though he said he had fun. She recognized that, in the future, she needed to stay calm and explain to Brad what she was thinking and feeling and what she wanted him to do, instead of raising her voice at him and asking him to return to the car without explanation. If she had done so then, Brad's behavior very likely would not have escalated.

Another NS spouse told us about a time when her husband was disturbed about a response he received in the mail about his application for Social Security benefits. After receiving a denial letter, he went to the local Social Security office, but was not able to communicate because of his frustration and anxiety. He looked highly agitated, so the police were called. When the police arrived, he was sitting in the parking lot rocking and still could not communicate. He did not resist when asked to come with the police.

He was taken to the mental health ward at the local hospital, and his doctor was called. Then the NS spouse was notified. Luckily, this did not escalate into behavior that resulted in the man being taken to jail since he experienced a shutdown (he could not communicate and went off by himself), not a meltdown, which often involves violent-looking physical behavior. Though the ASD spouse did not receive any additional support from the hospital staff, he was able to feel safe enough to start talking. His wife was called, and she was able to take him home. If the police had taken him to the police station, both his wife and the doctor feared the ASD spouse may have gotten agitated and/or violent, leading to an arrest and time in jail.

Substance abuse and addiction

Some individuals with an ASD report being in an almost constant state of anxiety. We have mentioned some soothing techniques (see the "Coping with stress" section in Chapter 6) that can help this at least temporarily. Meditation is another option, and is recommended by ASD author Chris Mitchell in his book *Asperger Syndrome and Mindfulness* (Mitchell 2008). Therapy is an option, too, although we have not heard of any cases in our research where ASD adults successfully continued with individual therapy programs for lengthy periods. In cases where the counselor and patient find a good "fit," and the proper techniques are used, evidence has shown that adults have had successful long-term therapy.

There are also a number of medications that can be prescribed for this purpose. Prescription medicine is an option that has worked for many ASD spouses we interviewed. Often prescribed by a family doctor in lieu of a specialist, such medication can come in the form of anti-anxiety drugs or antidepressants. One drawback is that many of these medications are addictive or have some sort of dependent effects on the body and/or brain. For ASD individuals with addictive personalities, this can be a real danger. When prescription medication is being sought, we strongly recommend that the couples or individuals seek out the help of a competent and experienced physician.

One drug used to treat anxiety is especially controversial. Although few states allow the use of medical marijuana (cannabis), there is some evidence that this trend may be changing. As of the writing of this book, 14 US states have created laws that provide for medical marijuana possession or usage by prescription only. It's possible, too, that the legalization of medical marijuana for Iraq War veterans suffering from post-traumatic stress disorder (PTSD) in 2010 may cause further changes in these laws across the states. However, the majority of the United States still views any association with marijuana as a criminal act, punishable by law.

A significant number of the NS partners we have spoken with over the past few years have voluntarily mentioned a concern that their ASD partners use illegal drugs. These spouses said their partners need marijuana to help control constant anxiety. What society may judge as abuse, those who know and care about or for someone with an ASD will often realize is a desperate attempt to soothe intolerable anxiety. Conversely, for spouses dealing with addiction, it is often a fine line between legitimate defense and enabling.

In addition to concerns about legality, cost can also be an issue. Partners report that the legal form of prescription cannabis is very expensive, often running at rates comparable to those found on the street, plus additional costs for sales tax, doctor's office fees and laboratory fees for blood work. In addition, these costs are not covered by health insurance (California State Board of Equalization 2009; Washington State Department of Health 2008). In the case of families with low to average incomes, this makes the use of cannabis difficult to impossible. A few NS spouses informed us that their ASD partners were trying to make "deals" with others so they could afford it, which basically meant they would help sell marijuana illegally in exchange for their own portions. Obviously, such actions run the risk of arrest and jail time. Worse, NS spouses who are aware of their partners' illegal activities can also be sentenced for possession of a controlled substance and may go to jail and/or lose their homes.

Another valid concern from several NS partners is that their ASD husbands function best on dosages of certain medications—such as stimulants that are considered controlled substances—that are much higher than US Food and Drug Administration (FDA) guidelines. The need for such high dosages is a problem, because most medical professionals will not prescribe the higher dosage. Some ASD partners we met take what is needed to function optimally for about half the month and then go without for the other half, until the prescription can be refilled. These scenarios describe self-medicating issues that are hard on both the ASD individual and the NS partner, and possibly other family members as well.

We have included next a rather lengthy description of substance use to illustrate concerns we often hear from NS spouses. This story was shared by one (anonymous) wife who was frustrated by her husband's long history of illegal drug use.

One NS woman explained that she feels at her wits' end and believes that to save her marriage and preserve her ASD husband's role as an active parent, he needs to be diagnosed and treated for his substance abuse problem. Her husband was diagnosed with attention deficit hyperactivity disorder (ADHD) as a child. In high school, he turned to almost every available recreational drug to help cope with his troubles. The man attempted to get off drugs when he joined the Army, but that did not work and he was soon discharged. He did enter a program at a local outreach center and got off all the drugs except marijuana—which he says he uses to stabilize his moods and think more clearly. He is now a card-holder for medical cannabis.

His wife, who met him many years after this, explains that he has always seemed unbalanced, but she attributed it to his ADHD and abusive upbringing. This man is extremely depressed, but believes the marijuana helps his depression. In fact, chronic marijuana usage can create extreme mood fluctuation and even promote depression, as well as create physical health risks, especially to the lungs (US Department of Health and Human Services 2008). He has trouble keeping a job and has been underemployed, mostly in restaurants. After unsuccessfully working five different jobs in two years, the NS wife and her husband decided that he would be a stay-at-home dad for their two children while she worked.

Unfortunately, during this time, her husband suffered a breakdown and began outpatient treatment at a mental health center. When he had a rage reaction to the medicine they prescribed, he refused to take more and now cannot access that center. This NS spouse continues to contact various agencies for assistance, but continues to struggle with getting the right help from experts who understand both addiction and Asperger syndrome in combination with ADHD, since those are her husband's challenges.

Lessons learned

- Carry a business-sized card that explains the nature of ASDs and offers the name and phone number of someone to call for further information—or place such cards in your spouse's wallet or pocket for quick access.

- Suggest that your ASD partner refrain from activities that annoy or frustrate him if he seems to be having a bad day or is going through an especially stressful period of time.

- Practice ways to let your ASD spouse know gently that he might need time alone; allow him his private space when you see that he needs it.

- Don't forget to use the above strategies when you are out in public with your partner or are socializing with others at home.

- Stay calm when you recognize a meltdown, especially when police or other security or rescue personnel are on the scene.

- Take time-outs for yourself as needed.

- Be sure to socialize without your partner, too, so that you do not feel overly responsible for him each time you are out. Join groups that let you focus on your own hobbies and interests.

- In the case of addiction to alcohol or drugs, consider self-help recovery groups such as Alcoholics Anonymous and Narcotics Anonymous (www.aa.org and www.na.org).

- Work with a counselor and/or a medical professional who is knowledgeable about the issues that ASD-NS couples face.

- Find reliable paths to legal medications as warranted.

- Encourage your ASD spouse to pursue exercise, meditation, massage therapy and any other positive means of relaxation.

- If possible, get written permission on file at your husband's doctors' offices (especially those of psychiatrists and counselors), so that you can provide a needed outside perspective on his health progress.

Chapter 9

Positive ASD Qualities vs. Negative Experiences

It is apparent that individuals with autism spectrum challenges possess many fine qualities. All the women we heard from had obviously fallen in love with men who possessed many positive attributes. They described an impressive list of characteristics, such as loyalty (lack of infidelity), devotion to spouse and family, brilliance in some academic areas and very firm principles, just to name a few. At some point in their relationships, however, all the partners we have spoken with have encountered significant struggles in their lives with their ASD partners. These struggles are of such a magnitude that these women were questioning their partners' true characters, their own sanity and their ability to stay in their relationships.

We felt the need to share some of "the best and the worst" in the same chapter, so as to spotlight better the rollercoaster emotions that all who spoke with us said they experienced.

Positive qualities of those on the autism spectrum

With all of the challenges those with ASD face, it may be hard for those outside of NS-ASD marriages to understand the draw that most of the NS wives we spoke with had to their husbands. However, most of these women were eager to inform us about the qualities they saw initially in their ASD partners. Many admitted that such traits were a big part of what kept them committed to their marriages even during hardships. Common descriptions included "real gentleman" with morals; intellectuals; men who were honest (almost to a flaw), trustworthy, attentive, charming, clever, doting, loyal, had unique senses of humor, were non-manipulative, kind, naive or child-like and handsome. Males on the autism spectrum may seem unlike other males in that they typically do not focus on otherwise "male" pursuits such as sports, cars and attractive women (unless one of these is a special interest, or obsession, to them). Instead, they are often described as quiet, kind and attentive with a strong sense of social and moral justice. It seems that NS partners have a unique ability to see through the challenges into the core of the "good person" inside—who just happens to have a developmental disorder, or ASD.

> NS Bonnie described how her ASD husband, Brad, was very vocal about women's rights and would often bring up the unequal pay issue between men and women in the workplace. Brad would likewise watch various documentaries about the oppression, abuse and/or the history of women's rights and would speak about these issues in conversation whenever possible.

Exceptional intellectual abilities and the pursuit of knowledge and truth that are so common in individuals with ASD are appealing to many partners. A child-like innocence, naivety, or "Peter Pan" quality is often seen as refreshing and endearing compared to the macho personality of many typical males.

In our experience, both the NS and ASD partners show little concern about age or cultural differences in their relationships. This is exemplified in the fact that the partners in many NS-ASD couples we met are from different cultures and/or their age differences are pronounced. For example, several of the NS wives shared that their ASD husbands were not originally US citizens, but had immigrated from other countries, and that English was not their native language. Several of the women were attracted to their ASD partners due to the "mystery" of their being from other cultures. In two cases, there was a significant age gap, with the ASD partner being more than ten years older than the NS partner. In a couple of partnerships, the NS partner was the one who was significantly older than the ASD partner. These differences often masked the oddities in the

ASD partner, as they were attributed to either cultural or age gaps or both.

As with "typical" relationships, ASD partners are often on their best behavior during the initial phase of a relationship. Just like the majority of NS men, ASD men can learn what women like and provide this while courting. In fact, they are often described as doing this even better than their NS peers. With their tendency to over-focus on one interest at a time, ASD men often make their future wives a special interest (see Chapter 1), and therefore excel at courting. They are often extremely loyal and dedicated to the relationship, which can be very attractive and appealing. Who does not want to feel special? It is understandable, considering this, that the wives may feel especially slighted after their ASD spouses suddenly revert to their other special interests, often almost immediately after the courtship has ended.

One NS spouse was struck by her husband's dedication to his daughter from his first marriage. Since having children and having a good father for the children was an important attribute in her mind, she saw their father-and-daughter relationship as proof that he would be a good father to their future children. In some ways, he was, and in other ways, he was not. When they did go on to have children, he was very kind to their children. However, he lacked the initiative she assumed he would have. She had observed him when he was a *non-custodial* father, and didn't realize his limitations in day-to-day parenting (see Chapter 7).

ASD individuals can have extraordinary abilities and are usually independent thinkers. They can be exceptionally hard workers when pursuing their special interests. When the special interest is a person, it can be very flattering. When the special interest is something lucrative or unique with money-making potential, that can be very exciting and enticing. Also, when sharing the special interest in some way, the NS-ASD couple can experience many relationship-building opportunities together.

Many of the NS partners we interviewed shared examples of how proud they were of their partners for their abilities in mathematics, computer technology, physics and music. As mentioned earlier, some of the ASD partners are very accomplished in their chosen professions of medicine, business or law. The NS partners in such couples had been attracted, in part, to partners with a successful careers.

Areas of exceptional knowledge can be a great attraction for both partners.

> NS Pam knew the area codes of all cities in her state, because of the job she had. ASD Jim was instantly attracted to someone with what he deemed a fascinating area of knowledge. However, it became a bit of a strain to the NS partner when the ASD partner wanted to spend an inordinate amount of time drilling her with questions on area codes.

Writer Kristi Sakai related a lovely story about her ASD spouse and how they appreciate and accommodate each other in their life together:

> Yesterday was Nobuo's and my 17th anniversary. I asked him if he wanted to do anything, or if I should cook something special. He was genuinely thinking about it for days, and then he finally said, "I know what I want. Starbucks." I laughed, "Have you ever HAD Starbucks?" He hadn't, but that's what he wanted: a cup of coffee from Starbucks, or rather a mocha latte. "Do you even know what that is?" I asked. "Nope, but it's what people order on TV."
>
> My only dilemma was how on earth to bring it home hot as it's at least 20 miles to the nearest Starbucks. I finally settled on going to a little gourmet cafe 3 miles away.
>
> I received a lot of criticism for marrying him because of his age (he is considerably older than me) and he hardly had two nickels to rub together. I didn't care; I was madly in love with him. He was funny and kind (and adored me in spite of the fact that I'm totally screwed up). I said people rarely stay married 20 years anyway, and that if we could have 20 years

together, we'd be luckier than most. When he was seriously ill [because the coffee aggravated his Crohn's disease] I said, "You can't die, you know; you haven't served your entire sentence—we haven't been married 20 years yet." When he began to get a little better, I bought him a gray silk hapi coat (Japanese formal wear—my husband is Japanese) painted with a fisherman and told him, "I've been thinking, you deserve a significant penalty for making me worry like that, so I've decided to make you serve another 20 years. And don't think you can get out of it because I intend to marry you all over again" (in his silk hapi coat). I hung it up in our bedroom and pointed at it every day to remind him he had to get well. It must have worked! Who knew you could spur on recovery simply by reminding a man he has no escape during his lifetime from his nagging wife? Statistically, they say married men live longer (which is, of course, frequently countered by men who say, "It only FEELS longer").

Well, it turned out a mocha latte was not the pleasant experience my husband had hoped for. He said it tasted great, but...let's just say drinking another might send him to the hospital, so he should probably lay off them from here on out.

Our anniversary was less than romantic and mostly consisted of me rubbing his tummy or giving him sympathetic looks while I made the kids frozen fish sticks (they were happy). But as most of you know, marriage isn't about the romance as much as it is about recognizing each other's challenges and loving not only in spite of them, but perhaps even because of them. Anyway, what could possibly be more romantic than my husband baking cookies with our daughter while I write this? He's a keeper. (Sakai 2007)

Kristi's tone of voice in this writing is an apt example of the endearing ways many of the NS spouses we met spoke of their ASD partners—even sometimes during their apparent exasperation with them. Another very positive view that NS wives consistently took was of their husbands as heroes of sorts, commonly revering them for their almost superhuman traits that made them different, such as a high ability to withstand physical pain or incredibly quick reflexes. Several NS wives also admitted outright that they felt they truly "needed" their husbands. This surely helps to keep them active in maintaining a functional, hopefully happy, relationship with their ASD partners, in spite of their unique challenges.

Negative experiences

Affective deprivation disorder

It is a sad truth that many NS women in a relationship with men who have an ASD experience a number of unique challenges that often give them decidedly negative outlooks on their relationships. In this chapter, we look at some of the most extreme examples of this, the main one being affective deprivation disorder.

The terms Cassandra syndrome, Cassandra affective disorder (CAD) and Cassandra affective deprivation disorder (CADD) have been used to describe an ongoing pattern of emotional deprivation experienced by many—though not all—NS partners in NS-ASD partnerships. This is especially true if the ASD partner is undiagnosed. These phrases are terms coined by Maxine Aston (Aston 2001), a professional counselor and researcher in England, on Asperger marriages. They are used to describe the extreme symptoms of stress that NS partners and other family members often experience in NS-ASD families. The stress of NS partners in such relationships is very real—just like the stress of the ASD partners that we have been discussing in prior chapters.

It is important to note that Cassandra affective disorder, no matter how it's phrased, is not currently a diagnostic category in the *Diagnostic and Statistical Manual* (DSM) of the American Psychiatric Association (APA 2000). However, it describes a phenomenon noted by many counselors who have worked with NS-ASD couples.

The terms CAD and CADD have roots in an ancient story. In Greek mythology, Cassandra was a princess who was given the gift of prophecy by the god Apollo. Apollo was infatuated with her, but she did not return his affection. As a result, he made it so that no one would believe Cassandra's prophecies, so that she would speak the truth, but never be believed. Cassandra's not being regarded seriously by others mirrors the situation in which many NS partners find themselves, especially when their partners have no diagnosis or even suspected diagnoses of autism spectrum disorders.

Aston compares the symptoms she sees in CAD or CADD to those of someone suffering from seasonal affective disorder (SAD) (Aston 2001). The symptoms of SAD and CAD are similar, including depression, anxiety and social dysfunction. Further, whereas SAD is caused by a chemical imbalance due to failure to receive sufficient sunlight exposure during the winter months, CADD (according to Aston) is caused by an emotional deprivation (Aston 2010). Whether or not the emotional deprivation is intentional, it usually seems intentional and/or unending to the NS partner (Aston 2010).

More recently, Maxine Aston and others have used the term affective deprivation disorder (AfDD) to label a relationship issue that results in chronic emotional deprivation for one or *both* partners. This deprivation is created because the partners are emotionally out of sync. Neither partner is described as actively or deliberately causing the emotional deprivation of the other. The difficulties in the relationship often develop because one or both partners have low emotional awareness, low ability to empathize and/or an inability to identify and describe their feelings. This term (AfDD) is also not an official DSM publication (APA 2000). In our research, we have learned that both partners can learn together to understand their differences and develop better ways to interact.

Self-doubt

Most of the NS partners we spoke with said that they felt at some point in time that they must be crazy. Outsiders saw the ASD partner as charming, intelligent and having other fine qualities. However, the NS partner also saw a rigid, demanding, immature and uncommunicative side that was rarely seen by the outsiders. When these NS spouses confided some of the problems in the relationship to such outsiders, they were told they must be exaggerating or causing the problems themselves, as others did not seem to recognize the behaviors and issues they described. As a result, many NS partners come to doubt themselves and often think they simply have to do more for their spouses or that they have to "fix" themselves.

In reality, many of the NS women who shared their thoughts, feelings and experiences may be described as exceptionally mature, understanding and sympathetic toward the perspectives of others. Most seem very socially aware and capable. This personality profile fits well in ASD-NS partnership, as the partner on the spectrum needs someone to model appropriate social behaviors, report expectations and take up the slack in various social situations.

NS partners often find themselves "running the show" with little or no social and emotional support from their partners. Many do not know why, and often no one else understands. Some wives attempt to resolve issues with counseling sessions, but if the counselor is not familiar with autism spectrum disorders, this usually does not resolve much and can, in fact, make matters worse.

Typically, the ASD spouse seems like a level-headed man who does not know why his wife is unhappy. The majority of NS spouses informed us that counselors saw the problem as theirs, suggesting that they find a job, a hobby or another focus in their lives. In some cases a child with an autism spectrum diagnosis was part of the family, and the counselor suggested that the NS spouse needed to let up some of the focus on the child and work on the marriage. In short, these frequently well-meaning but uninformed counselors did not take the wives' concerns seriously or understand the reality of the situation.

Several NS spouses told us that their counselors heard their concerns and suggested very quickly that they probably should leave the marriage; these counselors believed—from often only a few sessions—that the ASD spouses were willfully sabotaging the relationship. This, too, unfortunately shows the counselors' lack of understanding about ASD and how it can affect relationships.

Symptoms of affective deprivation disorder

All these misunderstandings—lack of professionals' knowledge about ASD and continued social-emotional deprivation experienced by the NS partner—can lead to a variety of symptoms now labeled alternately by professionals who are knowledgeable about autism spectrum disorders as AfDD, CAD, CADD or simply Cassandra syndrome. Common symptoms include:

- depression

- social dysfunction

- low self-esteem

- anxiety

- weakened immune system

- weakened libido

- lethargy.

(Aston 2010)

The great majority of NS partners we interviewed were still married to their ASD spouses. About 20 percent were either divorced or separated.

> One NS partner reported that now that she and her ASD husband were separated and had separate living spaces within a short commute from one another, they were much happier in their relationship. They still were close friends, but lived apart. They made "dates" and phoned each other at regular intervals. That way, the ASD partner could control his very limited social commitments and the NS partner could run an open, social household of her own. She said her strong, close friendships with other NS individuals made the situation possible and acceptable.

We now look at each of the AfDD, CAD and CADD symptoms individually.

Depression

Almost all of the NS partners we interviewed were on some form of antidepressant. Of those on antidepressants, over half reported that they no longer had any interest in sex or sexual intimacy. Some said they thought this lack of interest was due to the antidepressant itself. (This can be a side effect of many antidepressants, but not all.) Others said they just quit trying, because of their partners' lack of interest or true distress in situations involving sexual intimacy.

Many attributed their depression to being overwhelmed with responsibilities, especially those they considered to be typically the responsibility of the male in a partnership. Many of the spouses we interviewed were also the parent of one or more children, with at least one of the children having some form of ASD. On top of other responsibilities, those parents frequently had to be the peacemakers between their ASD spouses and their children. This was true regardless of whether or not the children were on the autism spectrum.

Still others felt they had "settled" and given up the hope of an empathic, lifelong relationship.

As one NS spouse put it:

> I was a very romantic person. I wanted to find my knight in shining armor who would be handsome, smart and courteous. I found him. I was thrilled. I was adored. Then after our marriage, I began to realize that the shining armor is never removed...that he does care about and even adore me at times, but beneath the armor, there is no empathy.
>
> I imagined long walks, talking about our future. My husband does try to take walks with me. However, since he is taller and more athletic, he walks faster than I. So we start out, [and] he won't hold my hand...doesn't like the feeling of that...and soon he leaves me behind. He is basically unaware that he is supposed to be with me. I usually just turn around and go home. When he returns, he can't understand why I'm mad or disappointed. I've been specific and asked him to walk more slowly and tried to talk to him. He doesn't seem able to walk and talk at the same time. He is a brilliant man who cares so much. He just simply can't do some things that would help me in feeling companionship.

When depression becomes severe or when low-level depression is long-lasting, it's important actively to seek solutions. Some examples include: counseling and medication; exercising (this can be as simple as taking a walk around the block a few times a week); rewarding yourself with healthy treats like fresh fruits and vegetables that please your palate; maintaining a regular sleep routine, so that you consistently get a minimum of seven hours of sleep each night, even on weekends.

SOCIAL DYSFUNCTION

A large number of the NS partners we interviewed had a social life separate from their partners. This let them socialize without the burden of worrying about their ASD partners' needs. The majority of NS partners who did not have much of a social life apart from their partners were much less happy and less well adjusted to their partnerships.

The rare few people whose partnerships involved a significant group of friends of both spouses reported that they chose open and accepting friends who found their partners' eccentricities endearing or humorous. One NS partner felt that several of their couple friends were there because of, not in spite of, their ASD partners. Some NS partners married to clergy or medical professionals said that they felt that those who claimed to be friends because of the partner actually wanted the status of that friendship.

LOW SELF-ESTEEM

Some NS partners find themselves apologizing for and excusing the behaviors of their ASD partners a large part of the time. Frequent episodes of public rudeness and strange behaviors can lead to a feeling of great social inferiority and gradually begin to drain the NS partners' self-esteem. They feel like failures at choosing a proper partner.

One NS spouse had resigned herself to being the brunt of her husband's humor. He had discovered that if he made fun of his wife's talking a lot and her cooking, their friends would laugh. Since this made him seem "cool" to their social set, she allowed it. Sadly, as time went on, she began to believe that she was less than those around her.

Some NS spouses also experienced a self-esteem drop over time as they began to question their own knowledge and authority over life matters.

> NS Kaye told us that when she first got together with her husband Pete, he would insist she was "wrong" about everything from how to groom their pets and do the laundry to how to spell certain words. Kaye recounted an incident when she brought him the dictionary to show multiple "acceptable" spellings of a word, but Pete responded, "That dictionary is wrong." Kaye began to doubt herself and started to feel like she was inept. She said that, until Pete's diagnosis, she spent several months turning to him as an expert in nearly every decision she made in life.

ANXIETY

Some NS partners shared their worries about possible upsets during vacations, parties, important meetings and other aspects of daily life, acknowledging that their worries made enjoying these occasions virtually impossible. Even award ceremonies for the NS spouse or family members can become sources of great worry.

The anxiety for ASD partners surrounding having "strangers" in the home also results in anxiety for the NS partner. A "stranger" could be anyone—such as a repair person, the friends of one of their children, a new neighbor or a delivery person.

Certainly, most families will need "strangers" to come to the home at some point. Crises like choosing between calling a plumber or living with only one working bathroom were common scenarios. That is, if the plumber or other repair person were to show up, the anxiety this would cause for the ASD partner would be tremendous and produce a strain on everyone in the household. The NS wives we spoke with had a tendency to anticipate such situations and to worry about them considerably. (See the "Meltdowns" section in Chapter 6.)

NS Kaye said that not only does she relate to this "stranger danger," but also she, too, can become just as anxious as her ASD husband Pete over "new people coming inside the house." And these feelings aren't just centered around strangers. Although Kaye had a very social upbringing and is herself a social person, she does most of her visiting outside of their home and often without Pete. She admitted that less than a year before our interview, she experienced a full-blown panic attack before her childhood friend came to visit her home, even though Pete was away at the time. She told us that it had been so long since she had entertained a friend at home that she suddenly became completely uncertain she could handle hosting duties properly, even for only one person.

Many NS wives shared that socializing caused anticipatory anxiety for them, whether they were to gather at their own homes or elsewhere. It seems that when their ASD husbands are preparing to socialize, they will often become demanding, setting clear and rigid boundaries in an effort to soothe their own nerves. Because these women often feel either verbally or emotionally abused by their husbands at such moments—often without the husbands' specific intention or awareness of doing so—NS wives frequently suffer from a specific anxiety that we have termed social buffering anxiety (SBA).

Social buffering anxiety consists of an NS partner's generalized anxiety before (and sometimes even after) social events with her ASD mate. While it can present differently in different individuals, SBA is due to an imagined need to anticipate the ASD spouse's wants and desires in an effort to make upcoming social events go as smoothly as possible for herself, her partner and the other guests at the event; combined with the NS spouse's own feelings of resentment or sadness or even guilt or shame at the somehow "broken" social component of their life as a couple.

Dinner parties are such a point of anxiety for Bonnie that she has stopped entertaining at home:

I not only endured Brad's rigid expectations of an immaculate house, a perfect dinner and the kitchen being perfect *before* and *during* serving the meal, but then I had to endure the embarrassment of his rudeness to our guests when he would insist on cleaning up the kitchen alone. If people offered to help him, he would be rude and snap at them while he complained about what a mess the kitchen was. It finally just became easier to take people out to dinner. This eventually led to fewer and fewer invitations for us to join our friends for parties and meals [at their homes, since we weren't reciprocating]. The only ones who continue [to socialize with us in this way] are those who truly accept Brad with all of these eccentricities revealed.

Bonnie concluded that it makes her overwhelmingly sad to think about this subject, and so she avoids it whenever possible; however, the sadness is preferable to her, compared to the anxiety and embarrassment she used to feel when she and Brad attempted to host dinner parties in their home.

Even award ceremonies for the NS spouse or family members can become sources of great worry.

NS Sheila once accepted a prestigious national award for her work without any family members present to congratulate her. She shared that she didn't ask her ASD son or her ASD spouse, because "our son would have been jealous of the attention given to me, and Harry [her ASD husband] would have just teased me about the whole thing. At least by going alone to the banquet, I could relax and enjoy my 15 minutes of fame." She said it hurt to know she was the only award recipient who didn't have family present, and that part of her dreaded the event in the days prior, just thinking about this aspect.

WEAKENED IMMUNE SYSTEM

Whether from depression and anxiety or from subsisting on their spouses' "odd" culinary requirements (often a rigid menu of favorites with a lot of meats and starches cooked a certain way and served at the "correct" temperature with little tolerance for a variety of fruits and vegetables or for trying something new), many NS spouses seem to have weakened immune systems. As one spouse put it, "I seem to get whatever is going around in the community." Considering the frequency of this complaint, we wonder if such illness might occasionally be a subconscious reaction to needing a break or to be taken care of and released from daily duties. These are anecdotal observations and not any part of a scientific study.

WEAKENED LIBIDO

The vast majority of the spouses we interviewed reported that their interest in and engagement in sexual activity had dropped to absolute zero. Many of the NS spouses and some of their ASD partners are on antidepressants; a side effect of some antidepressants is a weakened libido. That still can't explain the overwhelming numbers of people who report little or no interest in sex.

A few NS spouses informed us that, because of the caretaking relationship that was necessary, it left them feeling as if they were parenting their ASD mates, so intimate sexual relationships had become lost, and there was no interest in reviving sexual activity under those circumstances. Most felt that even when their partners attempted sexual activity, there was no foreplay and it was not a great experience. However, the small percentage of NS spouses who said their sex lives were "normal"—or even in two cases, considerably better than normal—reported that their ASD partners enjoyed sex and were good lovers. (A few NS spouses reported that sex was not important or in one case seemed aversive to the ASD partner, so that had put an end to sexual activity in the relationship.)

Depression can also weaken libido for both spouses. When feelings of sadness, grief or anxiety combine to overwhelm either the NS or ASD partner, a lack of interest in nearly everything that isn't considered immediately pressing may easily develop. It is not surprising in such times for one or both parties of the marriage to lose interest in sex specifically, especially considering the energy levels required to address unique challenges in this area. When antidepressants are used by, again, one or both members of the marriage, common side effects may include a lowered libido. Some spouses told us they could discuss a change in medication with their prescribing doctors to alleviate this issue; some said that the tradeoff for improving their depression was worth the lowered sex drive, and they had adjusted accordingly. (See Chapter 8 for more information on medications.)

> One woman shared that, when she first began to notice medication and life duties were slowing down both her and her ASD partner's sex drives, she decided to take the initiative and try something new. After many efforts to persuade her husband to initiate sex, she finally suggested they "have a make-out session." This took the pressure off her partner to perform. And the results were very satisfying for both of them, she shared.

Because sex increases pleasure-oriented brain chemicals like dopamine, finding ways to keep intimacy an active part of the marriage is one way to decrease depression symptoms. Another option for improving sexual relations would be working with a sex therapist. Sexologist and author Isabelle Hénault, PhD, says:

> In my practice, most couples are [NS]-ASD. Yes, I do sex therapy with some of them. Most of this work is about intimacy, exploring sexuality (gestures of affection, sexual script, dealing with inappropriate sexual behaviors, compulsive sexual practices, etc.) and educating spouses about sexuality. Most of them have been together for many years and have limited information and experience about sexuality.
>
> The other important issue is using the internet to get sexual stimulation (erotica, pornography and illegal sexual material). Many of my actual clients have sexual addictions—obsessions with regards to pornography. (Hénault 2010)

LETHARGY

About one-third of the NS spouses we interviewed experienced lethargy at intermittent intervals. Our reasoning is that it is part of general depression or an attitude of: "Why should I keep trying to be all things to all people when I usually fail?"

Lethargy can be the result of stress, lack of sleep, improper nutrition, depression and many other things. Many of the NS women we heard from describe themselves as neglecting their health after feeling overwhelmed with so much else they feel responsible to address. The stress they feel along with neglect of their physical needs would seem to add to the listlessness and mental fatigue they frequently described.

The seasons of a marriage

Most of the spouses we interviewed were middle-aged or younger. As with all couples, the entry into the senior phase of life brings with it changes for both partners in ASD-NS relationships. Depression can emerge for the first time in either or both partners. Monetary issues are often more challenging, as income has frozen or ceased entirely. Health is often on the decline. However, there is also the increase in wisdom and an ability to take a much longer-term perspective, even for spouses with ASDs in spite of their theory of mind challenges.

> One spouse describes her experiences as she and her husband continue to grow older:

>> I now look at some incidents that occur in our relationship and view them differently than before. When [my husband] was younger, I would see him doing something involving a really difficult "quirk" and think, "I'll find a way to help him control that." Or I would think, "How can I prevent this from happening again?" Now at those times, I often think, "Well, it's too late now. He is too old to change." In fact, some if not many of his habits, reactions and compulsions are becoming more exaggerated. I must also look at myself in all of this. While I'm younger than he, I am aging, too.

He has endured my hormonal changes, my illnesses, my pregnancies; none of those exactly were times when I was "Princess Charming." So, I largely view this latest stage as part of the yin and yang of a relationship.

I love him so much. When we said, "I do," it was "'til death do us part." That means forever. I will honor that. Yes, he is now more inflexible, but he never stops trying to make me happy...to be the best person he can be. I would do it all over again. I love him; he loves me. This is not the end of our story. It is just another chapter. I still would marry him all over again.

Certainly, the health and economic status of each partner will affect the severity of these issues. Good counseling and good healthcare are very helpful as these issues crop up in later life.

Lessons learned

- Strive for balance in your relationship. Focus on both your own and your ASD partner's strengths and interests, and build those as much as possible to strengthen the relationship.

- Continue to learn as much as you can about autism spectrum challenges. This will make it easier to know when and how to teach your partner about your thoughts, feelings, needs and wants.

- Exercise, eat healthy meals and do your best to keep a regular sleep schedule to avoid or alleviate depression.

- Join social groups and take part in hobbies and activities outside of your home as a means of temporarily alleviating social buffering anxiety.

- Validate your own feelings: Remember that the unique NS-ASD relationship struggles you face are real.

- Find others who acknowledge your challenges in this relationship, such as other NS women in relationships with ASD men and professionals who have knowledge of NS-ASD partnerships.

- Actively court intimacy in your relationship, as pleasurable activities like sex are a good means of fighting off depression.

- Work with your ASD partner to share thoughts and feelings, and don't assume understanding of each other's perspectives.

- Continue to seek outside help and support throughout the stages of life, especially as new issues arrive during later life.

Chapter 10

Successful Partnerships

All relationships take commitment and work, but when there have been misunderstandings and disappointments, an exceptionally strong level of commitment is needed. Author Marci can attest to this: After her husband was diagnosed, his acceptance of his AS diagnosis was crucial in helping them to begin fixing the problems in their relationship. Likewise, of course, it was important that Marci herself both accept and understand her husband's limitations and his strengths as someone on the autism spectrum. Equally important was the commitment of both spouses to their relationship. Several other NS partners echoed this important reciprocal perspective.

But a willingness to be committed to each other and recognition of ASD are often not enough to make a partnership successful without some tools. We discuss these tools—and diagnosis and commitment to success, as well—in more detail in this chapter.

Some of the NS spouses we interviewed reported that they either were using outside help in the form of counseling or that they had done so in the past with a variety of success rates and experiences. Many were looking for external support even if they had used it previously or were using it at the present. We acknowledge that, because many of the women contacted us, this sample may be more resourceful than the random NS spouse sampling.

Discussion of diagnosis

The majority of NS spouses we heard from started suspecting their husbands might have some form of ASD after a child in their families was diagnosed. Others had been looking for explanations of their spouses' unusual or aggravating behavior. In almost half of the marriages where a diagnosis was suspected, the husbands were open to learning more about ASD, and many of these husbands sought and obtained their diagnoses. In some marriages, the ASD partner was self-diagnosed or both wife and husband came to the conclusion together.

Reasons for pursuing a diagnosis were: to verify the suspicion of a diagnosis, to help the children or grandchildren better understand their father or grandfather and to find out how to address the challenges experienced by the ASD individual or the NS-ASD couple. The reaction to a diagnosis or the suggestion of ASD can range from relief and affirmation to fear, depression and anger.

NS spouses informed us that their ASD partners' reactions were varied. Often they expressed relief, but some of them did not agree with their diagnoses. Others, at least initially, were not interested in their diagnoses or in learning more about Asperger syndrome. Still some other ASD partners got defensive and/or depressed. However, immediately upon learning of their husbands' ASDs, most of the NS spouses told us they felt a sense of relief knowing that there was a name for their partners' behaviors and symptoms—and better yet, that information might be available to help them better understand their ASD partners.

The ASD partners sometimes react negatively, due to fears of being seen by society, friends and co-workers as being inferior, either in social status, competency or intelligence, and occasionally, all three. These partners sometimes contact experts and give scholastically oriented arguments about how they really aren't in any ASD category or they suspect that people are trying deliberately to categorize them as disabled to refute them in some way. One individual spoke with author Susan and said that his wife wanted to get him labeled, "so she can say she is always right."

Although disclosure is a complex issue and must be carefully considered by both spouses, the issue of disclosing and being diagnosed should be decided in finality by the challenged partner in almost every possible instance. One of the few exceptions might be when the ASD spouse is in trouble with the law or is in physical danger.

Author Marci's husband Phil initially experienced great relief and excitement when first diagnosed with high functioning autism. He felt that the diagnosis explained both the talents he enjoyed and the challenges he had faced throughout his life. He contacted family, friends and previous employers to tell them of his diagnosis. This lasted for several weeks after his diagnosis. Then, after about two months, Phil realized that knowing his diagnosis did not make his challenges in life disappear.

When this realization sank in, he experienced a clinical depression that lasted for months. Phil then slowly came to accept the reality of the diagnosis and began to learn more about himself, his diagnosis and strategies to optimize his abilities. For Phil, this acceptance and learning phase took years.

Successful partnerships require openness and honesty. Yet, more than 50 percent of the spouses we interviewed had not revealed to their partners that they thought the partners had ASDs. Some said they hide their ASD suspicions, because they don't want to hurt their partners' self-esteem. Others are certain that their partners will not believe this theory or else they have already approached their partners about the subject and have been rebuffed. Still others confessed a fear that their partners might indiscriminately disclose their ASDs, which could result in a loss of employment, friends or status within the community (such as for clergy members or doctors). Others negotiate with their spouses until their husbands agree to seek diagnoses.

This negotiation can range from overt to subtle: We heard stories about NS spouses leaving ASD-related literature out where their husbands could find it to read, as well as suggesting a spouse read "an interesting book" that happened to be about autism or Asperger syndrome.

One spouse shared that she described the *Diagnostic and Statistical Manual* criteria (used by the American Psychiatric Association (2000) to define specific diagnoses) of Asperger syndrome to her husband, initially telling him that it described a fascinating child in her sister's pre-school class. When her husband read it, he identified with every characteristic, and made his own decision to seek an official diagnosis, which later confirmed his wife's suspicions.

Sometimes, as mentioned, even if a diagnosis is given, the ASD partner rejects that diagnosis. In yet other partnerships, the subject is open and freely discussed between the two partners. This then extends to family and, in many cases, friends, employers and the community. It seems to be more readily accepted when broached calmly and dispassionately.

We found, as reported by the NS partners, that in the most successful NS-ASD partnerships, the husbands' ASDs are openly accepted by both partners, and they try to use this knowledge in coping with daily life. While an ASD diagnosis in children is made by direct observation and interviewing of parents and family members, the Health Information Privacy Act, which protects the privacy of health information (US Department of Health and Human Services 2001), prohibits interviewing anyone but the client in adult cases, unless the client agrees to such interviews.

Most clinicians will not make a definitive diagnosis of an adult on the autism spectrum without some developmental history, as well as specific information about social and communication skills. The clinician needs information from others close to the adult who can provide another perspective about interaction patterns.

Information about social and emotional reciprocity and patterns of behavior are best understood when someone close to the individual can answer questions and describe the differences and concerns encountered. If the adult will not give permission for others to be interviewed, this makes it difficult or in many cases impossible for a definitive autism spectrum diagnosis to be made.

When non-spectrum spouses are interviewed, they are sometimes judged harshly by the interviewer due to the Cassandra syndrome phenomenon (see Chapter 9). That is, professionals who haven't worked within the somewhat rare realm of more adapted people with an ASD may think the NS partner is negative, a "worry wart" or prone to exaggeration. They may fail to see the stress many NS spouses feel at having to be in charge not only of themselves but also of a challenged partner and often challenged children as well.

It is important to choose a clinic or professional carefully before approaching them for diagnosis or other support. Although there is no way to guarantee that the experience will be 100 percent positive—and it is likely (and normal) for both spouses to have at least some anxiety over obtaining a diagnosis and seeking treatment for the first time—asking questions in advance can help allay fears. We suggest that the NS (or ASD) spouse ask about the following areas: the clinic's (or professional's) experience in treating high-functioning individuals on the autism spectrum; the percentage of people on the spectrum who have been helped by the clinic or professional, plus how many of those were adults; what testing instruments or diagnostic criteria are used to confirm diagnosis; any specialized knowledge in the area of testing. If a professional or clinic is unwilling to answer questions up-front, this can be a sign of questionable methods or lack of experience, and we recommend looking elsewhere.

Support groups and books (see the Bibliography) make great resources. In recent years, more books have been written by adults with ASDs for adults with ASDs—about their own experiences in life, including relationships with NS partners. Conferences that provide speakers who themselves are on the autism spectrum are also highly informative resources. NS and ASD partners now provide sessions at both the yearly Autism Society and MAAP Services conferences. In recent years, workshops for NS spouses have been offered by Tony Attwood, Maxine Aston and the authors of this book, among others.

Knowledge is power. The knowledge that comes from an ASD diagnosis prompts ASD individuals and their spouses to read about ASDs, attend conferences and meet others on the spectrum and their families, and in the process, they gain important information and learn valuable coping mechanisms.

Commitment

Commitment is essential to most forms of success. This is certainly true in a marriage. Somebody who is prone to walk away from challenging relationships usually will not stay in an NS-ASD marriage or dating situation. As mentioned, once their spouse's diagnosis is confirmed, some NS partners feel relieved and confident that they can find solutions to the daily challenges they face. In other cases, once the ASD partner is diagnosed, the spouse feels vindicated in leaving the marriage, viewing the ASD diagnosis as synonymous with "failure." We strongly disagree with this viewpoint, as did the majority of partners who spoke to us.

Nevertheless, in some extreme situations, separation or divorce is indicated, primarily due to physical or mental abuse on the part of either partner.

> In one case we observed, the ASD partner was large and strong. He had a fast temper and was a threat to the safety of his children, each of whom had some form of challenge. The NS partner finally left the marriage and took the children with her.

Some couples decide that they love one another but are happier when living apart—even when abuse is not a factor. Such couples often live in the same town or neighborhood but maintain separate residences and friends. That is, they arrange regular or intermittent meetings or "dates," but live somewhat separate lives.

> In one case, the ASD partner was very uncomfortable with sexual intimacy and avoided such contact. The NS and ASD partners loved and respected one another greatly, were raising children together and were good parents. At one point, the NS partner developed a close friendship with another man. Eventually, this person moved into the household, where he was friends with everybody, and it was accepted that he and the NS partner shared a bedroom. Although this was quite socially unique, all parties seemed happy with this situation at the time of this writing.

Support

While a commitment to each other is an important part of any successful NS-ASD marriage, finding support outside of the home is just as vital. Some of the means to do this that are readily available include: reading books; attending conferences and workshops and couples' groups (especially for "mixed couples" where one partner has an ASD); seeking out kind and caring friends who know about the diagnosis; and building personal support systems. Both NS and ASD partners should ideally address their needs and seek ways to fulfill them. Joining online chat groups is a popular means of doing this (see the Useful Resources section).

Seeing a counselor (or counselors) is another important way to gain support. Although therapists and counselors who are unfamiliar with Asperger syndrome, especially in adults, can sometimes negatively impact couples, a qualified professional who has insight into adult ASD can provide many ideas, tools and other resources for couples to support themselves and each other. We have heard from spouses that individual therapy used alongside couples therapy is best for optimal support. Although, realistically, it can be a challenge to find more than one learned professional that each partner feels comfortable with, we recommend the ideal scenario: one counselor or other professional assigned to work with the NS spouse, one for the ASD partner and a third who works with the couple together. Proactive therapies, such as cognitive behavior therapy, frequently work best for men with ASD, we have seen. If money is a factor, resources are usually available to help with payment, such as finding counselors who offer sliding fee scales. Emailing the authors of this book (see our addresses in the Useful Resources section) can also provide support to NS-ASD couples and their families.

Often overlooked is the extreme importance of support for both spouses from family, friends and neighbors. In Chapter 11, we share some tips for those attempting to support the NS spouse.

Respite

Nearly anyone who has a child with disabilities, or who has been a caretaker for an elderly family member, is probably familiar with the term "respite." In such cases, it is used to define breaks from this often exhausting care via help from professional caregivers, family or friends. Respite is not necessarily a need that partners and spouses consider within their intimate relationships. However, the majority of the NS partners we have spoken with find that taking a break from giving care to others in order to restore personal balance is a key ingredient for the success of their lives with their ASD partners.

Respite can be defined in a variety of ways. Among the community of NS partners, respite can be described as a planned interval of time away from physical, emotional and cognitive contact with the ASD partner that allows some rest, relief and control for the NS partner. In cases where there is little personal contact with ASD spouses—such as when areas of special interest keep ASD husbands either away from the home or secluded in one space—respite can mean pure escape from the home, especially when no children are involved. As noted throughout this book, the NS partner often manages additional responsibilities, thanks to the ASD partner's communication, social and sensory processing differences and his executive functioning challenges. Separate vacations or personal days apart are helpful ways to achieve respite. We discuss these and other examples in greater detail in the following pages.

The ASD partner needs respite, too. However, it seems that all too often in many of these marriages, the ASD partner gets at least some respite time as needed, usually daily, as time alone or time to pursue special interests; the NS partner frequently does not.

NS partner Sheila described well the scenarios of finding respite at the grocery store for both herself and her spouse. Her ASD husband Harry finds respite away from crowded family gatherings by offering to go to the store for last-minute items. He knows the store well, and its consistent structure, routine and rules for conduct offer him comfort and refuge.

For very different reasons, the grocery store is often also a place for NS Sheila to escape for a little respite. At times, when Harry gets verbally abusive or when he and one of the kids "gang up" on her, Sheila uses the excuse of needing groceries to get out of the house. In these times, she says, she usually just walks around the store looking for snack treats or maybe some ingredients for something her husband and children might like. However, the main benefit of the trip to the grocery store for her is the bit of positive and predictable social contact with people she gets there. "It is just nice to be treated politely, even if it is just for a little while," she says. Then when she feels better, Sheila drives the long way home and allows herself a brief cry. "This may sound crazy, but it works," she sums up. Crying can be its own form of stress reliever.

Several other NS spouses described a similar short trip to a familiar store as a respite that they use at times. This same "shopping trip respite" is used by author Marci on a regular basis. NS partners need to escape from the volume of responsibilities and expectations that can often feel overwhelming.

Other forms of diversion can occur when one or both spouses join philanthropic groups (such as Meals on Wheels), bridge clubs, chess clubs, etc. Groups that have very clearly defined rules of conduct are especially helpful for ASD spouses. For example, Rotary Clubs often have strictly adhered-to policies and agendas that leave little room for social misstep once an ASD partner has learned the rules. When an NS-ASD couple joins a club such as this, the pressure to teach social cues and behaviors is alleviated, at least in part, from being the sole burden of the NS spouse. Also, attending a high school or college class reunion may help NS spouses reconnect with old friends who may be nearby and can provide deeper support and understanding.

Many wives not on the autism spectrum told us that money felt like a prohibitive factor in getting rest and time for themselves. However, we discovered that a little brainstorming and creative thinking went a long way in this area. For example, taking a walk or a drive, or going to a public place like the library for a little friendly social contact really does not have to take much time or cost anything. To women who are in the thick of exhaustion it may seem impossible to get away, but options like waiting until the children are in bed to take a break were methods that worked for the NS wives who tried them.

The important thing is for NS partners take a break! Longer respite breaks might be an option, such as a night or weekend away. But regular breaks were the most helpful and the easiest to implement for the wives we interviewed. An exercise routine, for instance, can be a creative respite option with additional health benefits. This exercise break can be done alone, at home, with others or just in the presence of others such as at the local gym.

Lessons learned

- Talk to him about your thoughts if you suspect your partner has an ASD. Even if the thought is initially rejected by your partner, it may stay in his subconscious long enough to ring true eventually.

- Discuss specific information about ASDs that you found in your research, as well as your own insights. Many individuals on the spectrum will not recognize general information in themselves, so pick out a description of an ASD trait, and pair it with the same trait you see in your partner.

- Keep ASD information in the house. Sometimes seeing literature lying around helps curiosity prevail, and your partner may pick it up to read.

- Discuss your thoughts about his possible diagnosis in a very matter-of-fact fashion and as positively as possible.

- When your partner with a potential ASD agrees to seek a diagnosis, choose the clinic or professional you visit for diagnosis or guidance carefully.

- Look for the following when considering a first-time visit to a clinic or specialist: experience diagnosing and treating a significant number of high-functioning individuals with various forms of pervasive developmental disorders; specialized knowledge in the area of testing; and a willingness to answer your questions up-front about what instruments (if any) and methods are used to test.

- If the diagnostician gives you a label, but no sources of networking or suggestions for therapy, ask for this information or where to find it. See the Useful Resources section of this book for information.

Note: Think long and hard before disclosing. This must be the ASD spouse's decision...or at least he should agree with your disclosing or know you are doing so.

- Keep in mind that, while it can be difficult to negotiate the challenges of living with someone on the autism spectrum, the rewards can be wonderful—especially when you both know the diagnosis, accept it and are willing to get the help and support you each need.

- Seek support along many different avenues.

- Ideally, see three separate counselors: one for you, one for him and one you see together as a couple.

- You can and must find family, friends and professionals who care and are supportive of both of you.

- Find a variety of "respite" options.

- Remember: You are not alone. *Do not give up* when it comes to finding supportive people in your life!

Chapter 11

Meeting the Needs of the NS Partner

In most committed intimate relationships, NS individuals can assume their relationships with their partners will provide the core of their social, emotional and sexual needs. However, in NS-ASD partnerships, the NS partners often need to find ways to address social, emotional and sexual needs in ways that do not necessarily directly involve their ASD partners. Additionally, we estimate that about two-thirds of the NS spouses we have spoken with have financial concerns over their partners' struggles to keep or find work that will support their financial needs. Thus, we have also included financial needs here.

Social needs

Many NS spouses report meeting their social needs through close (mostly same-gender) friendships, clubs, travel and community events. Most take separate vacations from their partners, though not necessarily exclusively.

> One NS partner noted that her ASD husband was heavily stressed by travel. He became nauseated the night before a trip and remained so until they arrived at their destination. He invariably made them late, because he repeatedly had to go to the bathroom on the day of travel. When the couple traveled with their two ASD sons, the one who was compulsive about time would become extremely upset about being late. This woman told us, "I absolutely love taking small trips on my own, as I only have to make *myself* happy.

It is a joy to set my own priorities for fun and relaxation and not to be the family referee for a change."

Most of the NS women we interviewed joined support groups to help them deal with issues surrounding parenting, their own depression or other health issues, and, specifically, ASD-NS marriages. Through these groups, they say they gain not only direction and support regarding exact needs, but also the bonding and fellowship of like-minded people. One spouses' support group even meets a few times a year for outings to allow NS wives true respite. They have met up for excursions such as shopping in Amish country and a weekend retreat at a tourist town.

Individual hobbies like quilting, gardening, crossword puzzles and other activities also provide respite from the typical caregiving role of the NS spouse, especially because these hobbies provide an opportunity for solo relaxation and socialization, such as quilting bees, gardener's clubs, competitions and classes. Book clubs were another popular means of respite-like self-care.

Emotional support

The main emotional need we hear from NS partners that often goes unmet is romance. Some get this vicariously through movies; others through books; still others via email "relationships." Many just decide to rid their lives of romance and appreciate the good things in their NS-ASD relationships.

> One NS spouse whose husband was incarcerated for over ten years eventually filed for divorce when she became romantically involved with a close friend.

A significant number of NS partners have pets or children with whom they connect emotionally. They realize this type of emotional support is different and limited, but find it important nonetheless. Most of the women who have participated in our workshops use humor to cope, finding relief from stress by laughing at common issues. Some NS women report joining women's groups and/or religious-based groups that help provide emotional support. Many with children on the autism spectrum join parent groups that they describe as also providing them with some emotional support. Indeed, many NS partners have found that networking with other NS partners has helped afford them some emotional support. We have listed some of these support groups in the Useful Resources section.

Sexual needs

To a significant number of NS partners, sexual needs (or lack thereof) is an area that does not receive much attention. The experiences of the NS partners we spoke with are varied, as illustrated in the following.

Celibacy

We were struck by the number of NS spouses who had stopped thinking about sexual intimacy in their relationship. Some had not had intimate sexual relationships in years. This was agreeable to both themselves and their ASD partners; hence there were no problems with the lack of sex lives in these relationships. Some NS partners attributed this to the prescribed use of antidepressants, whose side effects can include lack of libido (see Chapter 9 for more on weakened libido).

A few NS partners reported living like brother and sister, which they did not find acceptable. They were considering what to do, including ending the partnership to be free to move on to find intimate relationships that would include sexual relations. Those in this situation reported that they believed they would still be friends with their current ASD partners after the dissolution of the marriage. We heard from a couple of NS spouses that their marriages had indeed come to an end because of this issue. But in both cases, they remained very good friends with their ex-husbands and the NS partners felt free to date and look for other marriage partners.

Other NS spouses reported that, while not perfect, there was still some physical intimacy in their lives with their partners, just not very frequently. Several of the spouses said that it wasn't just their husbands; some of the wives, themselves, had less interest in intimacy than their husbands. This was attributed to various factors, including their ages, their levels of depression (and resultant antidepressant use with the side effect of lowered libido) and a need for foreplay that they did not receive from their partner.

Sex by appointment

A larger number of NS partners described having separate bedrooms and making "dates" to have intimate relations. Others explained they were presently taking breaks from their partners in terms of intimate sexual relations, and anticipated working through their problems before trying to resume sexual relations.

Healthy sex life

At least one-third of the spouses we interviewed reported having very satisfactory sexual relationships with their partners, focused on the mutual satisfaction of both partners. This indicates that there is hope for attaining sexual pleasure or at least tolerance, if mutual goals and beliefs can be established between the couple.

One couple, who asked to remain anonymous, reported that erotica and experimentation were both aids to their sex life together. Through exploring the visual images in magazines and reading fantasies in sex-based literature, this couple was able to have a frank discussion about their own likes and dislikes. The pictures were especially helpful for the ASD husband's understanding of what his wife meant when she explained her bedroom preferences.

Sex therapy (see Chapter 9) is another method that can be used to help improve romantic relations. Although none of the spouses we interviewed had visited sex therapists, the same couple above admitted to considering it.

The NS wife told us that her ASD husband was initially very rigid about his routines in the bedroom, often performing very mechanically and expressing confusion when she attempted to coach him to relax. She said she learned very quickly to show, rather than tell, what she wanted. When her husband suggested once in exasperation that he needed help from a professional, the couple sought out a sex therapist who could facilitate lessons on sexuality. However, the NS wife ultimately decided she was not comfortable with this. Instead, she proposed to her husband that she become a sex therapist of sorts to him whenever they were intimate. At this idea, he became much more vocal about his questions and his preferences until the two of them began to feel quite relaxed and satisfied with their relationship in the bedroom.

Erotic sex as a common interest

In one case, erotica and sexuality were described as an important interest for both partners. The focus was not pornography, but more of an interest in the history and mechanics of various aspects of sexuality. In a couple of cases, ASD partners shared that completion of the sex act led to a feeling of "normalcy" and a calmness of their brain, which was not obtained in any other way. The NS partners in these relationships appreciated this as a way to feel emotionally close to their ASD mates, which had not been possible for them in any other realm.

Of course, as with the example listed in the previous section, "Healthy sex life," visual erotica can also be used as a tool to "teach" the ASD partner ways to satisfy the NS partner and to convey his own sexual desires.

Alternative sex

A few NS spouses reported realizing that sexual experiences were important to them, but their ASD partners were not interested. Solutions they described included buying erotic "toys," finding sexual partners outside of the marriage or trying to develop a plan with their partner to increase sexual interest. Another solution involved one partner teaching another sexual foreplay or coitus techniques that appealed to him or her. This exploration can be very similar to other couples, although it often centers around communication and sensory issues. Another example of alternative sexual arrangements is illustrated in Chapter 10 at the end of the section on "Commitment."

Obsession with pornography

Several women we interviewed related stories of excessive pornography use by their ASD partners, which was making it hard for the NS partners to have a genuine sexual relationship. In one case, the ASD partner expected participation by his NS partner, which was not agreeable to her. In another situation, the pornography seemed to be the deciding factor in the breakup of the relationship.

Sex therapy

None of the NS partners we spoke with reported seeking professional help for this issue. Given the many negative experiences some NS-ASD couples have had with marriage counselors, we believe this reluctance to seek professional help is understandable. We also recognize that many people feel uncomfortable about being seen in the office of a sex therapist or discussing the intimate details of their struggles in this area with any strangers. Yet, we encourage partners reading this book who are unhappy with their sexual life to consider seeking the help of a certified sex therapist.

The American Association of Sexuality Educators, Counselors and Therapists (AASECT) website has information on this topic and provides a listing of accredited professionals in various local areas, including many professionals outside of the United States (see www.aasect.org).

It is important for therapists who work with NS-ASD couples to be properly informed about the sensory and theory of mind challenges associated with ASD, so that they can truly help such couples.

Financial needs

The vast majority of NS partners are the breadwinners in the family. Some live at near-poverty level. Others (about 30% of those we interviewed) have husbands who are highly compensated professionals or have a steady, reliable "techie" job.

Only a very small number of the NS partners we interviewed depend on their ASD partner to handle the family finances, as most have learned that the spouse (even if he is employed in a financial position) is seriously challenged by home budgeting and saving. There were remarkably few exceptions to this with the women we talked to. However, those who represented the exceptions were excellent budgeters and financial planners.

One scenario that was discussed among several NS partners we have heard from is the need to become the primary breadwinner. This transition was described as very difficult. Their ASD husbands had been employed in very well-paid positions, and then lost their jobs for a variety of reasons.

All the women say they try very hard to support their husbands in the search for comparable employment. In most cases, they are stay-at-home mothers who had not planned to work full-time until their children were older. Some women described having to work more than one job to help get the family's finances back on track— or to keep from sinking financially. Some of the women in the group, in fact, have started their own businesses or have hopes to do so at some point as a means of bringing in an adequate amount of money and to have some flexibility within the family. According to our research, trends like this have been common in ASD-NS relationships even prior to the present economic downturn.

Sheila recounted her experience to us:

> I never dreamed that one day I would be the person upon whom our income and financial wellbeing would depend. Harry has always been a very intelligent and hard worker. When he lost his job in his sixties and couldn't find another, it hit me like a sledgehammer: I was the breadwinner! I was scared to death. We both had worked for many years,

but my income was insignificant next to his. Now, I was consumed with worry: What if I fell seriously ill? What if the company I work for goes under? How can I find the energy to get a second job? My attitude was and is that Harry supported us well for as long as he could. When he retired and most of his pension was gone, it was my turn. I don't resent him for that. I just realize now how hard it is to be in charge of yet another huge responsibility.

Lessons learned

- Realize that your social needs are likely extremely different from those of your partner. Don't expect your partner continually to fulfill your needs for social companionship and a variety of social outlets.

- Respect your partner's needs and wishes, while you seek out opportunities to join friends who understand that you enjoy and need opportunities to socialize while your partner has other needs and interests.

- Your ASD partner may suggest you are out socializing too much. Discuss and agree on what activities you will take part in and how often you will be out with others.

- Perhaps without the pressure to be included, your partner will show some interest in trying new social experiences, particularly if a routine for the outings can be established, such as a weekly outing to play cards or meet friends for dinner.

- Seek out emotional support! Everyone who felt successful in their partnerships had found a way to get their emotional needs met.

- Keep working at it. A certain level of emotional support can be provided by the ASD partner, especially if you find a knowledgeable counselor who can help you work through some of the challenges you and your partner face.

- Establish and maintain as much intimacy as possible.

- *Don't assume that you will never be intimate again.* Give it your best try and assume that you can get this very basic human need across to your spouse.

- Discover what works best for you and your partner to meet your needs for intimacy. This area is one that needs to be addressed by the couple, and solutions are varied.

- Be prepared to assist your ASD partner in all facets of a job search, interview and ongoing monitoring of the work situation. If your ASD partner has the necessary skills for a lucrative job or career, be prepared to be instrumental in his finding a suitable job and keeping it.

- Consider that you may have to become the primary wage earner for the family at some point even though this is not what you both had planned.

Chapter 12

Final Thoughts

In this book, we have done our best to combine the wisdom, life experiences, opinions and dilemmas of over 100 women who are willingly committed to a lifelong relationship with partners on the ASD spectrum. A few are separated but have a commitment to a lifelong friendship with their former live-in partners.

Some equally wonderful women have made the agonizing decision to divorce. Those who have made that decision said they were still committed to offering information and advice to those who have either chosen to stay in relationships or who are trying to make decisions about the future of their NS-ASD relationships.

It is our hope that we have protected the identities of these couples well and that they will know how much we admire them for their commitment to family and faith. This book project started out as an exciting challenge. It ended up as a labor of love.

At the end of this leg of our journey through the ASD-NS partnership, we offer some heart-felt tips. The intention is to leave readers with important tools for the journey. Appendix I is a list of tips especially for those in a relationship that is often far from typical. Appendix II is a list of ideas for family and friends who want to support these couples, particularly the NS wives. Successful completion of this journey requires a lot of support. These pieces were written by three people who love several individuals on the autism spectrum as much as life itself and who respect all individuals with ASD as people who struggle to fit into an often unforgiving world. It is from such a perspective that we share advice in the following final pages.

To engage the reader further in the lives and the stories of the couples we have profiled, we have also added a third appendix, entitled "Couples Profiles." Although defining characteristics (such as names, ages, number of children, and so on) have been changed in most cases to protect anonymity, the sentiments and incidents shared are completely true. These couples exemplify the common themes present in the interviews we conducted with over 100 NS partners. Five of the ten couples profiled are actual couples; the other five are amalgams, used to illustrate the major situations revealed to us.

Ten Considerations for Non-Spectrum Partners

1. Learn about autism spectrum disorders and how they affect your partner

This will help you understand your partner better and help you resolve the issues you and your partner face. Learn from other NS spouses as well as from adults on the autism spectrum, but remember that not everything you hear and read will apply to your ASD partner. Use the knowledge you gain to ask and probe specific situations with your spouse. A better understanding of ASD and how your partner is affected is a useful tool and can help ensure that expectations of and support for him can be realistic and appropriate.

2. Do not assume you know the intentions of your partner's behavior

Always seek to clarify. NS partners cannot interpret ASD behavior through their non-spectrum filter and assume that they understand the meaning of a particular behavior of their ASD partner. As you learn more about autism spectrum disorders and what behavior is part of the challenges, you can be more realistic about expecting your partner to be able to change a behavior as you start to see life through his eyes.

It's important to note that this can be especially challenging at the beginning of a diagnosis. If you find yourself feeling that it's unfair that you show empathy to your partner who cannot often return the favor, know that you are not alone: Some of the other wives we spoke with also felt this way. However, once you begin to show compassion, you will likely be surprised at the ways your partner returns this to you.

3. Always prioritize

Some things must wait or be dropped. Decide what is important to address and when. This approach will help alleviate stress for you and your partner. Compromising can be a piece of prioritizing. Compromise is usually a two-way street. *However, for NS-ASD marriages, it is often a two-way, three-lane street!* What we mean is that *both* spouses may think they have more "traffic" than their partner. It may help you to remember that whether or not a person has an ASD has no bearing on who is right and who is wrong in a given situation. It takes extra energy to put yourself in the other person's shoes when making decisions. But it helps to remember to think, as the saying goes, "Great Spirit, before I judge a man, let me walk in his moccasins for ten days."

4. Keep your behavior practical, calm and predictable (PCP) as much as possible

Find other outlets to alleviate stress and use them! Encourage humor in your own life and in your life together. This will help keep your NS emotions in check, and your behavior more "PCP." Your spouse is still the same person you married. You can choose to make your knowledge of his diagnosis—or the symptoms of autism—as a weapon to justify grievances or as a tool to understand and encourage him and therefore enhance your marital relationship. When you choose to communicate with practicality, calmness and predictability, this "PCP" behavior can go a long way to furthering understanding and facilitating conversation between the two of you.

5. Establish clear boundaries in all major areas of your life together

The ASD partner needs clear and ongoing information about behavioral expectations. Think in terms of explanation instead of correction. This should be kept consistent, so frustration and confusion—on both your parts—is kept to a minimum. Individuals on the autism spectrum can and will do their best when appropriate expectations are explained and maintained.

6. Communicate with visuals

Use visual information (notes, email, even examples from movies or TV shows) to convey or supplement verbal messages. Be creative. Visual information is much easier for most individuals on the autism spectrum to process, and it can be used as a permanent resource when anxiety, sensory overload or executive functioning skills are causing challenges for your ASD partner.

7. Acknowledge and address sensory issues with your partner

These needs can change over time and even vary from day to day. Make sure you really hear your partner when he asks for a specific accommodation. Sometimes his senses get overloaded and he may have to shut down and not respond to avoid a "meltdown." As you learn what supports your partner's needs in these situations, overloads can be minimized.

8. State exactly what you need and learn to communicate in "autism spectrumese"

Make your "SOS" (sympathy or solutions) needs clear. Tell your partner that you just want to vent your feelings or would like any helpful suggestions he may have. Reveal your needs or feelings as openly and concretely as possible. Be direct, using a neutral tone, even if what you need seems obvious. The information processing and executive functioning deficits experienced by your ASD partner can "blind" him to your needs without this direction from you.

9. Find and develop your own social and emotional supports

This often means making friends outside of your relationship with your partner. Do what is necessary to get the support you need for social and emotional outlets. Also, be realistic and creative in finding ways that your ASD partner can learn to provide you with some social and emotional support.

10. Take care of yourself, while showing appropriate respect for your partner

Do not neglect yourself! Build in daily stress-free time as well as periodic longer breaks; even take separate vacations. Choose a trusted confidant (friend or professional) with whom you can share your worries, successes and problems. If that is not possible, or in addition, keep a diary or journal and/or "Tell it to the mirror." Most importantly, remember the "air mask allegory": Just as airplane travelers are instructed to put on their own oxygen masks before helping seatmates, so should you take care of yourself *first*, so that you are healthy enough to help tend to your partner's needs when necessary.

Advice from NS Spouses for Family and Friends

The wisdom shared here is the result of the collaborative thoughts of more than 100 NS partners. We hope our readers—those in NS-ASD relationships, as well as the family, friends and professionals who support them—will refer to this section often as they seek to understand and support especially the NS partners who are in committed relationships with ASD partners. These points are written from the perspective of the NS spouses we interviewed, representing the most common requests we heard from them of ways they wished their friends or family would respond. (See additional copyright information at the end of this appendix.)

1. Do not expect us to apologize for our partner. We did not do anything wrong. Having to apologize makes us feel bad

In many spouse support groups, women tell stories of family reunions, local outings and even important ceremonies being upset by a spouse behaving in rude or unconventional ways that cause hurt or embarrassment. Sometimes the women cannot think quickly enough in distressful situations. Holding a woman somehow responsible for her husband's actions really only adds insult to injury.

2. It's important to know that people with ASD often *appear* to be intentionally rude or unfriendly, when that is not the case

An ASD partner sometimes leaves a party, even leaving a spouse behind, because he can't take any more social pressure—perhaps because of a high noise level, because of an overwhelming smell or because of visual clutter or some other distressing overload. He may not tell anyone, but may just leave, knowing he is about to have a meltdown. He may commonly assume that others know this, too. In times like these, what the NS spouse really needs is for someone, kindly and without judgment, to provide transportation home at the end of the event.

3. People with ASD are often completely unaware of their effect on others

Some spouses have said that their ASD partners have been described as "awkward to relate to" by their NS friends and acquaintances. It can take years for this awkwardness to stop being a part of the NS-ASD friendship. The reality is that most ASD individuals are unaware of how they are perceived or how they otherwise affect those around them. Their primary focus is typically on meeting their own, unique needs—with none of the malice that their actions can connote to others. NS spouses may spend a lot of time explaining their partner's behavior or choose to detach themselves completely from it.

4. If our partners don't look at your face or eyes, please don't assume that they don't like you or that they are not listening to you

Many people with ASDs have a hard time looking into the eyes or even directly into the faces of others. As Margaret Dewey, an ASD person put it, "Other people send each other messages with their eyes and faces. I cannot decode these messages" (Dewey 1980). Many people on the autism spectrum say that they can process the speech of others better if they are not maintaining their gaze at the eyes or the face of the speaker. Some even describe feeling dizzy when looking directly into the eyes of the speaker.

5. Please don't assume that because we are involved in unusual partnerships, we are less socially skilled than you

Some NS spouses report being "talked down to" by people who know they have challenged partners. Others are subjected to pity. However, NS spouses enjoy varied social invitations and opportunities both with and without their ASD partners. NS spouses sometimes feel uneasy attending events for couples (like weddings or dinner parties) alone. But once they begin to accept their lives' differences and accommodate them, it is even easier for them to do so when those around them do too.

6. Don't offer us unsolicited advice

Typically, NS wives have known their husbands longer than those well-meaning individuals who would insert their advice into situations. The family members of ASD people know them in a different way than their spouses do. NS-ASD couples have their own special experiences and relationships. What may work as an appropriate relationship between an NS mother and her ASD son—or NS in-laws or co-workers and ASD individuals—will not usually translate to workable communication styles for NS-ASD partners.

7. Be aware that we often want to do things with you as couples, but our partners may back out at the last minute, may not find the proposed activities fun or may be upset or withdrawn during the activities we do share

This can occur even at very special occasions, such as weddings and holidays. The sad fact is that payment for unused reservations is not rare. NS spouses we met had this request: "Please do not offer to contact our ASD spouses and talk them into attending your functions." This type of "help" commonly backfires, creating more stress in the NS-ASD couple's household surrounding events.

8. Be aware that we may not be able to reciprocate dinner or party invitations because entertaining in our homes is often distressful to our partners

Many people in NS-ASD spouse groups indicate that they use the absence of their spouses—on business or some other occasion—as opportunities to entertain. For some, these are the only times they entertain. They share that they have had the most fun with friends and family members who will politely ask after their husbands' whereabouts, but "won't make a big deal" out of the fact that he is not present.

9. Remember that a bad day for our partners is a bad day for us, too

Even though we desperately need our friends and jobs (if we are employed), we may be overly grouchy or seem preoccupied or even drained if we have had a particularly distressful marriage dilemma that day. Fielding our partners' distress takes a toll on us, emotionally. We ask for your patience at these times.

10. Offer us unconditional friendship and include us without our partners when we seem to want it that way

An essential part of being a truly supportive friend to NS partners is knowing when to talk about their situation and when to avoid it. If unsure, it can help to ask if they'd rather discuss something else. Know that allowing an NS spouse to be around you, whether chatting or not, is preferable to their prevalent situation of loneliness and isolation. Distracting them with humor or activities you know they enjoy can help to refocus their attention and thus bring them out of their potential pessimism.

11. If you are not sure about how to act around our partners, feel free to ask us

Some spouses may say, "He's in a bad mood today. Just ignore him." Others may say, "He's having an Aspie day today. How about if we sit outside for a while?" In other words, spouses are often aware that those outside of their marriages may need guidance to understand how to respond to some ASD behaviors. While they don't have all the answers, most told us that they appreciate when friends and family ask them for pointers on how to respond to their ASD partners.

12. Understand that sometimes we want to talk about our special partners and other times we do not

Some NS spouses join religious study groups, place of worship groups, book clubs and other types of groups where other non-couples are present. This eliminates the need to talk about their spouses at length.

13. Know that sometimes we each need to know "safe" people and/or places to retreat to when our situations become overwhelming

Sometimes NS spouses escape to friends and family to laugh and forget their troubles or to hear about the troubles of those they love, rather than talking about their own worries. At other times, they really need to unload such worries without feedback (commonly called "venting"). At yet other times, NS spouses just need a safe and quiet place that allows them to be themselves and "escape." Sometimes this is done alone and sometimes in the company of others. There is really nothing different about these scenarios from any other average wife's, except that it can often be hard for NS wives' friends and families to relate to the unique challenges that NS spouses have.

14. Be aware that some of us experience extreme financial hardship

This does not necessarily mean NS-ASD couples want "handouts" or pity for their situations. However, outsiders to the marriages can understand when they do not want to join in expensive group outings or exchange birthday or seasonal holiday gifts.

15. Be *positive* in your interactions with us

NS spouses share: "We might have very low self-esteem and question our realities. We need to be *affirmed!*" In our groups and workshops, we often encounter brilliant women who think they are slow-witted or very attractive people who think they are ugly or interesting people who think they are boring. They often improve their self-esteem and reality testing from these group interactions. It is helpful to some NS partners to remember back to before they were joined to their partners. They can remember being popular or receiving awards or good grades or just being positively affirmed in their communities. Outside reinforcement can often help to mitigate the negative litanies that NS wives may be on the receiving end of at home—especially for those women who are vulnerable to affective deprivation disorder or social buffering anxiety. We try not to judge our partners negatively; we hope others will do the same, both with our partners and with us. Please be as positive as possible.

Note

Appendix II is based on the handout *Advice for Non-Spectrum Spouses of Individuals on the Autism Spectrum* © 2005 by Susan Moreno; 2nd edn © 2010 by Susan Moreno with additions by Marci Wheeler and Kealah Parkinson.

Appendix III

Couples Profiles

Although we interviewed over 100 people (mostly women) who were part of NS-ASD couples, for clarity of understanding and the sake of anonymity, we have condensed these people into an even ten profiles. Some of the profiles are true—such as that of Marci and Phil Wheeler. Some are truly based on specific couples or spouses we interviewed, with only a few identifying features and names changed to protect their identities. And some are composites of a number of couples we heard from and about, especially in instances where the stories overlapped repeatedly.

Because we three authors all resided in the US state of Indiana during the research and writing of this book, the majority of our participants did as well. But their life experiences were not limited to this state, nor were the sum total of the participating couples. We have tried to demonstrate in these profiles the various strong ties (upbringing, family connections or otherwise) to different parts of the United States and other countries that we encountered in our research.

In this book, we include a number of examples to illustrate each subject we examine. When sources are not named (for example, "One spouse told us…"), such examples are frequently word-for-word scenarios that were shared with us—especially when quoted. Again, easily identifying features were changed for protection. We have also drawn examples from the "couples profiles" outlined in this appendix, as explained above. For your ease of reading, we have included these profiles here in this appendix. We hope you identify with and come to love these couples—both compositional and real—as much as we have.

Marci and Phil

Marci and Phil both grew up in middle-class families with the expectation that they would go to college. Marci enjoyed the small northern New Jersey town just outside of New York City where she experienced small time life with big city benefits. She was the oldest of three daughters and at times was thrown into the role of parent as both her parents had demanding professional jobs, her father at one time working on Wall

Street. She enjoyed the fast pace and diversity of the people and cultures she was exposed to on a daily basis. Phil was very much at home in the rural part of northern Indiana where he grew up. One of seven children in a close-knit family, he also had aunts, uncles and cousins who were there for each other. Phil was the quiet middle child who found ways to be by himself and read or go for walks, befriending animals along the way—sometimes being talked into joining in with the others when they needed another "body" for the game they were playing.

Marci and Phil met while living at the same rooming house near the campus of Indiana University (IU). Marci was dating someone else at the time. Phil lived in a room in the basement that had no windows (the rent was very inexpensive). It never occurred to Marci that Phil enjoyed the darkness. She had a room that was on the main floor but somewhat tucked away from the "traffic" of people in the house. There was a small kitchen in the basement and a much larger kitchen on the main floor. They entered and exited the house through different doors. It is a wonder they met at all.

There was a front porch, complete with a bench swing. That is where they became acquainted. Phil enjoyed the motion of the swing. (It wasn't until years later that Phil revealed how he really preferred "rocking" furniture.) They ended up talking together one night. Marci had a dog that became fast friends with Phil. Marci was working and making plans to attend graduate school, for a master's degree in social work, while Phil had returned to IU to complete his undergraduate degree in physics. Marci was attracted to Phil's intellect and his commitment to his daughter from his first marriage. She also appreciated his views of the world, which were more "unique" than most of the men from the Midwest whom she had met. Phil seemed to feel comfortable with all people, regardless of their backgrounds. He was also very knowledgeable about a variety of subjects and liked to talk about what he had read and where he had been in his life (which included hitchhiking and moving with a friend to California).

As Marci finalized plans for graduate school in a different city, they realized their strong feelings for each other. Looking back, Marci realized that Phil almost seemed "lost" without her there during the week. Phil took care of Marci's dog. They spent many weekends together over the two years they lived in different cities, Marci always driving to Bloomington on Saturday mornings and leaving on Monday mornings. They would spend a lot of time in the same room reading; Marci read for school while Phil would read just about anything. They might spend time with friends from the rooming house in the evenings or walk downtown where Phil would enjoy taking on others at pool tables around town.

Phil's past history in the hospital for evaluation and treatment of mental health issues did not affect Marci's love or commitment to their relationship. It appears they were focused on the possibility that Phil had schizophrenia, which was not correct. The possibility of high-functioning autism was essentially unknown until many years later.

They were married just weeks after Marci completed her graduate work and two weeks before she started her job at IU. She is a social worker at the Indiana Resource Center for Autism at the Indiana Institute on Disability and Community. They have been married since 1983. Phil has been employed for about 12 years since they married, often part-time. For the first several years of their marriage, he was employed full-time as a technician at the IU Cyclotron. This required an extensive knowledge of physics. Over the years, Phil has tried several times to start his own business. His most successful business has been tutoring math and science and teaching math to homeschooled students. In later years, Phil has also been involved in speaking at autism-related workshops and conferences.

After six years of marriage, there were a variety of events that added stress for both Marci and Phil. They were raising two young sons at that time, along with Phil's daughter, who had come to live with them. Communication between the couple was breaking down. It was at this point that stress at work and home caused Phil to quit his job at the Cyclotron (thinking this was a way to get the employer to negotiate changes and supports he needed on the job). Phil, then unemployed, serendipitously read some material related to Marci's job that was written by a woman with high-functioning autism. Phil related instantly to what he read, saying this was the first person who ever shared some of the same experiences that he had gone through. This led to a discussion about the possibility of Phil's having autism. Within a year of quitting his job, he was formally diagnosed with high-functioning autism.

Their family life over the years has been a mixture of the traditional and not-so-traditional. Phil is much more comfortable when he and Marci spend time together each evening. He has a very difficult time during the Christmas holiday season. It is a rare and special occasion when Phil is able to travel for family vacations. Their daughter has been married since 1997 and has two children of her own that she and her husband are raising. At present, Marci and Phil's young adult sons still live at home. All three children and two grandchildren have received specialized supports in school and/or the community. Their older son has a diagnosis of Asperger syndrome and their grandson has an autism diagnosis.

Though the knowledge of Phil's diagnosis was enlightening and helpful for both him and Marci, they continued to struggle at times. They could not find a marriage counselor who was knowledgeable about autism spectrum disorders and could help them. Additionally, they have been seen as "experts" by others in the disability field and were told to "do what you already know to do." There have been some ups and downs, but their commitment to each other, their persistence in finding ways to communicate effectively with each other and the belief that they were both trying their best even though they did not always understand each other is what has saved their relationship and marriage. In fact, it is this commitment and persistence that continues to sustain their relationship and marriage as it continues to evolve and thrive.

Jane and Trevor

Jane and Trevor both grew up in suburban Midwestern towns in blue collar families where hard work was emphasized. College was considered an unnecessary luxury, though education and books were highly treasured. Trevor spent some time growing up in government housing and enjoyed finding treasures that others would discard, such as broken TVs, cameras and various appliances and electronics. He liked learning how things worked. He seemed to have a phenomenal ability to understand and enjoy computers. He and his two younger brothers never seemed to understand each other. Jane grew up in the country surrounded by woods and abundant wildlife. She was the middle child in a close-knit family of three children who also spent a lot of time with cousins who lived nearby. She spent her time outdoors or enjoying quiet pursuits such as drawing and reading. She was known for her creativity and imagination.

Jane and Trevor met at the wedding of Jane's cousin. Trevor was a close friend of the cousin. Jane was instantly attracted to Trevor's obvious intellect and humor, which put her instantly at ease. They felt as though they had always been friends. They ended up spending much of the weekend together. Jane had a serious boyfriend, however. Jane had gotten scholarship money to attend college and even spent a semester studying art in Europe. She had just returned home and was enjoying the reunion with her boyfriend. Trevor, on the other hand, had recently ended a seven-year relationship. He was very attracted to Jane and was convinced he could woo her away from her boyfriend. Trevor was a bit older and had a good job with a computer company. He also had a creative side and taught himself how to play the guitar.

Trevor invited Jane and her boyfriend to a Halloween party and to several group events, including skiing and caving with friends. Trevor would call Jane once in a while and they would talk like old friends. Trevor then took Jane on a solo "date" to the opera. Trevor was successful in winning Jane's heart. They dated less than a year before they were married. They quickly had their first child, bought a house in a suburb of Indianapolis and seemed to have a wonderful life ahead. Jane was a stay-at-home mom, and they were able to take vacations and enjoy time with family and friends. Jane did wonder when Trevor seemed to get so involved in projects for work that he did not come home or lost track of important family matters. They have been married since 1993, the first 12 years of their marriage seeming relatively typical and rewarding. During this time, they also welcomed two more daughters and a dog into their lives.

The past five years or so have been extremely challenging for Jane and Trevor. Trevor has a high school diploma and is a computer savant. He is currently unemployed, but was employed by IBM for 15 years, including the first ten years of their marriage. He was lured away from IBM by two colleagues who started their own business. Unfortunately, the business failed after a couple of years and Trevor was unable to return to his previous job or find another similar one. They lost their house when their savings and Trevor's unemployment benefits ran out. They now had three girls, the youngest an infant. The family had to split up and live with two different friends at this point. Friends and family helped to store some of their belongings. They struggled to find help. Jane began to wonder why Trevor had not found a job. Was he depressed? Who wouldn't be under those circumstances? But where, she agonized, could she get help? And besides, she could not get him help unless he wanted to get help too.

During this time when Jane was living at one friend's house and Trevor was staying with a different friend, Trevor had an accident and was admitted to the hospital. Jane worried that Trevor was trying to harm himself. At that time, due to the nature of the family circumstances and the nature of the accident, a referral was made to a psychiatrist. Luckily, after an evaluation, they had some answers. Trevor was given the diagnosis of Asperger syndrome. Jane had worked with some children with autism for a short time, so she had some knowledge of the communication and social difficulties people with this diagnosis face. More importantly, she now knew where to find more information. It helped her understand their communication difficulties and Trevor's lack of skill in being able to apply for jobs. Getting the correct diagnosis was a relief to both Jane and Trevor.

The financial troubles continued for the family, however. They found themselves homeless for a short time, dependent on friends and family until they could be reunited in one home. Though initially she was a stay-at-home mom, Jane has a bachelor's degree in fine arts with additional coursework in business. She currently works full-time as a secretary and also has some income from tutoring, freelance drawing and scrapbooking, as well as from donating plasma. While Jane works, Trevor spends his days "surviving the sensory onslaught" of living in a small space with three active children while trying to stay stabilized—a special challenge, because they cannot always afford the medication he has found that helps him sleep and cope better. He worries that he has not kept up on the latest in computers and has attempted to contribute to the family financially with little success. An application was made for social security disability income (SSDI), but follow-up is needed. Apparently, there was an interview appointment requested, but Trevor was not able to keep it.

Their oldest daughter is in high school and the other two are in elementary school. Because of their very limited income, they are focused more on survival, attending to getting the basics of food, shelter and medical care while trying to give their girls a healthy childhood. They have worked hard to make sure they have quality time as a family and figure out low-cost ways to celebrate birthdays, holidays and other important events. They have friends at school and cousins they see almost weekly. Jane's sister and her family live in the same town and provide a lot of emotional support. Other family members do not understand and sometimes add to the stress by suggesting Trevor is "no good" and not a "real man."

Jane and Trevor have limited time to focus on their relationship but do try to have time alone, as well as time for each of them to get the support that they need. Jane has contact with a couple of friends who are understanding of the diagnosis and can act as a sounding board. She goes out periodically with friends or her sister while Trevor enjoys the peace and quiet at home when he is there by himself. He needs time by himself, so he can get prepared truly to enjoy Jane and their three precious daughters.

Pam and Jim

Pam and Jim both grew up in Pennsylvania in families who were deeply rooted in their religious community. Their families focused on their faith with everything in family life centered around church and faith. They were both the oldest children, each having several much younger siblings.

Jim enjoyed intellectual pursuits. He spent time reading and learning the religious tenets, but also learned all about science and math. Pam was encouraged to be her mother's helper and, when she was not in school, helped with cooking, cleaning, sewing and other "womanly" pursuits. Pam also was very intellectually curious and enjoyed the companionship of books, but she felt she was discouraged from reading. She did enjoy helping her mother in the garden. She seemed to have a green thumb, making the family garden very prolific and beautiful.

Pam and Jim met while living in a religious community. Jim was going to college, studying math, and Pam was working for a social services agency that provided services for those in need. For a year, they lived communally within the same large household of 20 people. There were a lot of group activities that everyone participated in: camping trips and retreats, chores, communal meals and daily devotions. They found they were drawn to each other. They were not dating, but during this time they participated in a structured courtship process which included premarital counseling. Jim was attracted to Pam's beauty, intelligence and the fact that she knew numbers—especially zip codes. Pam was charmed by all the attention Jim showered on her and amused by the things that excited him, including her knowledge of zip codes. They also shared an interest in biology and nature, and both had the same deep ethical foundation and faith.

After about a year, they moved away from the religious household, each in a separate efficiency apartment in the same small complex. They continued the premarital counseling and faith-based activities while Jim finished school. Jim encouraged Pam to take classes. He said he believed in Pam's abilities and that she was very smart. They were married after a year. Jim found a job teaching at a small faith-based college and they were excited to start their married life together. Their older son was born during that first year of marriage. Pam enjoyed being a stay-at-home mom, and their second son came two years later. Jim was busy establishing himself at the college. With two young sons, who both seemed very active and strong-willed, Pam looked forward to time with Jim in the evenings to help her unwind.

It seemed to Pam that communication was breaking down. Jim did not understand Pam's feelings of being overwhelmed with the two boys during the day. Jim's job was to be the provider and he did not see the need to interact with Pam when he came home. Wasn't it enough that he came home, said goodnight to the boys before Pam put them to bed and spent time in the same room with his wife, where he worked on assignments for work and Pam could sit close by and read or sew quietly? They still did take walks together on the rare occasion that a friend offered to watch the boys for them. Jim was not able to communicate, though, even during these opportunities to get away with Pam and relax. He seemed to resent all Pam's questions and "jabbering."

Years went by and these patterns did not seem to change. Pam was in charge of the household and everything with the boys on a day-to-day basis. There were problems with the boys, especially the older son, who was not able to sit still in school. He was disciplined by the teacher in different ways. He was very bright; was he bored in school? Pam spent time at school volunteering, trying to help out and also to be in closer contact to try and understand her son's needs. In sixth grade (age 11–12 years), their older son was diagnosed with Asperger syndrome. Pam researched and studied every angle she could. It certainly explained a lot about not only her older son's behavior but also that of her younger son—and of Jim, too!

Pam and Jim have been married since 1981. The realization of Asperger syndrome in their lives came after 14 years of marriage. It took another ten years, however, to find the right help and supports for their marriage. They had gone to counseling during this time, but had not found the right counselor, one who truly understood their needs as an ASD-NS couple. Jim has never been formally diagnosed. They have both agreed, however, that he does have Asperger syndrome. While reading materials pertaining to their sons and filling out an Asperger syndrome assessment scale for one of their son's evaluations, Pam and Jim both realized this information also described Jim. He shared the information about his own self-evaluation with the marriage counselor they were seeing at the time, and the counselor agreed that Jim did have Asperger syndrome. Several years later, a second counselor helped Jim work from his strengths. She made much more concrete suggestions (instead of the traditional therapy of focusing on "fixing the deficits" and trying to develop empathy that wasn't there). This was much more successful for Jim and thus ultimately saved their marriage. Pam was able to reassess and reinvest in the relationship.

Currently, Jim finds great enjoyment in his work in risk management for a small financial institution. Pam was a stay-at-home mom for many years, raising their two sons. During these years, Pam was gradually completing coursework for a master's degree. Since graduating, she has enjoyed her work supporting families in difficult situations. Both their sons are grown and no longer living at home, though they both continue to need supports, at this time, to manage their lives. Pam and Jim feel that it is only in the last few years that they have been able to experience a truly strong relationship and marriage. They spend time each night together communicating and have learned truly to embrace their differences. Their commitment through the very hard times, the acknowledgment of Jim's Asperger syndrome and finding the right supports as individuals was crucial for transforming their relationship.

Molly and Sam

Molly and Sam grew up in Oregon. Sam's family lived in a college town and Molly lived about two hours away, in a more rural area, with her mother. Sam's dad was a college-educated professional who provided a middle-class living while his mother ran the household and did volunteer work at the schools. Sam's older brother and sister were one and two years older than he. While his siblings were quite social and involved in a variety of activities, Sam was a loner who enjoyed watching sports. He could remember many facts and statistics about the players and the teams. He amazed all who asked for him to recall details of a specific team or game. Sam also spent time fishing with his dad; he enjoyed going out at night, by himself, and finding worms for bait. Molly's parents divorced when she was a toddler and she lived primarily with her mother, a waitress, while her father struggled with mental health issues. She spent time riding her bike and babysat a lot when she was old enough. Molly had dreams of being a nurse like one of her aunts. She liked to learn, but school did not come easy to her. She was also very involved with youth activities at the church where her uncle was a pastor.

Molly and Sam met at the bookstore where they both worked while in college. Sam was studying to be an accountant and Molly a nurse. Whenever they would both work late, Sam would walk Molly to her dorm. Unlike other peers at school, Sam found it easy to talk with Molly, who listened eagerly to Sam's monologues about historical events. Molly enjoyed his passion for intellectual pursuits, his concern for her safety and his gentlemanly ways. Before long, they started studying together. Sam helped Molly with some of her assignments. Sam enjoyed Molly's ability to take charge, stay organized and socialize so easily. They felt very comfortable with each other and cherished their time together working and studying. Sam lived at home and would still routinely go fishing with his dad on the weekends. Molly enjoyed socializing with her friends when she had time.

Molly began to invite Sam to go with her to hang out with her friends, too. Sam readily agreed to activities that involved being outdoors. He did not like some of the other places they sometimes would hang out.

Molly didn't seem to notice this about Sam. They grew very close. Sam graduated and was offered a full-time job at the bookstore. They made plans to get married when Molly finished school. They both felt safe with each other and wanted to build a future together. Molly noticed Sam's lack of friends and his shyness around her friends. His strong work ethic and commitment to his family along with his other wonderful qualities were what she wanted in a life partner. She dismissed his quiet and somewhat odd style around others. Shortly after they married in 2003, both found jobs in a larger city. Sam was hired as the accountant for a family-run car dealer and Molly found a nursing position in a medical practice. They rented a small house and planned to save and buy their own house before having children.

After they were married and focused on work and their time together in a new city, Molly began to wonder about Sam. He did not seem to want to communicate with her. He would come home from work and immediately retreat to his computer. She would ask what she thought was a thoughtful question about what to fix for dinner or plans to do something together for the evening, and Sam would ask her not to bother him. She felt alone and frustrated. They were both lucky to get jobs that allowed them to spend time together in the evening, yet Sam was more focused on his computer and shutting her out. They joined a church and met a few of their neighbors. It helped Molly that Sam seemed interested in interacting with the new people they were meeting. Molly felt better, but was still puzzled by his behavior at home, especially after work in the evenings.

Molly was also concerned because Sam did not seem to have much common sense. She would ask him to help with things such as putting groceries away and then she could not find them anywhere logical. She tried to get his help in keeping the house clean, but he seemed totally lost. If she asked him to "get the dishes washed," he would stand at the sink with the water running but would not load the dishwasher. He could mow the lawn and help in the yard, but did not seem to notice when the work needed to be done. Molly would have to tell him to mow. She felt like Sam did not care and was deliberately not cooperating with chores around the house, which upset her because she felt like his mother and not his life partner. On several occasions, she would get very frustrated and cry about this, and Sam did not seem to notice.

After several years of marriage, Molly began to wonder if they should have children. Nothing much had changed. Molly did not know how to communicate with Sam about her frustrations. He seemed not to understand or simply disregarded her requests. She also now was seriously worried about his interactions around others. He did seem to enjoy activities at church and getting together with neighbors when there were outdoor cookouts and gatherings. But these activities were not as fun for her, because sometimes he would complain loudly about others when—in his mind—they had lied or misunderstood him. He could act very immature at times. She noticed that if she told him how to act and what to say, he did sometimes do better, but it felt like she was the adult and he was a child.

Molly decided that they needed go for counseling and discussed it with Sam. He agreed that he would go with her to talk with their pastor. About the same time, a teen with Asperger syndrome became a new patient where Molly worked. She went home and searched the internet. She was very intrigued to find that much of what she was reading described Sam's behavior. She shared this information with Sam, who thought the information was interesting. They had a few sessions with the pastor, which has helped a little. Molly continues to read and became connected with other non-spectrum spouses of ASD partners. Slowly, Sam is beginning to feel more comfortable with the possibility that he may have Asperger syndrome. He is not sure whether he wants to pursue an evaluation. They continue to discuss their plans for children. Molly feels it is important to know for sure if Sam has Asperger syndrome before they have a child. She is concerned about his ability to be a parent if he does not know how his brain works and how to be a true partner with her. Though Sam still does not understand Molly's frustrations with him, he wants to make her happy and continues to learn about Asperger syndrome.

Sara and Josh

Sara and Josh grew up in neighboring small Midwestern towns. They both had stay-at-home mothers, and fathers who managed small businesses. Sara's father managed a local chain restaurant and Josh's father ran a local auto parts store. Church and church-related activities were an important focus for both families. Sara grew up with a younger brother and Josh had an older brother and sister. Sara enjoyed drawing and making her own paper dolls. Her mother taught her to sew and together they would make dresses and other outfits for Sara. Josh enjoyed many hours watching television shows and recreating "scenes," as well as building with his Lego bricks and being active collecting bugs and rocks in the yard. He liked it when he could play by himself.

Sara and Josh met on an online dating site. They were both in their mid twenties at the time. Sara had a young son she was raising on her own while taking graphic design classes at the local community college. She was living with her parents, and her mother provided childcare for her. Josh was living at home and working in an electronics shop owned by a friend of the family. Sara felt online dating was an effective way to screen potential boyfriends. Josh was interested in dating, but had not been successful yet in having a long-term relationship with a woman. The service matched them and they started communicating by email.

They both immediately felt comfortable with one another and were excited to learn that they shared the same values and lived less than 30 minutes from each other. They arranged a meeting at the restaurant that Sara's dad managed. That night they stayed until the restaurant closed. Sara was struck by Josh's honesty and open, down-to-earth personality. He was shy, respectful and behaved like a "true gentleman." Josh was in awe of Sara's ability to go to school and raise a young son. He appreciated her "take charge" personality, intelligence and "practical" outlook on life.

The relationship got serious fast. When Sara introduced Josh to her son, Tommy, she was amazed at how well they got along playing together. They quickly became "best buddies." While working and living at home, Josh had saved a lot of money and he figured he had enough down payment for a small house. He quickly decided to ask Sara to marry him. Though Sara was in love with Josh, she did wonder why he seemed to get along well with her son and other young children, but sometimes felt uncomfortable and was even rude with other adults. He also did not seem to want to try going to new places beyond her church and the restaurant where they had their first date. She put her concerns aside, however, as most importantly they were in love and Josh had "proven" that he loved Tommy, too, and would take care of them.

They were married in 2000 and bought a small fixer-upper house with space for Sara's mother to stay with them as needed. Sara finished school and found a job with a small local business. A short time later, Josh switched jobs. Another family friend offered him more money to help manage the gas station and repair shop he had just bought. Unfortunately, the job seemed to overwhelm Josh. He could not seem to stay focused and organized with the various parts of the job. Josh was let go. He was able to find a part-time job doing data entry for another family friend. Life was stressful as they struggled financially and Josh seemed a bit on edge, at times, with Tommy. Though they still enjoyed playing together, sometimes Josh would suddenly go off to the bedroom to be by himself and would not want to play any more. All he could say was that Tommy was making a lot of noise. This did not make sense to Sara. Other behaviors Sara saw from Josh began to concern her.

Their son Ben was born just after their second wedding anniversary. Sara was alarmed that Josh was not helping with the added household responsibilities. Also, Josh seemed unable to help with the baby. He was relying on Sara to take care of all the household responsibilities despite their many discussions. Sara insisted they seek marriage counseling with their minister. The minister helped by discussing concrete examples of what Josh's responsibilities were as a husband and father. This helped some. Their minister referred them to an agency in town as he felt perhaps Josh had a learning disability and needed other assistance.

Josh was given a diagnosis of Asperger syndrome, which was a relief to both him and Sara. Most of their relatives, however, did not accept the diagnosis and were not interested in learning any more. They felt that Josh was using the diagnosis as an excuse for his behavior and he should just "be a man" and do what was expected of him. It doesn't help that the winter months from November to February are especially difficult for Josh. The doctor has suggested that Josh has seasonal affective disorder, and the various relatives feel that he is just fishing for more excuses for what seems to them eccentric and rude behavior. The attitude of relatives on both sides of the family has added a lot of stress that is especially noticed when the close-knit family members get together. Even when their son Ben was diagnosed with Asperger syndrome in elementary school, the relatives just thought Ben needed more discipline.

Sara and Josh have gotten involved in autism-related support groups and activities, and are educating the two boys about Asperger syndrome. Sometimes Sara is so frustrated she does wonder if Josh uses his disability as an excuse. They continue to be committed to each other and the boys. Some issues require consulting their church pastor or working with a therapist. Josh has tried to look into full-time work to help more with family finances, but nothing has worked out yet. He has agreed to seek help with employment-related skills.

There continues to be stress around parenting issues. Josh was more comfortable and successful parenting the boys when they were about four to eight years old, when he spent a lot of time as a "play buddy" to each of the boys. He does not seem to understand the true nature and changing roles of being a parent as the children age. Sara has involved her younger brother with the boys as an appropriate father figure and model for Josh on how to parent.

: and Pete

Having grown up in different parts of the United States—she in Indianapolis and he in Salt Lake City—Kaye and Pete met at a networking function in Chicago in their late twenties. Kaye felt an instant connection with Pete the minute they sat down at an open table together. The same age, they had similar backgrounds: Both grew up in large, multiethnic families (Kaye was the eldest, often mothering her younger sisters and brother, and Pete was a typically quiet middle child); each was considered "gifted," possessing higher IQs than many other kids at school. Kaye excelled particularly at reading and creative pursuits, and Pete at math and sciences. They also had both taken advanced placement classes through high school, and were encouraged to be active in their communities as student leaders by their liberal and supportive parents. However, their parallel paths stopped in their teen years. While Kaye went on to college to pursue a bachelor's degree in marketing, Pete was expelled from school when he not only grew bored with the curriculum but also met a group of delinquent teens who dared him to join them in bad behavior, like spray-painting the walls at school. As is typical of teens with ASDs, Pete was unable at that time to distinguish between friendship and manipulation. He later went on to pursue his high school diploma and community college, learning quickly not to trust everyone as he once had.

When they met, Kaye and Pete were both employed as event planners, although Kaye specialized in the creative elements, and Pete handled the technical aspects of events, such as lighting and sound.

Kaye was drawn to Pete's innate shyness and supreme intelligence. As the oldest of several children born to young parents, she is nurturing, which Pete benefits from and enjoys. Both grew up in homes with depression and hostility from one or both parents, and so learned to draw into themselves emotionally in various ways. They quickly became close friends, moving into a romantic relationship after just a few months.

During their courtship, Kaye and Pete frequented parties, weddings, networking functions, concerts and clubs. They often met up with friends (mostly Kaye's) and co-workers, and stayed out late dancing and socializing, although looking back, Kaye recalls now that Pete preferred to watch her on the dance floor most nights. After less than two years of dating, they married. Then Pete's personality "completely changed" only a few weeks after the ceremony, from Kaye's perspective. He became antisocial and withdrawn, refusing to go out to events, even the ones they had planned together. Kaye now goes alone or with friends to most social functions, while Pete accompanies her only to family events.

He was stressed on their wedding day by the pressures of socializing and his own misunderstanding of some of the traditions associated with weddings—like decorating the couple's car with "just married" slogans, which he took to be mean-spirited pranking. This put him in a foul mood for their honeymoon. He then insisted they not draw any attention to themselves, resulting in what Kaye calls the "secret honeymoon." Pete wasn't diagnosed until they had been married more than a year, when Kaye was insistent that he "get help or else" she'd leave him. He took the threat seriously, looking through the phone book for the most comprehensive and least expensive clinic in their area.

Pete can be emotionally volatile, and Kaye has a very sensitive reaction to this. During the early part of their marriage, before his diagnosis, the couple became more antisocial, rarely entertaining inside their home. Pete became more and more controlling in an effort to gain comfort in his new environment, while Kaye began to lose her sense of self-empowerment. Work with a counselor has helped to change this and restore balance, but more work remains to be done. Today, Pete can't tell the difference between his wife's shouting in anger and in joy, which leads to a lot of confusion when she's suddenly excited by something she sees on TV or out the window. He has since transitioned into a career as an audio technician; Kaye continues to work as an event planner.

They see a marriage counselor who specializes in working with people on the autism spectrum. This counselor helped invent the invisible "tool" Pete uses to "read" emotions—both his and Kaye's, all of which frequently overwhelm and confuse him. When Pete doesn't use his "emo-meter," Kaye feels pressured to be the core communications translator, not only between Pete and herself, but also between Pete and other people.

Kaye does a lot to soothe Pete, some of which she learned from the counselor and some she invented herself. As a creative person, she's learned to be very inventive. Pete also takes anti-anxiety medicine and sees a psychiatrist, which helps alleviate some of his emotional outbursts. His preferred means of being soothed is for Kaye to scratch his back, arms, chest or head in a stimming manner. Touching that isn't deep tissue, however, like the armbands and waistbands of his shirts, is a real irritant to Pete. On the other hand, he can stay very even-headed in reaction to crises that typically frighten non-spectrum people. Because of this, Kaye still calls her husband her "hero."

The couple has no children, but they do have a cat they adopted together. Although the pet-parenting responsibilities still fall mostly to Kaye, Pete continues slowly to adapt his routine around taking on more duties where the cat is concerned. He is genuinely interested in caring for his pet, but often forgets to or doesn't realize he should do things, simply because of the change in routine or his own lack of theory of mind.

Kaye and Pete are presently in their mid thirties and live in a small suburb outside of Chicago. They have been married since 2005, and credit the relative peace and understanding between them to Pete's diagnosis and to their shared willingness to adapt.

Sheila and Harry

Sheila and Harry are an active couple in their later years. Sheila is in her mid sixties and Harry is 11 years older. They have lived for many years in the suburbs of Minneapolis. Harry is from Europe and grew up in Germany, but Sheila grew up in the Midwest. Sheila had opportunities to travel and experience other countries and cultures while growing up. Their socio-economic backgrounds were quite similar. He is the son of a physician and she is the daughter of college-educated parents. Her mother is an artist and her father ran several small local companies throughout his life.

Sheila and Harry met while working in the accounts receivable department of a large Minneapolis publishing company. She was just out of college, working in an entry-level position, and he was already established as a manager. They were "fixed up" by colleagues who thought their love of music and the arts might be a bond.

On Sheila and Harry's first date, he discussed the economic pressures on Germany before the start of World War II. She was quite impressed by this, as her own knowledge of history was more limited. Also impressive to Sheila was Harry's nice, neat appearance and his great manners and complete focus on her. He would pick up her dry cleaning, bring wine and flowers when invited to dinner, offer to go to the store for her and many other things that women associate with caring and empathy.

Harry appreciated finding a woman who liked his sense of humor and attention, and who was well educated and happy to let him take charge. They dated for only three months before becoming engaged and were married within the year.

Just before their wedding, Sheila saw signs of Harry's meltdowns. During a discussion about a last-minute change to the guest list, Harry became so worked up that he broke the steering wheel of his car with his bare hands! Sheila was horrified and privately broke off the engagement until the next day, when Harry showered her with flowers, apologies and promises for the future. She felt very protective of him even though she was upset by his temper, and she kept this event secret for many years.

However, it was not the only time through the years that he lost his temper during emotional meltdowns, and Sheila was on the receiving end of his verbal abuse many times during their marriage. Harry has received counseling and medication, which have greatly helped these events.

They have been married since 1969 and have two children, now grown. Their older child, a son, has Asperger syndrome. He was diagnosed with high-functioning autism when he was six years old. Their younger son is not on the spectrum, and is married and has three children of his own.

The marriage has been rocky at times, but their love has prevailed. Before Harry got the diagnosis of Asperger syndrome, Sheila thought the communication differences were due to his not being a native speaker of English. Social events were often very frustrating, but she chalked it up to his long hours at work. Their marriage, though, has lasted through many traumatic events, both economic and health-related. They have survived Harry's losing his job of over 30 years, and Sheila's having serious and life-threatening health issues. They are both working past retirement age, due to economic necessity.

There are several couples with whom Sheila and Harry have been friends throughout their marriage. Sheila has a large group of friends from childhood, as well as college, to whom she is very close and spends time with on a regular basis. Harry is a bit unusual for someone diagnosed on the autism spectrum, in that he has several friends from youth. These friends have always realized he was somewhat unique, but have loved him for his kindness, loyalty and sense of fun. He also has friends from his former job.

Throughout their marriage, Harry prided himself in his ability to provide for his family and allow for Sheila to stay home and take care of the day-to-day responsibilities of raising their two sons. When the children were growing up, she enjoyed her various volunteer opportunities in the community and at church. She was also able to volunteer at the children's school and have the time to take their son to his various therapists. Sheila was also able to find music and art teachers willing to try and work with their son's unique talents and behavioral challenges. Their younger son was always a bright and social student who was often busy with activities at school and with friends; Sheila enjoyed supervising these as well. Harry eventually moved into the lead accountant role at the publishing company, but sadly was let go during corporate downsizing after more than three decades of work. He struggled for a while with job-searching after that, before joining an accounting firm. Sheila also returned to work after the children were grown. Currently, along with working, they love visiting their grandchildren and attending their ASD son's musical and art events. Sheila is still active volunteering when she has the time.

Bonnie and Brad

Bonnie and Brad both grew up in the suburbs of Columbus, Ohio. Brad grew up in a home with both parents and is the youngest of several brothers and sisters. His father made a good living while his mother was home raising the children. Brad is especially close to one of his older sisters and his mother. Bonnie's parents both worked, and she and her younger brother and sister spent a lot of time with their aunt, uncle and cousins who lived in the same neighborhood. Bonnie and her siblings would go over to their cousins' home most days after school as their aunt was there to provide supervision and a homemade snack. Bonnie took piano lessons and spent time in the evenings practicing piano.

Bonnie and Brad are both rather shy and non-assertive. Bonnie is several years older than Brad. They both enjoy intellectual pursuits and are passionate about music. Brad taught himself to play the acoustic guitar. He also played the trombone in the band at school. Bonnie has given piano lessons and she also earns money playing piano at various events in the area. Bonnie has a son and daughter from a previous marriage. She shares joint custody of the children with her ex-husband. Brad is a professor of math at a small college. Brad also likes to work out and runs every morning. They share a love of dogs.

They met when Brad attended an event where Bonnie was playing. He went up to her and asked if she could give him piano lessons. She agreed and they enjoyed their time together. They became good friends who enjoyed sharing musical interests and attending various performances together. Bonnie introduced Brad to another couple who enjoyed similar pursuits. Brad also enjoyed cooking for Bonnie. He had much practice growing up, learning from his mother and older sister, as well as occasionally taking cooking classes and experimenting on his own. Bonnie would help Brad organize and clean his house. She enjoyed Brad's "good heart" and his "pure" and positive outlook on life. Brad enjoyed Bonnie's patience with him and her "motherly" and "gentle" ways with him and with her children.

They never really dated, but enjoyed a friendship that eventually included Bonnie's son and daughter in many of their activities. Bonnie's son was diagnosed with Asperger syndrome when he was eight years old. When Bonnie and Brad began their friendship, her son was nine and her daughter was eight. One day, after about a year had passed, Brad declared he was in love and said, "Let's get married." Bonnie agreed. She felt she had found her soul mate and a partner her children adored and who would be there for them, too. They had a small civil ceremony with just family, and Bonnie and the children moved into Brad's house. The children began calling Brad, "Daddy B." They settled into what started out as a comfortable routine and family life.

Problems entered the relationship when Bonnie suggested changes to some of their routines. Brad did not want changes to any of their routines and nor did he want to change anything around the house, like rearranging furniture or accepting new clothes Bonnie bought to replace his old "worn out" items. They both enjoyed entertaining for small groups of friends, but Bonnie was frustrated with Brad's rigid expectations of how the events would be carried out. Though Brad always seemed to get along with people and have a positive attitude about life before they were married and lived together, Bonnie was concerned now that he would get angry with her at home when she would try to interact with him. He more often was interested in time alone in his den to tend to his musical or intellectual pursuits.

It was a close friend of Bonnie's who one day asked if Brad, like her son, might have Asperger syndrome. Bonnie immediately thought that made sense and wondered why she had not thought of that sooner. Bonnie quickly decided to share her thoughts with Brad and he quite quickly agreed that he probably did have Asperger syndrome. Though he was never formally diagnosed, this knowledge was helpful later on when they needed a knowledgeable therapist to work with Brad around issues of disciplining and coping with the children.

Since their marriage in 1996, Bonnie and Brad have been in love and deeply cherished their friendship. They continue to enjoy sharing a variety of musical and intellectual pursuits and attending small gatherings with friends. They are still involved in parenting their children as a couple, although the children are now young adults who are both focused on their own lives and are at colleges that are several hours away. Bonnie continues to struggle and cope with what she perceives as Brad's difficult, rigid routines and expectations. She does not see how, long term, they can both be satisfied living under one roof. She has discussed with Brad living separately, but staying married. That way they would each have their own space and along with that some control. Bonnie would not feel that she had no options for arranging and maintaining her living space in ways that work for her and she would not have to worry about upsetting Brad with adjustments she feels are important to her. Brad is open to exploring some sort of separate living arrangement.

Sally and David

Sally and David are both from the Northeast region of the United States, but they come from different backgrounds. Sally's family is from Taiwan and Sally and her brother were the first generation in their family to be born in the United States. Her family owns a restaurant. Sally and her brother were expected to do well in school, as well as help out in the restaurant. David's family is of Italian descent. His father is a plumber. His mother focused on raising David and his two younger brothers. Though David's two brothers were involved in sports from an early age, David did not enjoy or do well with baseball or basketball. At about the age of ten, David started bowling with his dad. He would also go along on his dad's bowling league nights. In high school, he joined a bowling league of his own.

Sally and David met in their second year of college when they both sang in the school choir. Sally was an elementary education major and David was studying accounting. They both found singing a pleasurable escape from their studies. They also enjoyed sitting together on the bus when the choir would travel. Sally was assertive in "pursuing" David, while David kept the conversation "buzzing" with his "lectures" on music and other topics of interest he had at the time. The bowling classes he took on campus for a couple of semesters were one such topic. They continued in their comfortable pattern for over a year before Sally suggested they go to her family's restaurant for a meal, so David could meet her family. This might have been considered one of their few "real dates."

They continued to see each other for choir practices and other choir-related events. When they both spent a semester off campus—Sally in student teaching and David as an intern for a business—they realized how much they missed each other. Sally saw David as very handsome and charming in his own way. She appreciated his work ethic and the fact that he respected her and her family's different culture, as well as the fact that she knew she could trust him to do exactly what he promised. David felt Sally was a hard worker, trustworthy and had strong family values. He also appreciated that she made him feel comfortable and took pride in her appearance. They got engaged during their last semester in school and were married right after graduation.

They moved into an apartment, and David began his job in a bank while Sally did substitute teaching. David joined a bowling league and Sally joined a women's book club. Sally was excited about meeting the neighbors and attending the various social events hosted by their apartment complex. David was reluctant to join her for these social events and it seemed when he did, he would sometimes make inappropriate comments and share private information. This was confusing and upsetting to Sally. She started attending social events by herself. They discussed starting a family as they were both eager to be parents, but they had problems conceiving a child of their own and chose to adopt.

It was after their son arrived that Sally's concern for some of David's behaviors truly escalated. David did not seem to be comfortable around the baby. She later discovered it was related to the sensory overload he was experiencing with all the new smells that the baby presented. David also seemed to get more rigid with his routines, especially around bowling and having visitors in their home. Sally had a talk with David and asked that they seek therapy together to discuss her concerns. David agreed. The first counselor they saw thought Sally was too demanding as a result of being a first-time mother. The second therapist thought Sally should consider separating from David as they worked through their issues. Luckily the third professional they saw recognized the possibility that David had an autism spectrum disorder. They were able to get the support they needed while working with this third counselor. The counselor also connected Sally with a network of other women who are married to men on the autism spectrum.

Sally and David have been married since 2001. They both enjoy various parenting activities with their son, who is now five years old. Sally is very grateful to have a network of women who can truly understand the blessings as well as the challenges of her unique life with a husband on the autism spectrum. David has been seeing the counselor on his own, as needed. He is still passionate about bowling, but is now better able to accept occasional changes in the schedule. He is also looking forward to teaching his son how to bowl and helping to support him in whatever sports or other activities he chooses as he gets older.

Joy and Frank

Joy and Frank both grew up in northern Michigan. They met through mutual friends who knew they both enjoyed the outdoors and liked to stay physically active. When they met, Frank was a successful financial planner who was divorced with a young son. Joy was supporting herself as a professional photographer. After being introduced, they spent many weekends together biking, hiking, boating and eventually camping together. Joy enjoyed taking pictures of their many adventures.

Frank also liked train watching, which he would share with his son, Drew. After many months, when Drew came to spend part of his school vacation with him, Frank introduced Joy to his son. It was at that point that Frank fell in love with Joy's "motherly" ways with both his son and him. Joy loved the way Frank insisted on taking care of her and Drew financially, and the way he would surprise her with new outdoor adventures. They married and within a year, their daughter was born. Frank and Joy "discovered" Frank's diagnosis, on their own, after their daughter was diagnosed on the autism spectrum.

They have been married sine 1985. They have had difficulty finding appropriate supports for their daughter, especially now that she is an adult. Recently, they have experienced financial hardship as they plan for later years. Joy and Frank continue to seek help working with therapists to resolve their marital issues. The main issue, in Joy's mind, is that Frank does not truly accept that he has similar issues to their daughter and therefore he is not truly committed to change.

Useful Resources

(All websites were accessed on 6 July 2011.)

Autism spectrum and Asperger syndrome
AANE (Asperger's Association of New England)
www.aane.org
An organization based in the USA, which provides support groups, conferences, seminars, workshops and other unique events and programs to foster awareness, acceptance, and support for individuals with AS, and related conditions, and their families.

ANI (Autism Network International)
www.ani.ac
A US-based organization founded by and for people on the autism spectrum which promotes self-help and advocacy and offering an online forum and unique yearly retreat for individuals on the autism spectrum.

ARC (Autism Research Centre)
www.autismresearchcentre.com
London-based Research Institute with a large focus on the biomedical causes and treatments of autism spectrum disorders.

ARI (Autism Research Institute)
www.autismresearchinstitute.com
US-based institute that conducts and encourages scientific research to improve diagnosing, treating, and preventing autism spectrum disorders; with a major focus on biomedical related issues.

The Asperger Marriage Web Site
www.asperger-marriage.inf
A married couple Chris and Gisela Slater-Walker provide a positive message and information about successful relationships where one partner has Asperger's Syndrome.

Asperger Syndrome Association of Ireland

http://aspireireland.ie

Provides support to those with Asperger syndrome and their families including a helpline, training events, research and support groups.

Asperger's Society of Ontario

www.aspergers.ca

Organization providing education information and support to individuals with AS, their families and professionals in their community.

Asperger's Syndrome Foundation

www.aspergerfoundation.org.uk

Organization providing seminars on Asperger syndrome for individuals, family members and professionals in London. Also has information sheets and email enquiry service.

ASPIA (Asperger Syndrome Partner Information Australia)

www.aspia.org.au

Mutual acknowledgment of the Asperger marriage experience for partners of adults with AS.

ASPIRES (Asperger Syndrome Partners and Individuals Resources, Encouragement and Support)

www.aspires-relationships.com

Internet-based support group for individuals with Asperger syndrome and their partners.

Maxine Aston

www.maxineaston.co.uk

London-based psychologist and author offers counseling, workshops, books and other resources for married couples affected by Asperger syndrome.

Tony Attwood

www.tonyattwood.com.au

Australian-based world authority on Asperger syndrome.

Australian Advisory Board on Autism Spectrum Disorders

www.autismaus.com.au

Members' organization representing individuals with autism and their families.

Autism Canada Foundation
www.autismcanada.org
Resources, information and conferences in Canada.

Autism Hangout
www.autismhangout.com
Internet resource dedicated to bringing timely news articles and information through webinars and a discussion forum.

Autism Society of America
www.autism-society.org
Local groups across the USA, information and conferences about autism, including Asperger syndrome.

GRASP (Global and Regional Asperger Syndrome Partnership)
www.grasp.org
Educational and advocacy organization for individuals on the autism spectrum.

Indiana Resource Center for Autism
www.iidc.indiana.edu/index.php?pageId=32
Develops and disseminates information, engages in research and provides training and consultation to support individuals with autism, Asperger syndrome and other pervasive developmental disorders.

National Autistic Society
www.nas.org.uk
Provides services, helplines, training, information sheets and an online directory of all autism and Asperger syndrome related services in the UK.

National Institute of Neurological Disorders and Stroke
www.ninds.nih.gov/disorders/asperger/detail_asperger.htm
Fact sheet about Asperger syndrome prepared by National Institute of Neurological Disorders and Stroke.

Naturally Autistic ANCA
www.naturallyautistic.org
Canadian-based organization that provides education and training to individuals on the autism spectrum, their families, and the broader community.

OAASIS (Office for Advice, Assistance, Support and Information on Special needs)
www.oaasis.co.uk/Home
UK-based organization providing information and support regarding autism, Asperger syndrome and learning disabilities for families; including those with partners on the autism spectrum, and professionals.

OASIS (Online Asperger Syndrome Information and Support)
Now includes MAAP Services for Autism and Asperger Syndrome
www.aspergersyndrome.org
Support for families and individuals with autism, Asperger syndrome and PDD-NOS.

Stephen Shore
www.autismasperger.net
Web home of author, presenter and advocate who provides much information about and for all interested in autism and Asperger syndrome.

Spectrum Mentor
www.SpectrumMentor.com/5-minute-mentor
Provides helpful and positive information for individuals on the autism spectrum on subjects ranging from child raising to relationships.

The Transporters
www.thetransporters.com
Provides information about a unique program to teach facial expressions and underlying emotions using real faces on animated forms of transportation.

Wrong Planet
www.wrongplanet.net
Online community and resource for autism and Asperger syndrome which features a discussion forum, articles and guides, blogging for all interested individuals as well as a chatroom exclusive to those on the autism spectrum or with related neurological differences.

Anxiety disorders

Anxiety Disorders Association of America
www.adaa.org
Support, therapist list and conferences.

Anxiety Disorders Association of Canada
www.anxietycanada.ca
Awareness, prevention and treatment of anxiety disorders.

Anxiety-Panic.com
www.anxiety-panic.com
Search engine for anxiety, panic, trauma, fear, phobia, stress, obsession and depression.

Anxiety Treatment Australia
www.anxietyaustralia.com.au
Provides information about anxiety disorders and treatment options along with psychologists in Australia who treat anxiety disorders and/or offer group therapy workshops.

Anxiety UK (formerly National Phobics Society)
www.anxietyuk.org.uk
Research opportunities, information on a wide range of anxiety disorders, helpline, private and NHS services available and treatment information.

Depression Bipolar Support Alliance (DBSA)
www.dbsalliance.org
Offers support and information for both consumers and caregivers on bipolar disorder and various forms of depression.

International OCD Foundation
www.ocfoundation.org
An awareness and advocacy organization that provides information on research and treatments for people with Obsessive Compulsive Disorder (OCD) and related disorders.

National Alliance for the Mentally Ill (NAMI)
www.nami.org
Support organization for anyone with or wanting to know more about mental illness in any form.

OCD Chicago
www.ocdchicago.org
Support organization whose website features an extensive library of resources on obsessive-compulsive disorders.

OCD-UK
www.ocduk.org
Support organization for children and adults affected by obsessive-compulsive disorder.

Dependency organizations

Alcoholics Anonymous
www.aa.org
Support organization helping people to recover from alcoholism.

Al-Anon
www.al-anonuk.org.uk
Support organization helping families and friends of people with a drinking problem.

Drink Aware
www.drinkaware.co.uk
Provides facts and figures about alcohol.

Narcotics Anonymous
www.na.org
Support organization helping people to recover from drug addiction.

Other resources

CHADD (Children and Adults with Attention Deficit/Hyperactivity Disorder)
www.chadd.org
US-based national advocacy, education and support organization for individuals with AD/HD and their families and interested professionals.

Irlen Method
http://irlen.com
The Irlen Method is non-invasive technology that uses colored overlays and filters to improve the brain's ability to process visual information.

LD OnLine
www.ldonline.org
International website with many resources and much information on learning disabilities and ADHD for adults and children.

Sensory Processing Disorder Foundation
www.spdfoundation.net
Provides research, education, and advocacy for individuals, families and professionals dealing with Sensory Processing Disorder.

Contact details for the authors

Susan Moreno, MA, ABS
C/o MAAP Services for Autism and Asperger Syndrome
PO Box 524, Crown Point, IN 46308
smoreno@maapservices.org

Kealah Parkinson
Communications Coach
PO Box 1346, Crown Point, IN 46308
kealah@kikiproductionsinc.com
www.speak-with-kealah.com

Marci Wheeler, MSW
C/o Indiana Resource Center on Autism
Indiana Institute on Disability and Community
2853 E. Tenth St., Bloomington, IN 47408
mwheeler@indiana.edu

Bibliography

American Psychiatric Association (APA) (2000) *Diagnostic and Statistical Manual of Mental Disorders* (DSM-IV-TR). Washington, DC: APA.

Asperger, H. (1944) "Autistic Psychopathy in Childhood." In U. Frith (ed.) (1991) *Autism and Asperger's Syndrome.* Cambridge: Cambridge University Press.

Aston, M. (2001) *The Other Half of Asperger Syndrome.* London: The National Autistic Society.

Aston, M. (2003) *Aspergers in Love: Couple Relationships and Family Affairs.* London: Jessica Kingsley Publishers.

Aston, M. (2008) *The Asperger Couple's Workbook: Practical Advice and Activities for Couples and Counsellors.* London: Jessica Kingsley Publishers.

Aston, M. (2010) 'Cassandra Affective Deprivation Disorder.' Available at www.maxineaston. co.uk/cassandra, accessed on 21 September 2011.

Attwood, T. (2003a) "Frameworks for behavioural interventions." *Child and Adolescent Psychiatric Clinics 12,* 65–86.

Attwood, T. (2003b) "Understanding and Managing Circumscribed Interests." In M. Prior (ed.) *Learning and Behavior Problems in Asperger Syndrome.* New York: Guilford Press.

Attwood, T. (2003c) *Why Does Chris Do That?: Some Suggestions Regarding the Cause and Management of the Unusual Behaviour of Children and Adults with Autism and Asperger Syndrome.* London: National Autistic Society.

Attwood, T. (2004a) *Exploring Feelings: Cognitive Behavioural Therapy to Manage Anger.* Arlington, TX: Future Horizons.

Attwood, T. (2004b) "Theory of Mind and Asperger Syndrome." In L. J. Baker and L. A. Welkowitz (eds) *Asperger Syndrome: Intervening in Schools, Clinics and Communities.* Hillsdale, NJ: Lawrence Erlbaum.

Attwood, T. (2006) *The Complete Guide to Asperger's Syndrome.* London: Jessica Kingsley Publishers.

Bailey, A., Palferman, S., Heavey, L. and LeCouteur, A. (1998) "Autism: The phenotype in relatives." *Journal of Autism and Developmental Disorders 28,* 369–392.

Baron-Cohen, S. (1995) *Mindblindness: An Essay on Autism and Theory of Mind.* Cambridge, MA: MIT Press.

Baron-Cohen, S. (2004a) *Mind Reading Emotions Library: The Interactive Guide to Emotions* [CD-Rom]. Available at www.jkp.com/catalogue/book/9781843102168.

Baron-Cohen, S. (2004b) *The Essential Difference: Men, Women and the Extreme Male Brain.* New York: Basic Books.

Baron-Cohen, S., Tager-Flusberg, H. and Cohen, D. J. (eds) (2007) *Understanding Other Minds: Perspectives from Developmental Cognitive Neuroscience,* 2nd edn. Oxford: Oxford University Press.

Bentley, K. (2007) *Alone Together: Making an Asperger Marriage Work.* London: Jessica Kingsley Publishers.

California State Board of Equalization (2009) Staff Legislative Bill Analysis. Bill No. AB 390, Marijuana Fee Tax. Ammiano (February 23, 2009).

Bibliography

Carley, M. J. (2008) *Asperger's from the Inside Out: A Supportive and Practical Guide for Anyone with Asperger's Syndrome.* New York: Penguin.

Cederlund, M. and Gillberg, C. (2004) "One hundred males with Asperger syndrome: A clinical study of background and associated factors." *Developmental Medicine and Child Neurology 46,* 652–661.

Coulter, D. (2008) *Manners for the Real World.* Coulter Video. Available at www.coultervideo.com.

Dewey, M. A. (1980) "The near-normal autistic adolescent." Paper presented at National Society for Autistic Children, Ann Arbor, MI (July 1980).

Edmonds, G. and Worton, D. (2005) *The Asperger Love Guide: A Practical Guide for Adults with Asperger's Syndrome to Seeking, Establishing and Maintaining Successful Relationships.* London: Sage.

Endow, J. (2010, 2011) *The Hidden Curriculum One-A-Day Calendar for Older Adolescents and Adults: Items for Understanding Unstated Rules in Social Situations.* Shawnee Mission, KS: Autism Asperger Publishing Company.

Frith, U. and Happé, F. (1999) "Self-consciousness and autism: What is it like to be autistic?" *Mind and Language 14,* 1–22.

Gagnon, E. (2001) Power Cards. Shawnee Mission, KN: Autism Asperger Syndrome Publishing.

Grandin, T. (1986) *Emergence: Labeled Autistic.* Novato, CA: Arena Press.

Grandin, T. (1995) *Thinking in Pictures and Other Reports from My Life with Autism.* New York: Doubleday.

Grandin, T. (2008) *The Way I See It: A Personal Look at Autism and Asperger's.* Arlington, TX: Future Horizons.

Hénault, I. (2005) *Asperger's Syndrome and Sexuality: From Adolescence through Adulthood.* London: Jessica Kingsley Publishers.

Hénault, I. (2010) Email to Susan Moreno, August 16 2010.

Hénault, I. and Attwood, T. (2002) "The sexual profile of adults with Asperger's syndrome." Paper presented at the first World Autism Congress, Melbourne, Australia (June 1999).

Jackson, L. (2002) *Freaks, Geeks and Asperger Syndrome: A User Guide to Adolescence.* London: Jessica Kingsley Publishers.

Jacobs, B. (2006) *Loving Mr Spock: Understanding an Aloof Lover—Could it be Asperger's Syndrome?* London: Jessica Kingsley Publishers.

Kana, R. K., Keller, T. A., Cherkassky, V. L., Minshew, N. J. and Just, M. A. (2009) "Atypical frontal-posterior synchronization of Theory of Mind regions in autism during mental state attribution." *Social Neuroscience 4,* 135–152.

Kleinhans, N. M., Johnson, L. C., Richards, T., Mahurin, R., Greenson, J., Dawson, G. and Aylward, E. (2009) "Reduced neural habituation in the amygdala and social impairments in autism spectrum disorders." *American Journal of Psychiatry 166,* 467–475.

Lantz, J. (2002) "Theory of mind in autism: Development, implications, and interventions." *The Reporter 7,* 18–25.

Lawson, W. (2005) *Sex, Sexuality and the Autism Spectrum.* London: Jessica Kingsley Publishers.

Matthews, J. and Williams, J. (2000) *Self-Help Guide for Special Kids and Their Parents.* London: Jessica Kingsley Publishers.

Mitchell, C. (2008) *Asperger Syndrome and Mindfulness.* London: Jessica Kingsley Publishers.

Moreno, S. (2005) *More Advanced Individuals With Autism, Asperger Syndrome and PDD/NOS: Advice and Information for Parents and Others Who Care.* Crown Point, IN: MAAP Services, Inc.

Murray, D. (ed.) (2006) *Coming Out Asperger: Diagnosis, Disclosure and Self-Confidence.* London: Jessica Kingsley Publishers.

Myers, J. M. (2006) "Aspie's Do's and Don'ts: Dating, Relationships and Marriage." In *Asperger's and Girls.* Arlington, TX: Future Horizons.

Myles, B. S. and Southwick, J. (2005) *Asperger Syndrome and Difficult Moments: Practical Solutions for Tantrums, Rage, and Meltdowns*, revised and expanded edn. Shawnee Mission, KS: Autism Asperger Syndrome Publishing.

Myles, B. S., Trautman, M. L. and Schelvan, R. (2004) *The Hidden Curriculum*. Shawnee Mission, KN: Autism Asperger Syndrome Publishing.

Newport, J. and Newport, M. (2007) *Mozart and the Whale: An Asperger's Love Story*. New York: Allen & Unwin.

Parish, P. (2002) *Merry Christmas, Amelia Bedelia*. New York, NY: HarperCollins.

Parish, P. (2003) *Good Work, Amelia Bedelia*. New York, NY: HarperCollins.

Parkinson, K. D. (2009) "Communicating intimately: The three Rs of marriage." Available online at www.selfgrowth.com/articles/communicating-intimately-the-3-rs-of-marriage, accessed on 29 August 2011.

Parkinson, K. (2010) *Speak Your Truth: How to Say What You Mean to Get What You Want*. Crown Point, IN: Lamp Post Press. Available to download in e-book format from www.speak-with-kealah.com, accessed on August 29 2011.

Ray, F., Marks, C. and Bray-Garretson, H. (2004) "Challenges to treating adolescents with Asperger's syndrome who are sexually abusive." *Sexual Addiction and Compulsivity 11*, 265–285.

Rodman, K. (2003) *Asperger's Syndrome and Adults… Is Anyone Listening? Essays and Poems by Partners, Parents and Family Members of Adults with Asperger's Syndrome*. London: Jessica Kingsley Publishers.

Sakai, K. (2006) *Finding Our Way: Practical Solutions for Creating a Supportive Home and Community for the Asperger Syndrome Family*. Shawnee Mission, KS: Autism Asperger Publishing Company.

Sakai, K. (2007) "Sanctuary: Making a sensory friendly home." Lecture given at the Autism Society of America Annual Conference (July 2007).

Shore, S. (2004) *Ask and Tell: Self-Advocacy and Disclosure for People on the Autism Spectrum*. Shawnee Mission, KS: Autism Asperger Publishing Company.

Slater-Walker, G. and Slater-Walker, C. (2002) *An Asperger Marriage*. London: Jessica Kingsley Publishers.

Snyder, R. (2006) "Maternal Instincts in Asperger's Syndrome." In *Asperger's and Girls*. Arlington, TX: Future Horizons.

Spezio, M. L., Huang, P. S., Castelli, F. and Adolphs, R. (2007) "Amygdala damage impairs conversations with real people." *Journal of Neuroscience 27*, 3994–3997.

Stanford, A. (2003) *Asperger Syndrome and Long-Term Relationships*. London: Jessica Kingsley Publishers.

Thompson, B. (2008) *Counselling for Asperger Couples*. London: Jessica Kingsley Publishers.

US Department of Health and Human Services (2001) *Protecting the Privacy of Patients' Health Information*. Available at http://aspe.hhs.gov/admnsimp/final/pvcfact2.htm, accessed on August 1, 2011.

US Department of Health and Human Services, Substance Abuse and Mental Health Services Administration (SAMHSA) (2008) *Health Effects of Alcohol and Other Drugs on Your Body*, Fact Sheet.

Volkmar, F., Klin, A. and Pauls, D. (1998) "Nosological and genetic aspects of Asperger syndrome." *Journal of Autism and Developmental Disorders 28*, 457–463.

Washington State Department of Health (2008) *Information Summary: Patient Access to Medical Marijuana in Washington State*. Olympia, WA: Health Systems Quality Assurance.

Weston, L. (2010) *Connecting with your Asperger Partner*. London: Jessica Kingsley Publishers

Zaks, Z. (2006) *Life and Love: Positive Strategies for Autistic Adults*. Shawnee Mission, KS: Autism Asperger Publishing Company.

Subject Index

Author Index